BY FAITH
ALONE

BY FAITH
ALONE

One Family's Epic Journey Through

400 Years of American Protestantism

Bill Griffeth

HARMONY BOOKS
NEW YORK

Published in the United States by Harmony Books, an imprint of the Crown
Publishing Group, a division of Random House, Inc., New York.
www.crownpublishing.com

HARMONY BOOKS is a registered trademark and the Harmony Books colophon
is a trademark of Random House, Inc.

Library of Congress Cataloging-in-Publication Data
Griffeth, Bill.
By faith alone : one family's epic journey through 400 years of
American Protestantism /
Bill Griffeth.
Includes bibliographical references and index.
1. Protestantism—United States—History. 2. United States—Church history.
3. Protestantism—History. I. Title.
BR515.G76 2007
280'.40973—dc22
2007006998
ISBN 978-0-307-33728-3

Printed in the United States of America

Design by Lauren Dong

10 9 8 7 6 5 4 3 2 1

First Edition

This is for my children, Chad and Carlee,
and for their descendants, with the hope that these and other
family stories are never forgotten.

Contents

List of Photographs

All photographs are by the author except photo of Washington, Kans., c. 1900, on page 234 (courtesy of Wichita St. University Archives).

A
FAMILY
of
FAITH
400 Years

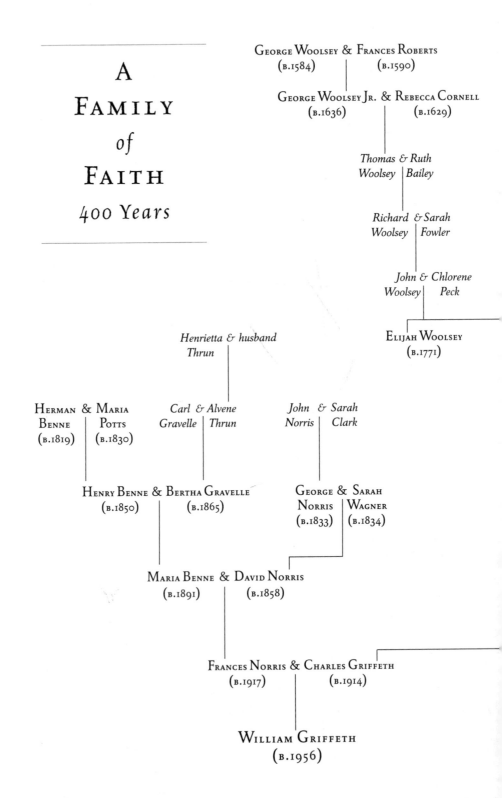

GEORGE WOOLSEY & FRANCES ROBERTS
(B.1584)   (B.1590)

GEORGE WOOLSEY JR. & REBECCA CORNELL
(B.1636)   (B.1629)

Thomas & Ruth
Woolsey | Bailey

Richard & Sarah
Woolsey | Fowler

John & Chlorene
Woolsey | Peck

ELIJAH WOOLSEY
(B.1771)

Henrietta & husband
Thrun

HERMAN & MARIA
BENNE | POTTS
(B.1819) | (B.1830)

Carl & Alvene
Gravelle | Thrun

John & Sarah
Norris | Clark

HENRY BENNE & BERTHA GRAVELLE
(B.1850)   (B.1865)

GEORGE & SARAH
NORRIS | WAGNER
(B.1833) | (B.1834)

MARIA BENNE & DAVID NORRIS
(B.1891)   (B.1858)

FRANCES NORRIS & CHARLES GRIFFETH
(B.1917)   (B.1914)

WILLIAM GRIFFETH
(B.1956)

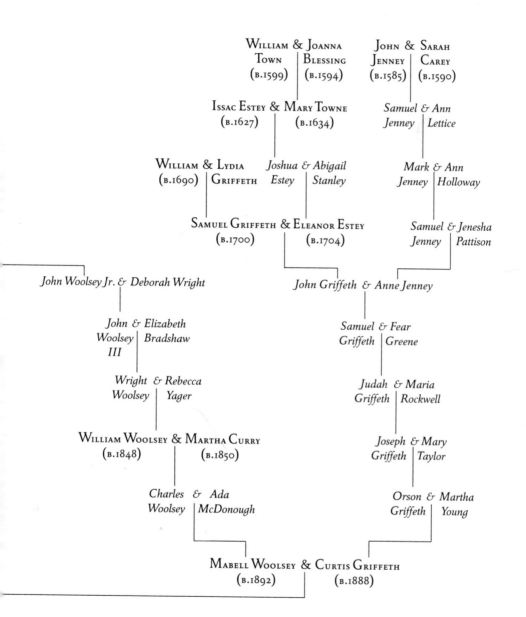

WILLIAM & JOANNA
TOWN | BLESSING
(B.1599) | (B.1594)

JOHN & SARAH
JENNEY | CAREY
(B.1585) | (B.1590)

ISSAC ESTEY & MARY TOWNE
(B.1627) | (B.1634)

Samuel & Ann
Jenney | Lettice

WILLIAM & LYDIA
(B.1690) | GRIFFETH

Joshua & Abigail
Estey | Stanley

Mark & Ann
Jenney | Holloway

SAMUEL GRIFFETH & ELEANOR ESTEY
(B.1700) | (B.1704)

Samuel & Jenesha
Jenney | Pattison

John Woolsey Jr. & Deborah Wright

John Griffeth & Anne Jenney

John & Elizabeth
Woolsey | Bradshaw
III

Samuel & Fear
Griffeth | Greene

Wright & Rebecca
Woolsey | Yager

Judah & Maria
Griffeth | Rockwell

WILLIAM WOOLSEY & MARTHA CURRY
(B.1848) | (B.1850)

Joseph & Mary
Griffeth | Taylor

Charles & Ada
Woolsey | McDonough

Orson & Martha
Griffeth | Young

MABELL WOOLSEY & CURTIS GRIFFETH
(B.1892) | (B.1888)

THE FAMILY TREE

THIS JOURNEY of mine began where all journeys end, in a graveyard.

One Sunday afternoon I persuaded my wife, Cindy, and our teenaged children, Chad and Carlee, to take a drive from our home in New Jersey to the far reaches of northern Westchester County, New York, because I had evidence that suggested we might have ancestors buried there. We were looking for members of the Woolsey family, which had been my grandmother Griffeth's maiden name.

Eventually we ended up in Bedford Hills, a town forty miles north of New York City, where residents are as likely to ride horses as to drive cars. After several twists and turns on dirt roads that took us past a number of horse ranches, we came upon an old cemetery in a clearing of trees. The sign at the front gate said Bedford Union Cemetery, and roughly twenty yards behind it we could see a large stone monument with WOOLSEY carved into it.

There were eleven headstones in this family plot, representing six generations of Woolseys. The oldest one read:

THOMAS
SON OF GEORGE WOOLSEY
BORN AT FLUSHING L.I.
1655   DIED 1730

The headstone next to it read:

RICHARD
SON OF THOMAS WOOLSEY
BORN 1697   DIED 1777

I looked at the notes I had brought with me, and found that they matched these names. The George referred to on the first headstone was my nine-times great-grandfather, which made him Chad and Carlee's ten-times great-grandfather. It meant that we were also direct descendants of Thomas and Richard. (The rest of the headstones represented a line of Woolseys separate from ours.)

Just like that, we had discovered our family had indeed lived in this area well before the American Revolution.

Cindy got out a pad of paper and began scribbling the names and dates carved on the other Woolsey headstones, and Chad and Carlee fanned out over the rest of the cemetery to see if there were any other family members buried here (there weren't). I took pictures of everything. Mission accomplished, I thought.

But the mission had only begun.

FOR SOME reason the really important moments in my life have happened while I was looking the other way.

In April of 1981, for example, I was a twenty-four-year-old single guy living in my hometown of Los Angeles, and I was obsessed with finding a job in television news. My friends were more interested in finding me a date. I was the fifth wheel attached to two married couples: Barb and Dave, and Tim and Deb. Only they never made me feel like a fifth wheel.

The moment occurred one evening while we were all having dinner and as usual the discussion got around to my social life, which had been in a slump. Just before dessert, Barb snapped her fingers and said, "I know who we can set you up with! Cindy Haas." It turned out Dave worked with this mystery woman, and he agreed enthusiastically.

I had never been on a blind date, and I really had no interest in one, but I called Cindy and invited her to dinner, mainly to please Barb. Long story short, Cindy and I were married one year later.

Four months later, in August of '81, while I was obsessing over my new girlfriend, another friend, Ben, called me about a job. He had read in one of the Hollywood trade papers that a new cable TV channel was being planned and they were looking for reporters. It was going to be called Financial News Network, or FNN.

Cable TV was just getting started in those days. CNN, MTV, and ESPN had only recently gone on the air, and more channels were being created. It was clear that this was where the jobs were. Even though I wasn't particularly interested in business news, I applied anyway. The executives who founded the network didn't think I looked old enough to have any credibility on camera, so they offered me a job as a producer, which I accepted, figuring I would continue to look for a reporter's job in the meantime. Six months later, when one of the anchors left, they put me on the air and I never left.

Cindy and I settled into a comfortable married life. We had a beautiful home, Chad was born in November of 1989, and by early '91 we learned that Carlee would join us in August. We had no reason to believe that we would soon be moving to the East Coast.

One evening in February of that year I got a call at home from FNN's president. The network was up for sale, he said, and chances were good that it would be moved to New York.

Cindy and I had sworn we would never leave Los Angeles. All of our family and friends were there, and we most certainly didn't want to live where it snowed.

In May of '91, NBC bought FNN and merged it with its own business channel, CNBC, which at the time was located in Fort Lee, New Jersey. They made me an offer that I simply could not refuse. And so, reluctantly, we moved. We fell in love with the East Coast and it became our home.

One afternoon in June of 2003 I received an e-mail out of the blue from my first cousin Donna. She was the oldest of Grandpa and Grandma Griffeth's eleven grandchildren, and I was the youngest. As it happens, we were born on the same date, August 7, twenty-two years apart, like bookends.

She wrote to tell me that her daughter, LeAnne, was working on a family tree. They had heard that I had some genealogical information about the Griffeths, and they were wondering if I would be willing to share it. What I had were four handwritten pages of notes from a cousin of my father's that took the family back two or three generations. I don't remember how I ended up with them, but I was happy to share, so I dug them out of the back of an old filing cabinet, made copies, and mailed them to LeAnne.

A few months later a file showed up in my e-mail box labeled FAMILY TREE. When I clicked it open, up popped a whole Broadway production: eight generations of Griffeths, ten generations of Woolseys, and dozens of other family names I had never heard before, going back more than three hundred years. It ran forty-four single-spaced pages in all.

Page one began with my own family: my father, Charles, who was born in Hastings, Nebraska, in 1914; and my mother, Frances, who was born in Washington, Kansas, in 1917. My three sisters were all born in the 1930s in Kansas. In 1939 the family moved to Los Angeles, hoping Dad could find work there. My brother was born soon after they arrived, in 1940. I was born in 1956. I am what the family delicately refers to as a "surprise."

LeAnne's family tree worked back from there. I casually thumbed through it, studying the different surnames—sixty-eight in all!—and tracing my ancestors' migration backwards to the East Coast.

The earliest Griffeths first appeared in New England colony records in the 1600s. The family patriarch, himself a William Griffeth, was my seven-times great-grandfather. All we know about him is that he was born around 1680 in Rochester, Massachusetts, and he died there in 1734. Over the next two hundred years my line of Griffeths migrated west, with stops in upstate New York, Illinois, Iowa, and finally in northern Kansas, where my great-great-grandparents settled in the 1870s.

On the Woolsey side, my nine-times great-grandparents George and Rebecca lived for many years in the New Amsterdam Colony in New York beginning around 1647. Succeeding generations migrated to Westchester and Ulster counties in New York, and then west to Ohio and into southern Nebraska, where my great-great-grandparents settled in 1870.

The tree helped me clear up a family mystery. My father insisted for years that we were somehow related to Alexander Hamilton. I searched the tree, and to my utter astonishment I found our nation's first secretary of the treasury. LeAnne had inserted a brief excerpt from a book called *The History of Jones County, Iowa*, published in 1879, which said the father of my four-times great-grandmother, Nancy Hamilton Stivers (1824–1908), was "a cousin of Alexander Hamilton, who was killed by A. Burr." That would have made Secretary Hamilton something like my great-great-great-great-great-cousin, if there is such a thing.

Then things started to get interesting, beginning with this startling revelation on page 29 of LeAnne's tree:

Mary Towne Estey was executed on September 22, 1692,
in Salem, MA, for witchcraft.

I went to my computer and entered the name in a search engine and up came hundreds of links to sites about the Salem witch trials of 1692. Nineteen people were executed that summer, all by hanging. Mary and her older sister, Rebecca, were among the nineteen.

But how was I related to this woman? I flipped back and forth through the pages of the tree and figured out that Mary and her husband, Isaac Estey, had had a granddaughter named Eleanor who married my six-times great-grandfather Samuell Griffeth on September 23, 1724, in Rochester, Massachusetts, which would make Mary Towne Estey my eight-times great-grandmother.

My great-great-great-great-great-great-great-great-grandmother was one of the legendary Salem witches. I didn't know whether to be horrified or jubilant.

I plunged further into the family tree, spending more and more time online studying maps of England, matching names and dates with places. Ever so slowly the names on the pages of this tree my cousin had compiled were turning into real people, and after hours spent connecting the dots, I was able to piece together the stories of their lives.

I figured out, for example, that the Woolseys, the Townes, and another pair of ancestors—John and Sarah Jenney—had all been Puritans who fled England in the early 1600s during the persecution of the English Protestants under the Stuart kings James I and his son Charles I. The three families eventually settled in different American colonies.

Amazingly, the Woolseys and Townes came from the same town, Great Yarmouth, a fishing village on the east coast of England, and—incredibly—George Woolsey was baptized in the very same Anglican church where Mary Towne's parents were married and where many of the Towne children were also baptized.

Around 1620, the Woolseys sailed across the English Channel to Rotterdam, Holland, before George junior continued on to New Amsterdam in America, sometime in the 1640s. The Townes settled in the Massachusetts Bay Colony in the 1630s.

The Jenneys, who were from the English village of Norwich, were members of the legendary congregation of Pilgrims that lived in Leiden, Holland, for twelve years before settling the Plymouth Colony in New England. John and Sarah didn't sail on the *Mayflower*; they migrated on another ship three years later, in 1623.

I had to know more. I bought dozens of books about the Puritan movements in England and Holland and in the American colonies, and books about the Salem witch trials (and there are plenty). I spent count-less hours combing the Internet, and I joined a couple of genealogical societies and explored their extensive databases. I also wrote letters and e-mails to distant relatives I had never met, looking for still more information.

The tree became my obsession. For the next two years I retraced three hundred years of my family's journey from England and Holland to America's heartland, hopping on a plane or jumping in the car when-ever I could find the time and visiting the places where they had lived.

In England I went to Great Yarmouth and worshipped where the Townes and Woolseys had worshipped. In the Netherlands I spent time in the town of Leiden, where the Jenneys had lived with the rest of the Pilgrims, and I walked the narrow cobblestone streets of Rotterdam's Delfshaven district near where the Woolseys lived for a number of years.

Back in the United States, I made frequent trips to Massachusetts. In Topsfield I worshipped in the Congregational church that was begun in the 1680s by a group of Puritans that included members of the Towne and Estey families. In Salem, my family and I tried to under-stand the causes of the bizarre witch trials. And in Plymouth, I met a couple who run the grist mill John Jenney built in 1636.

In New York City, near where I live, I visited the neighborhoods in Manhattan, Brooklyn, and Queens where George and Rebecca Woolsey and their children lived for more than fifty years. And I stumbled upon the bizarre story of the death of Rebecca's mother, my ten-times great-grandmother Rebecca Cornell, and I read the court records of the investigation and trial that resulted, a trial with an unbelievable twist ending.

During one memorable Sunday morning in a small town in New Jersey, I stood in the pulpit of a tiny Methodist church founded in 1802 by my five-times great-uncle, a Methodist circuit rider named Elijah Woolsey, and read excerpts from his journal to the members of the congregation.

Finally, I completed the journey by returning to the place where my parents and my sisters had been born: the farmlands of northern Kansas and southern Nebraska, where all of our ancestral lines converged in the late nineteenth century.

When all was said and done, I had traveled more than ten thousand miles by plane, train, and automobile. I kept a journal along the way, which filled five large spiral-bound notebooks, and I took hundreds of photographs.

This book is more than just a history of my family. At some point during my research I realized that in order to fully appreciate the world my ancestors lived in, I needed to understand the Protestant Reformation that profoundly changed the course of Western civilization and shaped my ancestors' views of God, the Church, the English monarchy, and—most critically—themselves.

Most of the people you will read about here happen to be relatives of mine, but the journeys they undertook were not unique. If you are an American Protestant of European descent, chances are good that your ancestors lived in the same colonies, fought the same battles, and pursued the same dreams. All of them took enormous risks and overcame unbelievable obstacles.

For that we can all be grateful.

Part One

EUROPE

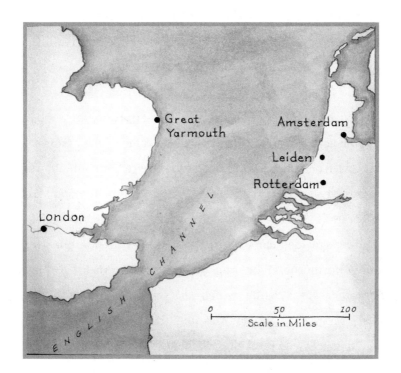

BEGINNING AT THE
BEGINNING

I SAT IN THE PASSENGER LOUNGE AT NEWARK LIBERTY INTERNATIONAL Airport one Friday evening, sipping a beer and scribbling notes to myself as I waited to board a flight to London. I jotted down the surnames of my English ancestors, boldly retracing the letters over and over again.

TOWNE . . . WOOLSEY . . . JENNEY . . .

In the days before the Norman Conquest in 1066, the people who lived in the land we know today as England came by their names pretty casually. Each person would, of course, be given a first name at birth, but last names evolved over time based on various criteria: a person's particular skill or trade (Miller or Cooper, for example), where they hailed from (my mother's maiden name, Norris, was a very common English name meaning "northerner"), or some physical characteristic (my maternal grandmother was a Benne, which *The Oxford Dictionary of English Surnames* says was a nickname meaning "the plump, lumpish one").

The name Towne (and all of its many variations, including Town and Townes) was derived from the Old English word *tun*, which meant "homestead" or "village." A twelfth-century Englishman named William who lived in the village might have been referred to as William de tun. By the thirteenth century, surnames not only became more common, but also hereditary, with names passed on from one generation to the next. By that time, William de tun would have become William Town, or, in my family's case, Towne.

Woolsey was originally spelled variously as Wulcy or Wulsi. It was derived from the nickname "wolf's eye," which was common in Suffolk.

It is not exactly clear where Jenney came from. It was either from an old Cornish name, *Genn,* from which names like Jennifer, Gene, and Jean are also derived, or it may have been from an old French name, *Jene,* which the Normans brought with them.

When my flight was called, I finished my beer and headed for the boarding gate. As I was taking my seat on the jet a flight attendant greeted me, took my drink order, and handed me a dinner menu and a small gift bag. After I stowed my luggage and got myself situated, I opened the bag. Inside I found a pair of black socks, a sleeping mask, lip balm, toothpaste, a toothbrush, and some breath mints, everything to make a transatlantic flight more comfortable.

It was all very nice and luxurious, but it made me feel self-conscious, because all I could think about were the hardships my seventeenth-century ancestors endured when they made their own journeys across the Atlantic. Conditions on the merchant ships they sailed on were difficult, the food was horrible, and there was the very real possibility that during the two months they were at sea, one could fall ill and maybe even die. Here I was, with black booties and breath mints on board a luxury jet that would take only seven hours to get to England. I tucked the bag in the seat pocket in front of me, unopened.

These ancestors of mine were members of history's holiest generation, the Puritans. They were among the tens of thousands of English men and women born between 1590 and 1610 who passionately took a stand for their faith, sought to transform England into a community of godly people, and when that failed they made the decision to start from scratch and form their own holy community on the American continent.

What would my ancestors think of their holy community today? One that explicitly separated church from state, that banned prayer in the classroom and displays of the Ten Commandments outside courthouses, and debated dropping "under God" from its national pledge and currency.

The Puritans, who punished members of their own community for missing a single worship service, would no doubt be dismayed to know that by the early twenty-first century, church attendance in America had eroded to roughly fifty percent of the population. Even more alarming, attendance in their English homeland had fallen below five percent.

I had packed lightly for my trip, making do with a small suitcase and a shoulder bag. In addition to clothing and a shaving kit, I packed a soft four-by-eight-inch notebook with zippered pouches just large enough to carry my journal, maps, and train schedules. At the last minute, I threw in a pocket-sized Bible.

A Bible might have been the first thing a Puritan family would pack, if they could afford one. The art of printing hadn't yet progressed to the point where books could be affordably mass-produced. In fact, in the early seventeenth century, Bibles sometimes cost more than houses. But they were still an essential part of a Puritan household. Literacy rates were extremely high among the Puritans because reading the Bible was as important as eating and breathing. Children were taught to read expressly so that they could read the Bible. Today, of course, while the Bible is the best-selling book in the world, it is unclear how many are actually read.

My plan was to visit two countries. In England, I was very anxious to see the seaside resort of Great Yarmouth, where the Townes and Woolseys had lived during the early 1600s. In the Netherlands I would spend time in the university town of Leiden, where the Jenneys lived with the rest of the famed English Separatist congregation until they sailed to Plymouth, Massachusetts, in 1623. And in Rotterdam I would visit the area where George and Frances Woolsey had moved with their children sometime before 1620.

These ancestors were products of the Protestant Reformation, which began quietly on the evening of October 31, 1517, in Wittenberg, Germany, when the young Augustinian monk Martin Luther tacked a laundry list of theses, ninety-five in all, to the front door of the village church for public display. In them Luther took issue with various Church practices, including the number of sacraments the Church sanctioned (Luther pared the list from seven to the only two mentioned in the Bible: baptism and communion); the growing number of saints, which Luther felt needlessly diverted attention from Jesus; and the pope's controversial practice of selling indulgences to finance the construction of St. Peter's Basilica in Rome.

Luther had intended only to stir debate among his fellow theologians in town. But when someone reproduced the list and distributed it throughout Germany, it set off a chain reaction of protests that eventually splintered the Church and positioned the passionate Luther as the Protestant movement's first spokesman.

The Protestants preached *sola fide*—by faith alone—an idea taken from the Apostle Paul's letter to Christian converts in Rome that said each person could achieve salvation simply by having faith in the teachings of Jesus Christ, as opposed to performing the many rituals the Church required. They also believed that the Bible, not the Church, was the sole source of God's Word—*sola scriptura*. Because the newly invented printing presses allowed the mass production of Bibles, people were able to read the scriptures for themselves, bypassing the Church's interpretation.

At about the same time, England experienced its own reformation, but under very different circumstances. It wasn't about an idea. Instead, it was the result of a power struggle between a king and a pope.

In 1528, Henry VIII asked Pope Clement VII for permission to divorce his wife, Catherine of Aragon, who had failed to produce a male heir, so that he could marry his mistress Anne Boleyn. When permission was denied, the explosive king retaliated by seizing control of all Church assets on English soil and having Parliament proclaim him the head of the new Church of England.

After Henry VIII died in 1547, England experienced an identity crisis that lasted roughly a decade. Henry's sole male heir, ten-year-old Edward VI (by his third wife, Jane Seymour), was greatly influenced by a group of Protestant theologians who steered the Church of England away from Catholic traditions. Their most ambitious project was to make the Bible accessible to all of the people by having an English translation placed in pews. But when Edward died six years later, in 1553, he was succeeded by his half-sister Mary, the daughter of the very Catholic Catherine of Aragon.

Mary Tudor immediately reversed all of the Protestant reforms, returning England to the customs dictated by the Church of Rome. In 1555, Pope Julius III declared that all English heretics were to be burned at the stake, and Mary complied. For the next three years almost three hundred Protestants, including Archbishop of Canterbury Thomas Cranmer, were executed, earning the queen the nickname "Bloody Mary."

Hundreds of Protestants fled England for the Continent, most no-tably to Geneva, Switzerland, where a community had been formed by John Calvin (1509–1564), the French theologian widely regarded as the most influential member of the Protestant movement after Luther. It was in Geneva that the English Protestants were exposed to Calvin's ideas about predestination and the relationship between church and state.

Queen Mary's reign was a short one, lasting only five years until her death at the age of forty-two in 1558. Because Mary was childless when she died, she was succeeded by her half-sister Elizabeth, the daughter of Henry VIII and Anne Boleyn.

Elizabeth I had been raised an Anglican, and she reinstated Church of England traditions. But she also realized how splintered her country had become theologically in the eleven years since her father died. Most of her subjects embraced the Anglican Church's Catholic/Protes-tant hybrid model. There were also a growing number who sought to "purify" the Church of England by eliminating all Catholic rituals, saints, and relics—thought to be false idols—and all sacraments not specifically mentioned in the Bible. In 1563 the queen sought to appease the growing number of Puritans by giving her blessing to the creation of a list of thirty-nine broad statements of faith that formed the foundation of the Church of England. The Thirty-nine Articles, which are still in use today, agreed with Luther by recognizing only two of the Roman Church's seven sacraments, and it condemned the use of "Images as of Reliques, and also invocation of Saints," calling them "vainly invented, and grounded upon no warranty of Scripture, but rather repugnant to the Word of God."

By the time of the Virgin Queen's death in 1603, England had become a prosperous political powerhouse, but it remained divided theologically. The division between Anglicans and Puritans became more pronounced when Elizabeth's second cousin, Scotland's James VI, succeeded her and became England's first Stuart king, James I.

In Scotland, James, who was a devout Anglican, had had to deal with the Presbyterian form of Protestantism, which used a decentralized style of governance begun by a disciple of Calvin's named John Knox. When he came to England, James was very happy to embrace the Church of England's more-centralized Episcopalian form of governance, which made him the head of the Church. In 1605 he abolished the Presbyterian Assembly in Scotland and imposed the Anglican ways on his homeland. He also took on the handful of congregations made up of radical Puritans who had separated from the organized Church—the so-called Separatists—by requiring all English citizens to attend Anglican services on Sunday.

When James died in 1625, he was succeeded by his son Charles I, a young man who was susceptible to the ideas of his advisers, most notably Archbishop of Canterbury William Laud, a zealous Anglican theologian who sought to rid England of all religious dissenters. Laud's campaign caused the Great Migration of the 1630s that brought my ancestors to America.

After my jet from Newark to London reached cruising altitude and the flight attendants had finished serving dinner, I asked for a cup of coffee and got out my journal. Underneath the three ancestral names I had written I added a line:

TOWNE ... WOOLSEY ... JENNEY ...
BY FAITH ALONE

Chapter One

GREAT YARMOUTH, 1600–1630

The Puritans

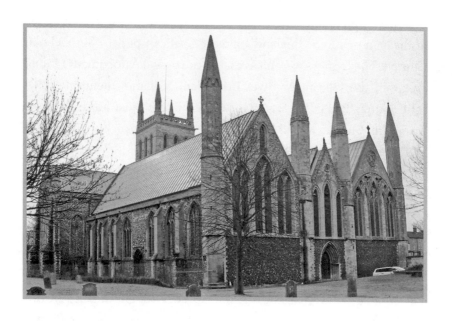

I TOOK THE afternoon train from Liverpool station in London for the 120-mile trip to Norfolk, on England's east coast, where the Townes, Woolseys, and Jenneys lived in the sixteenth and seventeenth centuries. My goal was to see where it all began for my family. That would be easy when it came to the Townes and the Woolseys. According to records quoted in my cousin LeAnne's family tree, both families lived in the ancient fishing village of Great Yarmouth and worshipped in the same church, England's largest Anglican parish, St. Nicholas Church. The Jenneys weren't as easy to pin down. A document I found online in the Pilgrim Archives in Leiden, Holland, mentioned that John Jenney had come from Norwich, the town just north of Great Yarmouth. But that was all I knew. So I would wait to pick up the Jenney trail when I got to the Netherlands.

All three of my ancestral families were Puritans, a label that has become a caricature that obscures our view of the individuals who embraced it. The journalist H. L. Mencken's flippant characterization that a Puritan's greatest fear was "that someone, somewhere may be happy" distorts them like a reflection in a fun-house mirror.

There is no question the Puritans were strict disciplinarians. They had to be. They were agents of change. They sought drastic reforms from top to bottom in an ancient institution with deep-seated traditions and beliefs that extended back more than a millennium. They took on the two most powerful forces in England, the monarchy and the Church. The courage of their convictions came from the sincere belief that they were backed by the most powerful force of all: God. Were they religious fanatics? You bet, but they had to be. They had set the bar very high, and their goal of purifying the Church of England of all vestiges of the Church of Rome would not be achieved with a casual attitude.

"They quarreled with the Stuart monarchs about playing games on the Sabbath," wrote Edmund S. Morgan in his *The Puritan Family*, "and with Anglican churchmen about vestments and ceremonies. They wrote hundreds of books explaining the exact conduct demanded by God in every human situation. They had, in fact, complete blueprints for a smooth, honest, civil life in family, church, and state."

Not all Puritans were equal. The moderates who made up the majority of England's Puritan population were determined to reform the Church of England from within. They worshipped beside their Anglican neighbors even as they complained about the elaborate decorations and formal ceremonies. The more-radical minority separated from the Church altogether and formed smaller independent congregations. One of the first of the so-called Separatist communities was founded in Norwich in 1580 under the radical cleric Robert Browne, who was imprisoned thirty-two times on heresy charges before being exiled in 1582. For many years, the Separatists were called Brownists.

The Jenneys were Separatists. They were members of what was by far the most famous Separatist congregation to emerge from England. It was formed in the 1590s in the village of Scrooby and was led by two Cambridge alumni, Scrooby's well-to-do postmaster, William Brewster, and a former Anglican priest named John Robinson. John and Sarah Jenney joined this congregation not long after it left England for the Netherlands in 1609. Eleven years later, in 1620, roughly a third of the group sailed to America on the *Mayflower* and formed the Plymouth Colony. The Jenneys sailed with their children three years later on the *Little James*.

The Townes and Woolseys appeared to be moderate Puritans, since they were willing to worship in an Anglican church. George and Frances Woolsey crossed the English Channel with their children around 1616 and settled in Rotterdam, where they joined a Dutch

Reformed congregation. The Dutch Reformed Church had been founded on the same Calvinist beliefs that inspired the original Puritans. Years later, probably in the 1640s, my eight-times great-grandfather George junior sailed to the New Amsterdam Colony, where he and his family eventually became Presbyterians, the Protestant denomination begun in Scotland by the Calvinist John Knox.

William and Joanna Towne probably left Great Yarmouth around 1634 during the height of the so-called Great Migration, when tens of thousands of Puritans left for America to escape persecution during the reign of Charles I. The Townes settled in Topsfield, Massachusetts, where some members of the family eventually became part of the Congregationalist Church, a form of Protestantism that leaned toward the Separatists' desire for independent congregations.

My late-afternoon train from London to Great Yarmouth was packed with people heading home from work. It passed through Suffolk and into Norfolk, making frequent stops along the way at towns with names unfamiliar to me. I scribbled them in my journal each time we stopped: Chelmsford, Witham, Colchester, Stowmarket, Diss, to name a few. At each stop, several passengers got off and hurried to their cars. It was a long three hours by the time we pulled into the station in Great Yarmouth, when the sun was at its lowest point on the horizon, casting the longest shadows of the day. Just before I put my journal away, I recorded the name of our final stop. Next to it I wrote: HOME.

GREAT YARMOUTH's recorded history goes back to the first century A.D., when Britain was a northern outpost of the Roman Empire, an occupation that lasted from A.D. 43 to 433. At the time, that portion of the eastern shore of Britain was a massive estuary of salty North Sea water mixed with three freshwater rivers: the Yare, the Waveney, and the Bure. To protect themselves from invasion by the Saxon, Angle, and Jute tribes of the European continent, the Romans in A.D. 50 built fortresses at the northern and southern tips of the estuary.

The spiritual leaders in that part of Britain were the Celtic Druids, the mysterious sages who have since vanished into history. Since they left no written material behind, what we know about them today is largely legendary. It is believed they preached that the soul was immortal and at death it was passed on from one body to the next. If a warrior died a hero in battle, his spirit would have the special honor of being passed on to a higher being. Each time a child was born, the Druids mourned the passing of that soul from the netherworld as it returned to earth.

Soon after the Romans left the area in the middle of the fifth century, Saxon, Angle, and Jute warriors did indeed invade, and over the course of two centuries they gradually drove the local tribes of Britons to the west, to the land that is now Wales. Angleland, as the country became known (a foreshadowing of England), was divided into seven small kingdoms: Northumbria, Mercia, Kent, Essex (for East Saxon), Sussex (South Saxon), Wessex (West Saxon), and the largest and most powerful of them all, East Anglia, which was divided into two regions: Norfolk (where the Northern Folk dwelled), and Suffolk (for the Southern Folk).

The Anglo-Saxons were pagans. They worshipped gods of nature who influenced the quality of the annual harvest, the outcome of war, and their ability to bear children. Their belief system was based largely on ancient Germanic and Norse mythology, which included gods still familiar today.

There was Woden, the father of all gods. In Norse mythology, he was the leader of the hunt who flew across the sky with his hounds. The fourth day of the week was named for him. Today, we know *Wodensday* as Wednesday.

Woden's wife, Frigga, was the mother of all gods, who oversaw the success or failure of childbirth. The sixth day of the week, Friday, is named for her. One of Woden and Frigga's sons, Thor (Thursday), was the god of thunder, who was responsible for the weather and the success of all crops. Another son, Tiw (for Tuesday), was the god of war.

Warriors would paint his symbol, an upward-pointing arrow, on their shields to protect themselves in battle.

Philosophically, the Anglo-Saxons viewed life through a concept called Wyrd, a word loosely translated as "fate," which suggested that past actions affect the future. In *Macbeth,* Shakespeare used the three witches—the Weird Sisters—to predict various characters' fates. Today, Wyrd is thought to have been an early influence on the Calvinist and Puritan concepts of predestination.

In 597, Pope Gregory I sent an emissary, named Augustine (not to be confused with the more famous Augustine of Hippo), to convert Anglo-Saxons to Christianity, and by the eighth century most pagan practices had been abandoned. There obviously were a few holdouts, though, because a decree was issued in the tenth century requiring priests to "extinguish" practices that were viewed as magical and super-natural. The Church's witch hunts continued on and off for centuries afterward throughout Europe, and it spread briefly to America, most famously in the small village of Salem, Massachusetts, in the summer of 1692.

By the time Augustine arrived in England in the sixth century, a sand bar had begun to form at the mouth of the great estuary in the coastal area that borders Norfolk and Suffolk. It gradually became a long, narrow island measuring roughly eight miles from north to south, and eventually enough sand built up on the northern tip that the island attached itself to the mainland, forming a peninsula. The early settlers in the area founded a town on the west bank of the Yare River, which they named Jiermud, which translates into modern English as Yarmouth. It was later renamed Great Yarmouth to distinguish it from a smaller community to the south called Little Yarmouth.

Great Yarmouth grew rapidly for one reason: the herring, more specifically the Atlantic herring, the most abundant fish on earth. Giant schools made up of hundreds of thousands darted about in the waters off the coast of New England, north toward the southern coastlines of Greenland and Iceland, and into the area of the North Sea around

Norway and the British Isles. Thousands of fishermen were drawn to Great Yarmouth, where a thriving industry sprang up. Each fall, merchants from all over Europe journeyed to Great Yarmouth for the annual Yarmouth Fair where the fisherman sold their harvest. Great Yarmouth became a boomtown.

I GOT off the train at the Great Yarmouth station with the handful of passengers who were left from our long three-hour ride from London. Most of them got into cars parked in the station's lot. I hailed one of the cabs idling at the terminal entrance.

Great Yarmouth today is a seaside vacation spot for middle-class tourists. There are no luxury resorts, but only a line of modest inns, bed-and-breakfasts, and motels along a winding boulevard that borders the beaches facing the North Sea.

My driver was a cheerful young man named Keith. I gave him the name of the motel where I would be staying, and asked if it was within walking distance of St. Nicholas Church. He said it was, and he drove along the route I would need to take between the two. We passed a large cemetery and he pointed out the tall steeple of St. Nicholas in the distance.

My motel was at the north end of the boulevard that borders the beach, away from all the action. Just before he dropped me off, I mentioned to Keith that I would be taking the early train back to London two days later. I asked how I could go about making arrangements for another taxi. He casually said he would make sure one picked me up. Just like that.

"The train leaves at six-twenty-two," I said. "What time should I be ready?"

"I would think six o'clock should be enough time," he said as he lifted my bags out of the trunk.

The next morning I got up before sunrise, dressed warmly, grabbed my camera and journal, and headed to the beach across the street.

An early-morning marine layer on the horizon kept me from actually seeing the sun emerge from the horizon. I stepped onto the beach and found the sand was coarse and damp, which made it easy to walk on. Pale green beach grass, some of it waist-high, stood waiting quietly for the morning's first breeze. The sand was dotted with pale blue and white stones. The closer I got to the water, the more colors there were: blues, whites, oranges, browns, and grays. The Puritans would have celebrated this moment. Their disciplined ways called for prayers to be recited first thing in the morning and just before bedtime in the evening.

I recited the first prayer that came to mind.

"Our Father, who art in heaven . . ."

As part of his Sermon on the Mount in the Gospel of Matthew, this was the prayer Jesus taught his disciples when they asked him the proper way to pray. During the Middle Ages it was known as the *Pater Noster*, recited exclusively in Latin, and after the Reformation all members of the Church of England were allowed to recite it in English. In his Book of Common Prayer, Archbishop Thomas Cranmer included it in his instructions on the proper way to conduct Morning Prayers (the "Our Father" was to be recited near the end) and Evening Prayers (in which it was the very first prayer recited).

In the Geneva Bible, which the Puritans used for many years, even after King James brought out his Authorized Version in 1611, this is how the prayer read in Matthew 6:9–13:

> *Our Father which art in heauen, hallowed be thy Name*
> *Thy kingdome come, Thy will be done euen in earth,*
> > *as it is in heauen.*
> *Giue vs this day our daily bread.*
> *And forgive vs our dettes, as we alfo forgiue our deters.*
> *And lead vs not into tentation, but deliuer vs from euil:*
> > *for thine is the kingdome, and the power,*
> > *and the glorie for euer. Amen.*

I continued walking north along the shore, teasing the small waves each time they rushed toward me. What was it like, I wondered, when the Townes and Woolseys boarded ships in this area and began their journeys away from England? Would there have been a ceremony with their neighbors on hand to wish them well, or did they slip away quietly?

The best-known account of a Puritan congregation's departure from England was written by William Bradford, who was a seventeen-year-old member of the Scrooby Separatists when they fled England for the Netherlands in 1608. His journal, *Of Plymouth Plantation: 1620–1647*, immortalized the people history remembers as the Pilgrims.

Bradford wrote that before and during the Great Migration of the 1630s, emigrants were required to obtain permits before they could leave the country. But the Scrooby congregation faced a classic catch-22: in order to secure their travel permits, they had to state their reason for departure, but if they admitted they were Separatists in search of a more tolerant land, they would have been jailed for being religious dissenters.

They could have lied, of course, but apparently they chose not to. Instead, they secretly contracted with an unnamed shipmaster in the English seaport of Boston to take all of them—probably close to one hundred congregants—to Amsterdam.

Sometime in the fall of 1607, they made the journey south from Scrooby to Boston, where they quietly boarded late one night with all of their supplies and belongings, only to find that the shipmaster had betrayed them to the local authorities, who confiscated everything and threw them in jail for a month.

Several months later, in the spring of 1608, they tried again with another, more trustworthy, shipmaster who agreed to pick them up somewhere on the banks of the great Humber River, north of Scrooby. But things did not go well this time, either. During the boat trip from Scrooby, many of the women became seasick in the Humber's rough waters. And just as the first group of men was loading the ship with supplies, a posse of bounty hunters appeared on the scene. The ship-master immediately weighed anchor and headed out to sea, leaving a handful of men and all of the women and children behind. William Bradford writes that the men were frantic to get back to their wives and children, but the shipmaster pressed on to escape capture.

They encountered a terrible storm at sea that, according to Brad-ford's dramatic account, lasted for seven days. Everyone on board gave up hope of ever reaching land.

"When the water ran into their mouths and ears and the mariners cried out, 'We sink, we sink!' they cried . . . 'Yet Lord Thou canst save! Yet Lord Thou canst save!'

"But when man's hope and help wholly failed," Bradford wrote, "the Lord's power and mercy appeared in their recovery; for the ship rose again and gave the mariners courage again to manage her.

". . . Shortly after the violence of the storm began to abate, and the Lord filled their afflicted minds with such comforts as everyone cannot understand, and in the end brought them to their desired haven, where the people came flocking, admiring their deliverance."

Back in England their wives and children were detained by authori-ties. Because they were homeless, and because all of their menfolk and worldly belongings had left for Holland, leaving them with no financial support, they were allowed to make the trip across the channel where they were reunited with their husbands in Amsterdam.

Not all Puritans experienced the same degree of hardship that the Scrooby Separatists did, but all of them faced a great deal of risk because of the dangers at sea and the uncertain conditions they would encounter when they arrived at their various destinations. Their willingness to endure great hardship showed how resolute—maybe even desperate—many Puritans were to live a godly life, no matter where.

I continued along the shoreline, picking up some of the stones that littered the beach and stuffing them in my pocket. Behind me there was the sound of rustling in the tall beach grass. I turned and saw a woman walking toward me with her dog. The day was beginning. It was time to move on.

I crossed the street and headed west along a narrow side road, retracing the route my cabdriver had taken until I came to the town cemetery. I entered through the nearest gate and waded into the ankle-high grass that was wet with morning dew.

The cemetery was enormous, a vast sea of vine-covered headstones and monuments that extended for several city blocks. According to a history of Great Yarmouth, written in 1619 by town clerk Henry Manship, the town had been devastated by the Black Death in 1348.

"It pleased the Almighty to send such a great mortality within the township," he wrote, "that there died in one year the number of seven thousand inhabitants," or roughly 70 percent of its population.

"Scarcely the number then living sufficed to bury the dead, much less to proceed in the building" of the town.

I wandered through the cemetery, stopping here and there, reading some of the headstones, taking a few pictures. Pretty soon I spotted a tall spire through the trees.

The first photo I took of St. Nicholas Church from that spot is still my favorite of all the pictures I took. It is difficult to describe adequately what I felt standing before the church my ancestors had called home four hundred years ago. This was where it had all begun for my family ten generations ago, and I was in awe.

St. Nicholas Church was founded in 1101 by Herbert de Losinga, the first bishop of Norwich parish, who went on to serve King Henry I as Lord Chancellor of England from 1104 until his death in 1119. He named it for St. Nicholas, a fourth-century bishop born in Turkey.

All that is known for sure about Nicholas of Myra is that he was imprisoned by the Roman emperor Diocletian during one of the many Christian persecutions, he attended the Council of Nicea in 325, and he died on December 6, 343.

There are also many legends about him. The most famous involves

a father with three daughters who didn't have enough money to provide them a decent dowry. So, in one version, Bishop Nicholas climbed on the family's roof three consecutive nights and threw gold coins down the chimney so that they would land in the girls' stockings as they hung drying on the fireplace. It established his reputation for charity that spread throughout Europe, where he was called Sankt Nikolaus in Germany and Sinter Klaas in Holland. A tradition of giving gifts eventually developed on his feast day, December 6, but after the Reformation the German Protestants insisted on the tradition being moved to the feast day of the Christkindl (the Christ child), December 25. It was, but Santa Claus wasn't exactly forgotten in the process.

Another story is told about a trip Bishop Nicholas took to the Holy Land. During his voyage back to Turkey, his ship was caught in a storm that threatened to capsize it. The bishop prayed calmly during the crisis, and to the amazement of the sailors on board, the winds suddenly died down. That would help to explain the number of St. Nicholas chapels built in many European seaports, including Great Yarmouth.

I continued to take pictures of the church's exterior, amazed at how large a building it was, given the size of the community it served, and I slowly made my way around to the south entrance, which was padlocked. A sheet of paper was posted on the gate. It listed upcoming events, including last Sunday's services. At the bottom it read, TUESDAYS: HOLY COMMUNION 8:15 A.M. I looked at my watch. It was 7:55. A communion service was to begin in twenty minutes? Where was everybody?

Almost on cue, a man dressed in black and a cleric's collar walked into the courtyard carrying a briefcase. He was about my size, had gray hair cut fashionably, and he wore glasses. I guessed he was probably a few years older than me.

"Good morning," I said, extending my hand. "I'm an American."

He smiled and took my hand. "No kidding," he said. "Could have fooled me."

"And here's something you've probably never heard before," I said, "My ancestors are from Great Yarmouth, and they attended St. Nicholas."

"Wonderful," he said. "You probably want to come in and take a look around."

He unlocked the outside gate and headed for the front door.

"You'll have to excuse me," he said as he opened the door. "I have to prepare the communion. You're welcome to join us."

I followed him in.

Like many of the great medieval cathedrals, St. Nicholas Church was built in the shape of a cross, positioned with the top of the cross where the altar sits facing the east. The members of the congregation traditionally enter doors at the west end and, during services, face the east so that they can see the rising sun shining through the stained-glass windows onto the altar. At St. Nicholas, the entrance is situated at the southwest corner of the sanctuary.

Inside, the center aisle and two columns of pews where the members of the congregation sit is called the nave. The origin of the word is not exactly clear, but it is thought to be derived from the Latin word for "ship." Traditionally, there will be two narrow aisles on either side of the nave, but St. Nicholas is unusual—indeed, a church brochure claims it is unique—in that the side aisles are actually wider than the nave, making it an especially large area for worshippers. The cross's crossbeam, called the transept, is where the elevated pulpit and lecterns are located, accessible by climbing small circular staircases. Behind them is the chancel area, where the choir and organ are positioned, and beyond that, at the top of the cross, is the high altar.

A booklet published by the church, called "The Priory and Parish Church of St. Nicholas," described its splendor just before the Reformation:

> It was then open from end to end; the windows were filled with stained glass, tapestries hung on the walls and the walls were covered with polychromatic decoration and the floor enriched with sepulchral brasses.
>
> Candles burned night and day before the images of saints, which were dispersed throughout the church.
>
> In 1465 it was noted that twenty pence was paid for making a ship which was suspended from the roof as an emblem of St. Nicholas.

That same year, a magnificent organ was installed.

But the early years of the Reformation were not kind to St. Nicholas Church. Great Yarmouth's close proximity to the Netherlands, where Calvinist traditions were strong, exposed it to early Protestant influences, which resulted in sometimes violent clashes.

In 1535, for example, as an Anglican mass was being said, a riot broke out, led by Protestant chaplain William Swanton, who loudly proclaimed, "No honour should be given by lights to saints or pictures and images within the church." Swanton also famously mocked the holy water being used during mass, saying it made a good sauce for capons. Then, in 1541, four local merchants disrupted communion just as the host was being elevated. Each of them was fined two shillings for their outburst.

As the sixteenth century progressed, and the Reformation movement gained traction, things only got uglier. The stained-glass windows
were smashed, all images of saints were destroyed, the gold chalices
were melted down, and the tall steeple was dismantled. In the cemetery
many headstones were removed because the Protestants believed their
elaborate decorations smacked of idol worship.

By the middle of the seventeenth century, the interior of
St. Nicholas had been divided into three separate areas, partitioned by
brick walls, to accommodate the various Protestant sects. The chancel
area was used by the so-called Independents, the Presbyterians took
over the north aisle, and the larger Protestant congregation used the
south aisle and the nave. For the next two hundred years, as congregations came and went, parts of the church were abandoned and fell into
disrepair. Then, in 1844, the brick walls were taken down and an effort
was begun to restore St. Nicholas to its previous glory, this time of
course as an Anglican parish.

In the early morning hours of June 25, 1942, a German bombing
raid badly damaged the church. Yet another reconstruction project was
begun after the war, and it was completed in 1961.

Today, St. Nicholas has the look and feel of a museum because
of the number of memorial plaques hanging everywhere. The dates
on them range from the early 1700s to the present. Above the doorway
to the vestry, I spotted the plaque I had been looking for:

WILLIAM TOWNE AND JOANNA BLESSING
WERE MARRIED IN THIS CHURCH ON 25 APRIL 1620
AND SIX OF THEIR EIGHT CHILDREN WERE BAPTIZED HERE.
THEY FOUNDED THE TOWNE FAMILY IN AMERICA.
TWO OF THEIR CHILDREN, REBECCA AND MARY,
WERE EXECUTED DURING THE SALEM WITCHCRAFT DELUSION
IN THE 1690S.

Members of the American Towne family had had the plaque placed there in 1961 to commemorate the family's close ties to this parish, which extended back more than four hundred years.

My cousin LeAnne's family tree said patriarch William, my nine-times great-grandfather, was born March 18, 1599, in Great Yarmouth. His wife Joanna Blessing's birth date is not known. As the plaque in St. Nicholas Church said, they were married April 25, 1620, and six of their children were christened there:

> Rebecca: February 21, 1621
> John: February 16, 1623
> Susanna: October 20, 1625
> Edmund: June 28, 1628
> Jacob: March 11, 1632

Their sixth child, my eight-times great-grandmother Mary, was christened August 24, 1634. Two more children, Sarah and Joseph, were born and baptized after the family moved to New England.

George and Frances Woolsey's three sons were also christened at St. Nicholas:

> John: October 27, 1611
> Robert: March 13, 1613

My nine-times great-grandfather, George junior, was christened May 15, 1616.

Did the Woolseys and the Townes know each other? Great Yarmouth was a pretty good-sized town in the early seventeenth century, so it is possible that they didn't. But still, they did attend the same church and the youngest Woolsey child was baptized only four years before the Townes were married. At the very least, I have to believe that a Woolsey and a Towne passed each other in the marketplace; maybe they tipped their hats to each other or exchanged pleasantries as they shopped for fish or produce.

The time grew closer for the communion service to begin. A few people had gathered in the chancel area of the church near the high altar. A middle-aged woman in a cleric's collar was standing with the other people, engaged in animated conversation. One of the men in the group leaned toward her and said something and she threw her head back and howled with laughter. The sound echoed into the rafters. She was about my height and wore her brown hair quite short. When she spied me, she beckoned to me to sit next to her in the front row.

"Welcome," she said as we shook hands.

The priest who had greeted me out front appeared wearing a cream-colored robe and a lime green stole. I glanced around me. There were only eight of us. I noticed that the man sitting in the pew behind me was also wearing a cleric's collar. That made three priests in attendance. A few rows back, I saw another. That made four. Only later did I find out that these seven people made up the St. Nicholas clerical and administrative staff, and this was their private weekly communion service that I had crashed.

The priest leading the service began without any great ceremony. He welcomed the American who was in Great Yarmouth searching for his roots, and then he joked that after he had rushed to church to prepare for the service, he looked at the schedule and realized that he wasn't scheduled to lead this service, his lovely wife was.

The lady priest next to me howled again. This was his wife.

The priest continued, "This morning we are to remember Saint Alphege, who was martyred on this date almost one thousand years ago."

He told the story of a young man born into wealth who had given it all up to become a monk. In 984 Alphege became Bishop of Winchester, and in 1005 he was made Archbishop of Canterbury, where he was revered for his austere lifestyle and his great charity. In September of 1011, when the Danes invaded southeast England, they took

Archbishop Alphege prisoner and placed a ransom of three thousand pounds on his head. But Alphege forbade anyone from paying it, knowing that the money would have to come from the poor people of his parishes. After seven months in captivity, Alphege was executed by his captors on April 19, 1012.

The priest said, "Let us pray:

"Merciful God, who raised up your servant Alphege to be a pastor of your people and gave him grace to suffer for justice and true religion: Grant that we who celebrate his martyrdom may know the power of the risen Christ in our hearts and share his peace in lives offered to your service; through Jesus Christ your son our Lord, who is alive and reigns with you, in the unity of the Holy Spirit, one God, now and for ever."

By now my mind had begun to wander. I looked past the priest at the altar behind him. Presumably, this was where William Towne and Joanna Blessing were married. The priest would have conducted the service as outlined in the Book of Common Prayer, the same service used in Anglican churches today:

At the day appointed for Solemnization of Matrimony, the persons to be married shall come into the body of the church, with their friends and neighbors. And there the priest shall thus say:

"Dearly beloved friends, we are gathered together here in the sight of God, and in the face of his congregation, to join together this man and this woman in holy matrimony, which is an honorable estate, instituted, of God in paradise in the time of man's innocency, signifying unto us the mystical union, that is betwixt Christ and his Church . . ."

Then shall the curate say unto the man:

"Wilt thou have this woman to thy wedded wife, to live together after God's ordinance in the holy estate of matrimony? Wilt thou love her, comfort her, honor and keep her, in sickness, and in health? And forsaking all others, keep thee only to her, so long as you both shall live?"

. . . Then the priest shall say to the woman:

"Wilt thou have this man to thy wedded husband, to live together after God's ordinance in the holy estate of matrimony? Wilt thou obey him and serve him, love, honor, and keep him, in sickness, and in health? And forsaking all others, keep thee only unto him, so long as you both shall live?"

. . . Then shall the minister speak unto the people:

"Forasmuch as William and Joanna have consented together in holy wedlock, and have witnessed the same before God and this company, and thereto have given and pledged their troth either to other, and have declared the same by giving and receiving of a ring, and by joining of hands: I pronounce that they be man and wife together . . ."

Near the end of the service, the priest would recite the following prayer:

O merciful Lord and heavenly Father, by whose gracious gift mankind is increased: We beseech thee assist with thy blessing these two persons, that they may both be fruitful in procreation of children, and also live together so long in godly love and honesty, that they may see their children's children, unto the third and fourth generation, unto thy praise and honor.

MY ANCESTORS George Woolsey Jr. and Mary Towne would have been baptized following the service described in the Book of Common Prayer. After a number of prayers and readings, the book instructed the priest

to take the child in his hands and ask the name, and naming the child shall dip it in the water so it be discreetly and warily done, saying,

"I baptize thee in the name of the Father, and of the Son, and of the Holy Ghost. Amen."

Then the priest shall make a cross upon the child's forehead, saying,

"We receive this child into the congregation of Christ's flock, and do sign him with the sign of the cross, in token that hereafter he shall not be ashamed to confess the faith of Christ crucified, and manfully to fight under his banner against sin, the world, and the devil, and to continue Christ's faithful soldier and servant unto his life's end. Amen."

It was time for communion to be served in our small private service. We approached the altar in pairs and knelt at the railing.

The priest handed me the wafer. "The body of Christ," he said, "given for you." I placed it in my mouth, and allowed it to melt on my tongue. Then he lifted the chalice to my mouth, and I took a sip. "The blood of Christ, given for you," he said.

After everyone had been served, we read the closing prayer together:

"God, who gave us this holy meal in which we have celebrated the glory of the cross and the victory of your martyr Alphege: By our communion with Christ in his saving death and resurrection, give us with all your saints the courage to conquer evil and so to share the fruit of the tree of life; through Jesus Christ our Lord. Amen."

The priest disappeared into the vestry and the rest of the staff dispersed to begin their day. His wife stayed back to chat with me for a few minutes. I told her briefly about the Townes and the Woolseys, then we shook hands and I thanked her for the hospitality and headed out the south entrance back to town.

THE DATES in my cousin's family tree indicate approximately when my ancestors left England, but they don't tell why. Were they threatened or maybe even attacked? I have no way of knowing.

After James I ascended to the throne, he met with Puritan leaders during the Hampton Court Conference in 1604 and rejected all but one of their ideas about reforming the Church of England. (The one idea he agreed to was a new English translation of the Bible, which was published in 1611. Today we remember it as the King James Bible.)

Relations between the monarchy and the Puritans deteriorated further when James died in 1625 and his twenty-five-year-old son became King Charles I. By then the Puritans had gained a majority in the House of Commons, and they often found themselves at odds with the king on a number of issues, especially when it came to funding his military campaigns in Spain and France. In March of 1629, Charles forced the adjournment of Parliament and did not call for another session until 1640.

In 1633, William Laud became Archbishop of Canterbury, the most powerful clergyman in the Church of England. He was a very conservative Anglican who began a campaign to rid the church of "dissenters," as the Puritans were known.

Laud instructed all churches to conduct services in strict accordance with the Book of Common Prayer, which the Puritans opposed. He required all priests to wear the formal gowns called surplices and all church members to bow at the mention of the name of Jesus Christ. And he called for a curtailment of sermons, or "lectureships" as he called them, which the Puritans regarded as the centerpiece of all worship.

The archbishop did not tolerate opposition. He was quick to imprison and execute such prominent Puritan leaders as Alexander Leighton and William Prynne.

William Bradford, writing years later about that period, described the difficult conditions English dissenters faced.

"Religion hath been disgraced, the godly grieved, afflicted, persecuted, and many exiled; sundry have lost their lives in prisons and other ways. On the other hand, sin hath been countenanced; ignorance, profaneness and atheism increased, and the papists encouraged to hope again for a day."

The Puritans had a choice: abandon their efforts to reform the Church of England and become strict Anglicans, or leave the country.

My guess is George and Frances Woolsey, who probably moved to Rotterdam soon after their third son, my nine-times great-grandfather George junior, was baptized in 1616, chose to leave England for economic reasons. George senior, who would have been in his early thirties around that time, had been a merchant. Public records referred to him variously as a grocer and a tobacconist. And since Rotterdam had become an important trading port, it is entirely possible that the opportunities for a young businessman with a growing family would have been greater there than they were in Great Yarmouth. The fact that George junior later migrated to the New Amsterdam Colony in America, probably as an employee of the West India Trading Company, supports that notion.

The Towne family is a different story. My guess is they left for religious reasons not long after their sixth child, my eight-times great-grandmother Mary, was baptized in 1634 while Archbishop Laud's campaign was in full swing. Leaving England for America in the seventeenth century must have been a daunting task for anyone. Leaving England for America with six children must have been next to impossible, but that is what the Townes did, and for that reason I have to believe they felt they had no other choice.

MY ALARM clock's bell sounded at five-thirty the next morning, but I was already awake. It had been one of those nights when I woke up every hour because I didn't want to oversleep. I had a long morning ahead of me. My train from Great Yarmouth would arrive back at Liverpool Station in London at 9:00 A.M. From there I would take a cab to City Airport, where I would catch the ten-thirty flight to the Netherlands. But first I had to catch a cab to the train station.

I jumped out of bed, caught a quick shower, threw my clothes on, and headed out the door. Outside the air was chilly and the marine layer covered the horizon the way it had the day before. I looked at my watch—5:55.

Off in the distance I heard the sound of a car heading my way. When it was close enough, I could see the taxi light on the roof. It stopped in front of me and out jumped Keith.

"Good morning, Mr. Griffeth," he said as he grabbed my bags and threw them in the trunk.

"Good morning, Keith. Right on time."

"Yes, sir," he said as we both climbed into the car. "Did you find what you were looking for?"

"Yes," I said. "I did, actually."

And we drove off to the train station with the sun rising behind us.

Chapter Two

THE NETHERLANDS, 1608–1640

The Separatists

IN THE SPRING, when the snow pack in the northern Alps melts, the water is pushed along by a network of rivers to the European continent's low-lying northern shores, where it combines with the rainwater that blows in off the North Sea. It lingers there in giant pools of swampy marshland, submerging tens of thousands of acres of land like an *über* high-tide.

The earliest inhabitants of the region, who were descendants of the Celts from the north and various Germanic tribes from the south, took control of the flooding cycle and reclaimed the land in ingenious ways, rerouting the water through a complex network of dikes and canals. They planted crops in the fertile soil and raised their livestock, and when the floods overwhelmed the canals, which happened frequently, they simply dealt with it. It was a risk they were willing to tolerate patiently.

Tolerance and *patience*. Those are the words most often used to describe the people of the Netherlands. Their English neighbors to the north insisted on calling them Dutch, an anglicized corruption of the German *Deutsch* they mistakenly believed them to be. Tellingly, rather than correct the mistake, the Netherlanders simply tolerated it and adopted the nickname.

It was this tolerance that attracted religious refugees during the seventeenth century: Jews who had been driven from Spain, Catholics who found conditions difficult in Protestant Germany, French Walloons who left what is now Belgium, and Separatists who fled King James's England.

The group from Scrooby arrived in Amsterdam in August of 1608.

According to William Bradford, they were overwhelmed by the culture shock:

"They heard a strange and uncouth language, and beheld the different manners and customs of the people, with their strange fashions and attires; all so differing from that of their plain country villages . . . as it seemed they were come into a new world."

They realized right away that their biggest challenge would be to find work. A city the size of Amsterdam offered myriad opportunities for skilled laborers, but most of the members of the congregation were farmers, so it became clear that they would have to start over at the bottom of the economic ladder.

"But they were armed with faith and patience," wrote Bradford, "and though they were sometimes foiled, yet by God's assistance they prevailed and got the victory."

They had expected to be a part of a larger outpost of English expatriates. But after six months, many of them wanted out because of theological conflicts that persisted. Without the uniformity of a centralized church, the Puritans and Separatists were left to form their own traditions and doctrines, and inevitably the personal freedom that Protestantism allowed led to differences of opinion. Who was to say, for example, that one congregation's decision to delay baptism until adulthood was more or less correct than another's decision to baptize infants?

So most of the Scrooby congregation decided to move on. In early February of 1609, John Robinson sent a letter to officials in Leiden, a bustling village twenty-two miles south of Amsterdam, requesting permission for his flock to settle there:

To the Honorable the Burgomasters, and Court, of the City of Leyden:

With due submission and respect, John Robinson, Minister of the Divine Word, and some of the members of the Christian Reformed Religion, born in the Kingdom of Great Britain, to the number of one hundred persons or thereabouts, men and women, represent that they desire to come to live in this city by the first of May next, and to have the freedom thereof in carrying on their trades, without being a burden in the least to any one.

They, therefore, address themselves to Your Honors, humbly praying that Your Honors will be pleased to grant them free consent to betake themselves, as aforesaid.

Almost immediately, a letter dated February 12 returned with welcome news:

The Court, in making a disposition of this present Memorial, declare that they refuse no honest persons free ingress to come and have their residence in this city, provided that such persons behave themselves, and submit to the laws and ordinances: and, therefore, the coming of the memorialists will be agreeable and welcome.

And so, in May of 1609, they headed south to the village that would be their home for at least the next eleven years. Some would never leave.

LEIDEN

The morning I flew into Amsterdam, a thick blanket of clouds hid the landscape. Seconds before the jet landed, it emerged from the clouds to reveal the lush green fields and miles of canals that characterize the Dutch landscape. As we taxied to our gate, a heavy rain splattered against the windows.

After clearing customs, I took the escalator to the train station directly below Schipol Airport, where I caught a train for the fifteen-minute ride south to Leiden. Outside the Centraal Station there, I jogged the few hundred yards in the rain to my hotel on the outskirts of town. I checked in, changed into dry clothes and slept for a few hours. When I woke up around noon, the skies had cleared so I headed into town.

From the air, Leiden looks like a giant pretzel. The canal that surrounds it defines its distinctly elliptical shape, and the two strands of the Rhine that enter from the east converge almost precisely in the middle of town before exiting as a unified river to the west.

Walking south from my hotel, I crossed a few bridges, dodging cars and bicycles as I made my way toward the center of town. I was immediately charmed by its beauty. Leiden is a city of cobblestones and canals that is still laid out almost exactly the way it was when the Scrooby Separatists arrived more than four hundred years ago.

I walked along the Rapenburg Canal on the west side of town, where rows of very handsome brick apartments line both sides, and where rows of small cars sit parked at the water's edge. Bradford wrote glowingly of his new home, calling it "a fair and bewtifull citie, and of a sweet situation."

Leiden forever earned its place in Dutch history when Spanish forces surrounded the city on October 31, 1573, cutting it off from the outside. The plan was to force a surrender by starving the people. And starve they did, but they also held their ground at the behest of their beloved leader, William the Silent, the legendary Prince of Orange considered the father of the Dutch Republic.

By the following summer, with both sides stubbornly holding their ground and hundreds of people dying from starvation, the decision was made to flood the area by destroying some of the dikes, which would drive the invaders away and allow Dutch boats to bring in badly needed supplies.

Easier said than done. The first dikes were breached on August 1, but the water level only rose by a foot. On September 11, more dikes were pierced, but water levels still didn't rise enough to accommodate supply boats until early October, when Mother Nature intervened to complete the mission. Gale-force winds from the south pushed the water level high enough to allow the boats to enter the city from the south via the Vliet River on Sunday, October 3.

According to Dutch lore, thousands of citizens immediately paraded their rescuers to St. Peter's Cathedral, or Pieterskerk, where they gave thanks for their good fortune and triumphantly sang the words of Psalm 9:

> *I will give thanks to the Lord*
> > *With my whole heart;*
> *I will tell of all your wonderful*
> > *Deeds.*
> *I will be glad and exult in you;*
> > *I will sing praise to your name,*
> > *O Most High.*
> *When my enemies turned back,*
> > *They stumbled and perished*
> > > *Before you.*
> *For you have maintained my just cause;*
> > *You have sat on the throne*
> > > *Giving righteous judgment.*

(Psalms 9:1–4)

Afterwards, the whole town enjoyed a day of thanksgiving, which included a feast of fish and vegetables and breads, an annual tradition the Separatists would take with them to New England.

After the year-long siege was over, William the Silent rewarded the people of Leiden by offering them a choice: they would no longer have to pay taxes, or they could be home to a new university. The people chose the latter. The University of Leiden was initially housed in old convents that had been seized during the Reformation, and within a generation it became a world-class institution, drawing professors and students from all over Europe.

I turned left off the Rapenburg Canal and headed east on Kloksteeg, or Bell Lane, into the Pieterskerk courtyard. Before me stood the great Gothic cathedral built in 1390.

On the north side of the courtyard was a row of small apartments that once housed a group of French Walloons. Around the corner from them was the Latin School where the young Rembrandt studied around 1615 to 1620. But I was most interested in the building facing the cathedral from the south side of the courtyard. It was here that John Robinson and some of the members of his congregation lived and where all of them worshipped during their time in Leiden.

In 1611, Robinson and three members of his congregation pooled their funds to buy the private residence called Groenepoort, or Green Door. There were many reasons to like it. First, it was centrally located in Leiden, making it accessible for the Separatists no matter where they lived in town. Second, the primary home on the property was large enough for Robinson to accommodate his growing congregation during worship services. Third, and most important, the estate included a parcel of land in the back large enough to build twenty-one cottages for members of the congregation who couldn't afford to live anywhere else in town. Robinson and company paid the hefty sum of 8,000 guilders for the property by first making a down payment of 2,000 guilders and promising to make annual payments of 500 guilders thereafter. It had to be a great financial burden for the English newcomers, who right away had to take low-paying jobs for unskilled labor. In those days a skilled cloth dyer earned roughly 400 guilders a year, and a journeyman potter earned more than 500 guilders a year.

The building on the site today was built in 1680, and next to the front door there is a plaque that reads:

ON THIS SPOT
LIVED, TAUGHT AND DIED
JOHN ROBINSON
1611–1625

Even though they obviously enjoyed a good relationship with the Dutch Calvinists in Pieterskerk, Robinson and his congregation did not worship there. Instead they chose to worship privately in Robinson's home, under his direct leadership, which they had been forbidden to do in England.

Bradford wrote fondly of that time:

"So as they grew in knowledge and other gifts and graces of the Spirit of God, and lived together in peace and love and holiness, and many came unto them from divers parts of England, so as they grew a great congregation."

That would include my nine-times great-grandparents, John and Sarah Jenney. Neither of them was from Scrooby, and records don't indicate when they joined the congregation in Leiden. John was born in 1585 in Norwich, just north of Great Yarmouth in Norfolk County. Sarah was born in Suffolk in 1590.

Their marriage certificate, which is part of the Pilgrim Archives in Leiden, says they were betrothed on Friday, September 5, 1614, and married almost a month later on Saturday, November 1. Theirs was a civil ceremony, a Dutch invention made law in 1590 to accommodate religious refugees who couldn't set foot in Dutch Reformed churches.

I have no way of knowing for sure, but based on the information I have gathered, I suspect John Jenney may have been one of the many young Englishmen from Norfolk who moved to the Netherlands to join the so-called Scottish Brigade, the militia formed during Elizabeth's reign and continued under James I to protect the Dutch from Spanish invasion.

The Jenneys' marriage certificate says that John had been a resident of Rotterdam at the time of the wedding. John's hometown of Norwich had developed a strong connection with Rotterdam in the late 1500s because of the influx of Dutch refugees, the Elizabethan Strangers who fled Spanish persecutors and took up residence in Norfolk, many of them in Norwich, where they jumpstarted the area's textile industry.

At some point he was drawn to Leiden, perhaps because he had known John Robinson at St. Andrews parish in Norwich, where Robinson had served before joining the Separatist congregation. During a visit to Leiden, the young Sarah Carey must have caught his eye.

The Jenneys eventually settled in a home on Veldestraat, or Field Street. Most of the homes in Leiden were of modest size, usually with two rooms each measuring roughly twenty by twenty feet. The front room would have been used as a sitting room furnished with chairs, tables, and a cabinet for dishes or clothing. Most often, a small alcove was built near the fireplace for a bed, usually for the adults in the family. The backroom would have been the home's private quarters, another Dutch invention, inaccessible to guests. This is where the meals would have been cooked and eaten, and most often where the children slept near the hearth, unless there was room above for a loft.

Almost immediately the Jenneys began a family. Their oldest, my eight-times great-grandfather Samuel, was born in 1616. A daughter named Ann followed in 1618, but she died shortly after birth and was buried in Pieterskerk on June 16. Another daughter, Abigail, was born a year later, in April of 1619.

The Jenneys were devout Christians. Nathaniel Morton, who was ten years old when he accompanied them to America in 1623, later described John as a godly man "singular for his publicness of spirit." And Edward Winslow, in his memoir published years later in Plymouth, remembered that the Jenneys were comfortable worshipping—even taking communion—with the Calvinists in Pieterskerk.

The Jenneys' marriage certificate listed John's occupation as a brewer's mate, so it is likely that during his time in Rotterdam, he apprenticed in that trade. Brewing had long been a thriving business in Holland, and the beer and ale made there was a very popular and profitable export. In Leiden, John found work as a brewer. Because of the inconsistency of the quality of water, beer was consumed by adults and children, so qualified brewers were always in great demand.

At least twice a week, the Jenneys gathered with the other members of their Separatist congregation at John Robinson's Groenepoort to worship and to listen to his teachings. The other members included people who would later become well known as Mayflower Pilgrims:

- William Brewster, the congregation's ruling elder. Next to John Robinson, Brewster was the congregation's most important member.
- John Carver, an astute businessman who may have arrived in Leiden before the Separatists, but he became a Deacon in the congregation. He married a French Walloon, Mary de La Noy, whose name was later anglicized in America to Delano, and carried down through the generations to her most famous descendant, Franklin Roosevelt. Carver and his first wife, Sara, had a son, Thomas, the year before the Separatists migrated to the Lowlands. Two other children born in Leiden died in infancy and were buried in Pieterskerk. Sara died in 1615.
- Robert Cushman, born in 1577 in Kent. He had worked as a grocer in England, but in Leiden, as so often happened to the expatriates who took whatever job they could get, he found work

as a wool comber in the city's prosperous textile industry. Robert married Mary Singleton in 1617.

- Isaac Allerton, a highly ambitious tailor from London who was a very bright, enterprising, aggressive entrepreneur—maybe too aggressive. His organizational skills made him a valuable member of the congregation when they journeyed to Plymouth, but his push for a profit got him into trouble. By the time he was forced to leave Plymouth in 1633 on charges of financial misconduct, he had become the colony's wealthiest citizen. He first moved north to the larger Massachusetts Bay Colony, and later he headed south to the New Amsterdam Colony, where he owned a large warehouse managed by his assistant, my ancestor George Woolsey. (Much more about that later.) Allerton and his wife, Mary, had three children, Bartholomew, Remember, and Mary, all of whom journeyed to Plymouth on the *Mayflower*.

- Edward Winslow, the diplomat and writer, who discovered the Separatist congregation during a tour through the Low Countries. In 1618 he married Elizabeth Barker and set up shop as a printer.

These and many other members of John Robinson's flock no doubt felt they had found a suitable home in Leiden where they could achieve the holy lifestyle that had been denied them in England. But the greatest adventure of their lives was still ahead of them.

ON SUNDAYS the doors to St. Pieterskerk open to the public at 2:00 P.M. My watch said 1:55 as I arrived in the courtyard. I decided to walk around the cathedral's perimeter first. Much to my dismay, most of Pieterskerk's exterior was covered with scaffolding because of an extensive renovation that was under way. The roof, all the windows, and some of the wooden eaves were being replaced, and the stone walls were being scrubbed clean. I was disappointed that I wouldn't get to see this great Gothic cathedral in its natural state, but at the same time

I was encouraged to see that the city was taking good care of it. Like most of the great European cathedrals, Pieterskerk has a long, unpredictable history.

A small chapel was first built on the site around 1100 for use by the ruling counts of Holland who lived in the area. In 1268 the chapel became a parish church to accommodate the city's growing population, and a larger structure was begun. In 1350 an enormous 330-foot tower was built at the foot of the church. Even though Leiden is five miles inland from the North Sea, the tower was visible to the fishermen at sea. It was called Coningh der Zee, or "King of the Sea." The tower collapsed in 1512 and was never replaced.

In 1390, work was begun on the cathedral that stands today. Construction was completed 180 years later in 1570. The completed Pieterskerk served the Church in Rome for only two years before the Reformation came to Leiden in 1572 and it was converted to a Dutch Reformed Church.

By 1971 the size of the Reformed community in Leiden had declined enough that it could no longer support all three of the parish churches in town, so Pieterskerk was closed because it was the oldest and most in need of repair. But what to do with such an important piece of history? A debate raged for three years. One faction advocated selling the building to the university, while another argued for turning it into a parking garage. In the end, a foundation was formed and funds were raised to preserve the cathedral and turn it into a venue for concerts and conventions.

I had completed my walk around the church and returned to the large wooden doors on the north side just as they were being opened by two elderly women in matching powder blue sweatshirts. I followed them in and began my tour.

Pieterskerk had once been a typical medieval Roman Catholic cathedral with thirty-five altars and images of more than fifty saints hanging everywhere. When the Reformation arrived, it was stripped bare, just as St. Nicholas had been in Great Yarmouth.

Today, because it serves as an assembly hall, the ceiling has been painted white and huge golden chandeliers hang throughout to give it a bright, cheery feel, but there are still plenty of things to remind those assembled of the great cathedral's sacred past. There is the splendid dark wooden pulpit, built in 1532, that towers over the center aisle of the nave. The octagonal sounding board above it was installed in 1604. The Bible verse carved into it reads, "I am the way, the truth and the life."

Pieterskerk once housed five altars dedicated to the trade unions or guilds that were so important to Leiden's booming economy in the sixteenth century. During the Reformation the altars were replaced by plaques called Guild Boards, each bearing its own biblical text. The carpenters' board, for example, begins "He who buildeth on sand is foolish." The tailors' board reads, "If thou seest a naked person, so dress him."

During the Middle Ages, European congregations began to bury their local clergy and nobility inside the churches so that they could rest eternally near the remains of a saint who might also be buried there. But over the centuries this practice became a source of income for the church, and any sufficiently wealthy person could pay to be buried inside.

The skeletal remains of all who had been buried in Pieterskerk were removed in the nineteenth century, but the stone grave markers were carefully restored so that today the floor in Pieterskerk is a patchwork of carved black stone. Only the wealthiest could afford stone markers with their names on them. Most of the graves were covered by plain slabs.

Many members of the English Separatist community were buried in Pieterskerk, a number of them children. There is a plaque on a wall outside that lists some of the members of the community who buried loved ones inside, including Robert Cushman, who buried his wife and child in 1616, and Isaac Allerton, who buried a child there in 1620. John and Sarah Jenney buried their second child there, an infant daughter they named Ann, on Saturday, June 16, 1618.

And a few famous people from that era were also buried there, including the painter Jan Steen (c. 1625–1679), a prolific contemporary of Rembrandt's known for his many festive paintings of large feasts and celebrations. Despite being a devout Catholic, Steen's popularity in his hometown earned him a place in Pieterskerk when he died.

And there was the controversial Dutch Reformed theologian Jacobus Arminius (1560–1609). Arminius had served in the ministry from 1588 until 1603, when, at the age of forty-three, he became a professor of theology at the University of Leiden, where he taught a more liberal interpretation of Calvinist doctrine, especially on the important issue of predestination.

John Calvin believed that God's will and authority were absolute, and to make his point he theorized that God decided which humans would achieve salvation (the so-called Elect) and which would suffer damnation. And there was nothing any human could do to change that. According to Calvin, the course of everyone's eternal journey is predetermined. And just as Luther had turned to the Apostle Paul for guidance, Calvin cited a passage from the letter to the Romans to justify his position:

"For those whom he foreknew he also predestined to be conformed to the image of his Son, in order that he might be the first-born among

many brethren. And those whom he predestined he also called; and those whom he called he also justified; and those whom he justified he also glorified." (Romans 8:29–30)

But second- and third-generation Protestants were willing to embrace the power and independence of the human being that blossomed during the Renaissance. Arminius modified Calvin's doctrine of predestination by theorizing that humans had some control over their destinies by exercising their free will, and, just as important, God was merciful enough to allow it.

After Arminius's death in 1609, a group of forty-five ministers who agreed with him submitted a document known as the Remonstrance to the Dutch government for its approval. It sparked a debate that resulted in one of the most important theological conventions in Protestant history. A council of churches known as a synod was convened in Dortrecht in November of 1618 largely to debate the merits of the movement that had come to be known as Arminianism.

The Calvinist viewpoint was presented by a former colleague of Arminius at the University of Leiden named Franciscus Gomarus, and the Remonstrants, or protesters, were represented by Simon Episcopius, a liberal Dutch theologian who had carefully systematized the Arminian view.

When the synod ended in May of 1619 the Arminian view had been rejected and a document called the Canons of Dort was produced, detailing the Reformist view on a number of issues. Along with two other documents—the Belgic Confession and the Heidelberg Catechism—the Canons formed the belief system for the Reformed churches in Europe and later in the United States.

As for the Arminians, initially they were expelled from the Netherlands altogether, but by 1630 Dutch tolerance prevailed once again and Arminianism was acknowledged as a legitimate wing of the Dutch Reformed Church. More than a century later its doctrine would be embraced by a group of theological students at Oxford University in England. Their leader, John Wesley, borrowed from it liberally, most especially the beliefs about God's unending mercy, for what would become the Methodist movement in England and in America.

In its most basic form, the Reformed doctrine that emerged from the Synod of Dort is represented by the acronym TULIP that Presbyterian and Reformed Sunday Schools still teach today:

TOTAL DEPRAVITY. The Reformers believed that humans were inherently sinful, incapable of goodness and devoid of spiritual tendencies without God's help. As Paul wrote to the citizens of Rome: "There is none righteous, no, not one; there is none who understands; there is none who seeks after God. They have all turned aside; they have together become unprofitable; there is none who does good, no not one." (Romans 3:10–12)

UNCONDITIONAL ELECTION. Did God choose to save certain people because of their faith, or did the people have faith because they had been chosen? The Reformers said "neither." They believed that God did not attach any conditions to those selected for salvation. And while it was always assumed that anyone among the Elect would be a godly person of faith, that was not an automatic tip-off. Salvation was God's gift, not something to be earned.

LIMITED ATONEMENT. The Reformers did not believe in a universal salvation; instead they believed that Jesus had died on the cross to atone for the Elect only. As brutal as it may sound, all others were condemned to eternal damnation.

IRRESISTIBLE GRACE. What if someone didn't want to be saved? Too bad, the Reformers said, because the grace God bestowed on the Elect could not be deflected.

PERSEVERANCE OF THE SAINTS. This one was pretty clear. Once someone had been chosen for salvation, it was impossible for him or her to fall from grace. Just as damnation for the non-Elect is eternal, so is salvation for the Elect.

John Robinson was asked to contribute to the debate at the Synod of Dort, and, not surprisingly, he sided with Gomarus. Robinson and his Separatist flock were strict Calvinists. They believed themselves to

be among the Elect that God had chosen for salvation. It was this belief
more than anything else that gave them the confidence to pursue their
risky journeys, first to the European Low Countries and later to the
American wilderness.

As strict Calvinists, the Separatists recognized only two sacraments,
baptism and communion, and like all Protestants they rejected the
elaborate religious rituals and symbolism found in Catholic churches
as the invention of mortal men and not of God, and opted instead for a
plain meetinghouse devoid of any decoration or symbolism. That
would explain their willingness to continue worshipping in John
Robinson's Groenepoort during their time in Leiden.

In Pieterskerk's baptistery, in the southwest corner of the cathedral, there is a tribute to Robinson and the Pilgrims.

The plaque reads:

In Memory Of
JOHN ROBINSON
Pastor of the English Church in Leyden
1609 1625
His Broadly Tolerant Mind
Guided and Developed the Religious Life of
THE PILGRIMS OF THE MAYFLOWER
Of Him These Walls Enshrine
All That Was Mortal
His Undying Spirit
Still Dominates the Consciences of
A Mighty Nation
In the Land Beyond the Seas

This Tablet Was Erected By the General Society
of Mayflowre
Descendents in the United States of America A.D. 1928

Robinson had obviously gained the respect of his fellow scholars at the university, but this charismatic preacher had also become indispensable to the members of his own congregation. This is how Bradford characterized the relationship between the shepherd and his sheep:

> Yea, such was the mutual love and reciprocal respect that this worthy man had to his flock, and his flock to him, that it might be said of them as it once was of that famous Emperor Marcus Aurelius and the people of Rome, that it was hard to judge whether he delighted more in having such a people, or they in having such a pastor. His love was great towards them, and his care was always bent for their best good, both for soul and body. For besides his singular abilities in divine things (wherein he excelled) he was also very able to give direction in civic affairs and to foresee dangers and inconveniences, by which means he was very helpful to their outward estates and so was every way as a common father unto them.

Next to it is a photograph taken on July 17, 1989, close to the anniversary of the day the first wave of Separatists left Leiden for the New World. The photo is of the first President Bush speaking to a gathering inside Pieterskerk that day. Next to the photo hangs a diagram outlining the president's family tree back to the Pilgrims. It was here that I discovered that George Bush's "Pilgrim ancestor" was my nine-times great-grandfather John Jenney.

By 1617, Leiden had begun to wear on many of the Separatists. The years of hard labor were taking their toll, and the Dutch tolerance for diversity that had been an attraction almost a decade earlier now began to irritate. For example, some of their Dutch neighbors thought nothing of pursuing leisure activities on the Sabbath, which included an odd ball-and-stick game imported from Scotland, which the Dutch called *kolf.* This didn't sit well with the English whose children were growing up and sometimes succumbing to these temptations. They may have separated themselves successfully from the popish influences of the Church of England, but they worried that they were losing their identities as Englishmen and were instead being absorbed into the Dutch culture.

And there were other reasons to worry: they found the growing Arminian challenge to their Calvinist beliefs a troubling development, and the end of the twelve-year truce between the Dutch and the Spanish was only three years away.

So, as Bradford recalled, "Like skillful and beaten soldiers [they] were fearful either to be entrapped or surrounded by their enemies so as they should neither be able to fight nor fly. And therefore thought it better to dislodge to some place of better advantage and less danger, if any such could be found."

Deacons Robert Cushman and John Carver were dispatched to London to find someone willing to finance their move, beginning with the group of investors called the Virginia Company, who had underwritten the Jamestown settlement.

To show how determined—or desperate—they were to leave the Low Countries, Cushman and Carver carried with them a document signed by Robinson and Brewster that offered seven statements of belief about the Church of England. It is hard to believe that the compromises offered here were genuine, since they endorsed the Anglican Church's Thirty-nine Articles and acknowledged the authority not only of King James I but also of the English bishops. Clearly the Separatists believed that these white lies were worth it if they succeeded in securing them passage out of Leiden and enough funds to begin their own separate colony.

❊ ❊ ❊

The Seven Articles

Seven Articles which the church of Leyden sent to the Council of England to be considered in respect of their judgments occasioned about their going to Virginia.

1. To the confession of faith published in the name of the Church of England and to every article thereof we do, with the Reformed Churches where we live, and also elsewhere, wholly assent. *[This one must have been especially hard for Robinson to profess since he had been dismissed from St. Andrew's parish in Norwich for refusing to follow the Thirty-nine Articles to the letter.]*

2. As we acknowledge the doctrine of faith there taught, so do we the fruits and effects of the same doctrine to the begetting of saving faith in the land (conformists and reformists) as they are called, with whom also, as with our bretheren, we do desire spiritual communion in peace, and will practice in our parts all lawful things.

3. The king's Majesty we acknowledge for Supreme Governor in his Dominion in all causes and over all persons, and that none may decline or appeal from his authority or judgment in any case whatsoever, but in all things obedience is due unto him, either active if the thing commanded be not against God's Word, or passive if it be, except pardon can be obtained.

4. We judge it lawful for his Majesty to appoint Bishops, civil overseers or officers in authority under him in the several provinces, dioceses, congregations or parishes to oversee the churches and govern them civilly according to the laws of the land, unto whom they are in all things to give an account, and by them to be ordered according to godliness.

5. The authority of the present Bishops in the land we do acknowledge so far forth as the same is indeed derived from his

majesty unto them, and as they proceed in his name whom we will also therein honour in all things and him in them.

6. We believe that no Synod, Classes, Convocation, or assembly of Ecclesiastical Officers hath any power or authority at all, but as the same by the magistrate is given unto them.

7. Lastly, we desire to give unto all Superiors due honour, to preserve the unity of the spirit with all that fear God, to have peace with all men what in us lieth, and wherein we err to be instructed by any.

❖ ❖ ❖

The Virginia Company made an initial offer, but to their credit Cushman and Carver had the fortitude to turn it down since they did not believe the terms were favorable enough. Negotiations continued on and off for another couple of years.

Meanwhile, back in Leiden, William Brewster and another Separatist, Thomas Brewer, set up a printing press in a shop a block east of Pieterskerk on the charmingly named Stink Alley. (Today it is known as Brewstersteeg or Brewster Alley.) The press was set up ostensibly to publish theological treatises promoting Separatist ideas that could be smuggled into England. They included such titles as *A Full and Plaine Declaration of Ecclesiastical Discipline* and *Certain Reasons of a Private Christian against Conformitie*.

They also published a number of scholarly works by John Robinson. A copy of one of the most famous, called *Justification for Separation*, found its way back to Norwich, where he was roundly criticized by his former colleagues at St. Andrew's parish.

This didn't sit well with authorities in London, so the English ambassador to The Hague, Sir Dudley Carleton, was dispatched to find the source of the rogue texts. On July 27, 1619, he wrote to King James, "I have seen within these two days, a certain Scottish book . . . written with much scorn and reproach . . . concerning the affairs of the church. It is without name either of author or printer; but I am informed it is printed by a certain English Brownist of Leyden as are most of the puritan books sent over of late days into England."

A few days later, on August 1, he wrote that he had determined the identity of the culprit:

"I believe I have discovered the printer . . . that is one William Brewster, a Brownist who hath been for some years an inhabitant and printer at Leyden but is now within these three weeks removed from thence, and gone back to dwell in London." That wasn't entirely the case. Brewster had in fact returned to London in May, but he had gone there with Robert Cushman merely to resume negotiations with the Virginia Company. The timing was merely fortuitous. If he had been in Leiden when the press on Stink Alley was raided by Dutch authorities on behalf of the English, Brewster would most certainly have been returned to English soil and sent to prison. Instead, he went into hiding somewhere in England.

In early September, authorities in Leiden informed Carleton that they had arrested Brewster, and the ambassador wrote triumphantly to his king. A few weeks later, though, Carleton was told that there had been a mixup of names. Mr. Brewster was not arrested after all. It was Mr. Brewer who had been taken into custody.

On September 22, a red-faced Carleton wrote, "In my last letter, I advertised . . . that Brewster was taken at Leyden, which proved an error in that the [bailiff] . . . being a dull drunken fellow, took one man for another. But Brewer . . . is fast in the University's prison."

Brewster never returned to Leiden. He remained in England until the following July, when he met his fellow Separatists in Southampton and continued on with them to America on the *Mayflower*.

By early 1620 it had become known around Leiden that some of the English who worshiped in Robinson's Groenepoort were eager to leave. So a group of Dutch traders made them an offer: free passage to the New Amsterdam Colony on Manhattan Island and enough provisions to help each family get a fresh start. As tempting as the offer may have seemed, the Separatists probably would have turned it down eventually. After all, their intent was to leave the Dutch culture and reestablish their English identities in a colony of their own.

Some members of the congregation had argued for going farther south, to the warmer climates in Guiana. As Bradford remembered it, they made it sound like a new Garden of Eden:

"Those for Guiana alleged that the country was rich and fruitful, and blessed with a perpetual spring and a flourishing greenness, where vigorous nature brought forth all things in abundance and plenty without any great labour or art of man."

Those who argued against Guiana reasoned that a group of Englishmen wouldn't be suited to the warmer climates, that they would be more susceptible to disease there, and that even if they were able to build a successful colony, the Spanish would probably take it from them just as they had taken Florida from the French.

Before they could respond to the Dutch offer, an aggressive English businessman named Thomas Weston showed up in Leiden with an offer of his own. He represented a group of investors who already held a land patent in the New World from the Virginia Company in the name of John Pierce. These investors, whom history remembers as the Merchant Adventurers of London, were willing to bankroll the group's journey to Virginia in return for a share of whatever the colony was able to produce.

This offer, too, was tempting, but the Separatists knew they would still need the king's approval. When James I was told that the colonists would make their living by fishing the waters off the coast of Virginia, he famously responded, "So God have my soul, 'tis an honest trade, 'twas the Apostles' own calling."

When approval arrived from London, Robinson and company accepted the offer and began to make plans for a group to leave.

But who exactly would go? Edward Winslow wrote in his memoir that it was decided the youngest and strongest of the congregation would leave first, and others would follow later. Eventually it was decided that William Brewster, who in 1620 was already fifty-three years old, would lead the departing group, and Pastor Robinson, who was forty-five, would stay behind with the rest of the congregation and make the journey on some future date.

There is no record of whether John and Sarah Jenney wanted to go or stay. John was about thirty-five years old at the time, and Sarah was about thirty. They had two small children: Samuel would have been three years old and Abigail would have been one. Obviously the Jenneys—and indeed all of the members of the congregation—had a number of options. For example, the man of the house could choose to go and leave his family behind, as Samuel Fuller did. Or a husband and wife could go and leave some of their children behind, as Edward and Mary Winslow did. Or the whole family could go, as the Carvers did. Or the whole family could remain in Leiden—which, for whatever reason, is what the Jenneys did.

Preparations got under way immediately. Cushman and Carver went back to England to secure a ship for the trip across the Atlantic, and those who had chosen to go sold their homes and generally got their affairs in order. They also began salting down beef, baking hard-tack, and securing barrels of beer and water for the voyage.

The plan was to depart Leiden in July and journey south to the port of Delfshaven, outside Rotterdam, where they would board a small merchant ship called the *Speedwell* that would take them across the English Channel to Southampton. There they would meet the larger ship full of other English families. Together they would all depart some-time in August. The trip would take roughly six weeks, which meant they would arrive in Virginia in mid-September, giving them plenty of time to set up camp before winter.

As their date of departure approached, they gathered at Groene-poort and held a day of public fasting, which was the custom in the Old Testament in times of mourning, and Robinson preached his final ser-mon to his full congregation, based on chapter 8, verse 21 of the book of Ezra, which, in their beloved Geneva Bible, read:

"And there at the River, by Ahava, I proclaimed a fast, that we might humble ourselves before our God, and seek of him a right way for us, and for our children, & for all our substance."

The full text of Robinson's sermon doesn't survive. Thankfully, Edward Winslow provided an account in his memoir:

Amongst other wholesome instructions and exhortations he used these expressions, or to the same purpose:

"We were now, ere long, to part asunder; and the Lord knoweth whether ever he should live to see our faces again. But whether the Lord had appointed it or not, he charged us before God and his blessed angels, to follow him no further than he followed Christ. And if God should reveal anything to us by any other instrument of his, to be as ready to receive it, as ever we were to receive any truth by his Ministry. For he was very confident the Lord had more truth and light yet to break forth out of his holy Word."

And then this charismatic shepherd, who had so skillfully guided his flock through the Dutch wilderness, brilliantly prepared them for what was to come by commanding them to continue their spiritual journey without him. According to Winslow's account, Robinson reminded them that the Lutheran Church ceased to grow spiritually without Luther, and as for the Calvinists, "they stick where he left them, a misery much to be lamented.

"For though they were precious shining lights in their times, yet God had not revealed his whole will to them; and were they now living, they would be as ready and willing to embrace further light as that they had received."

Winslow also remembered that Robinson told them when they encountered Puritans in the New World, they should work to unite with them rather than divide from them. And finally, perhaps with tears in his eyes, Robinson made one final request:

"Be not loath to take another Pastor or Teacher, for that Flock that hath two Shepherds is not endangered, but secured by it."

When the time of fasting and worship had concluded, Winslow wrote, "We refreshed ourselves after our tears, with singing of Psalms, making joyful melody in our hearts, as well as with the voice."

It was the last time they would all be together.

I FOLLOWED the Rapenburg Canal to the southwest part of town, where it connects to the Vliet River, crossed the bridge there, and walked south a few blocks. On the west bank of the river, in a cluster of forsythias, stood a small statue, maybe three feet tall, of a human of indeterminate gender facing south. Below it was a concrete slab with a list of names carved into it, including the most familiar from the Sepa-

ratist congregation: BRADFORD . . . BREWSTER . . . CARVER . . . CUSH-
MAN . . . FULLER . . . GOODMAN . . . WHITE . . . WINSLOW . . . And
near the bottom of the left column was JENNEY.

The figure is in the midst of a single step, with its left foot in the lead.
Its left hand is extended straight ahead as if reaching for something or
someone. The figure looks as though it is passing through an invisible
doorway, its back half rough and dull, like unpolished stone, and the
front half smooth and shiny. The symbolism is clear: this spot where
the Separatists boarded the boats for their journey south to Delfshaven
was the first step of their transformation.

They had fled their homeland because they were called criminals by
the Crown. In Leiden, despite the welcome extended to them by city
officials, they never ceased being refugees, and most of them were still
marginalized citizens stuck with menial jobs. Their only alternative, as
they saw it, was to move on to uncharted territory and risk the dangers
posed by the natives and the elements.

Bradford's account of their departure unwittingly gave them their
eternal label:

"So they left that goodly and pleasant city which had been their resting place near twelve years; but they knew they were pilgrims and
looked not much on those things, but lift up their eyes to the heavens,
their dearest country, and quieted their spirits."

Pilgrim. Bradford had gotten it just right. The dictionary defines a
pilgrim as "one who embarks on a quest for something conceived of as
sacred." Two hundred years later, on December 22, 1820, during a ceremony marking the bicentennial of the Separatist landing at Plymouth,
Daniel Webster seized on Bradford's word:

"Let us rejoice that we behold this day! We have come to this Rock
to record here our homage to our Pilgrim Fathers."

The label stuck and helped to shape and focus our understanding of
their journey and its significance to our country's own identity.

The Separatists didn't call themselves Pilgrims, but they most certainly understood the sacredness of their journey. The risks they were

willing to take defied all logic, and in fact many of them would be dead within the year. But I suspect that even if they had known that ahead of time, they would have taken that first step out of Leiden anyway. It was their destiny, it was God's will that they continue their search for their own promised land. They knew the importance of the journey was bigger than any of them.

I stood before this small statue that marked the first step of that sacred journey, angling for just the right photo. When I had finished, I noticed that the forsythias next to me were in the midst of their own transformation from the bright yellow of spring to the green of summer. I reached for one of the yellow leaves and plucked it off its branch.

I walked farther south to the bridge closest to the statue, hoping to get a good view of it from above for another photo. When I reached the middle of the bridge, I looked south. The river was visible for roughly a mile before it veered out of sight, heading southwest toward Rotterdam. I leaned over the stone wall on the bridge, listening to the quiet. The morning's rain clouds had moved on, the sky was a spectacular blue, and a breeze blew gently through the trees nearby. I released the yellow forsythia leaf, and a tiny gust carried it slowly to the water. Right away, it spun in place as though it were caught in a small whirlpool. The river's current took it up and I watched it float away until it was out of sight.

ROTTERDAM

I arrived in Rotterdam around noon. It had been raining there the day before and all that morning, but by the time I arrived the skies were clearing. I grabbed a cab and headed downtown.

Rotterdam and Great Yarmouth have much in common. Both cities were formed out of great estuaries, and both prospered a great deal from their proximity to the herring fishing trade in the North Sea. And just like Great Yarmouth, Rotterdam had been hit by German bombs during World War II. In fact, during the Luftwaffe bombing raid of May 14, 1940, which caused the Dutch to surrender to the Germans, much of the city was destroyed, which means virtually all of the bustling trading port my ancestors George and Frances Woolsey came to call home is now gone.

I checked into my hotel, one I had chosen because it was located in the heart of downtown, which made it easy to walk to the spots I was most interested in seeing. After a quick lunch in the lounge, I walked several blocks east toward my first destination, the only medieval building in town still standing.

I made my way through the massive exchange market, an outdoor mall where stores with high-end luxury goods stand next to fast-food

joints. Off in the distance, I could see the steeple of the church that had miraculously survived the German bombing.

St. Laurence Kerk was completed in 1525 after more than a century of construction. It is a massive Gothic cathedral built in the same cruciform style as St. Nicholas in Great Yarmouth and Pieterskerk in Leiden. It was named for a Roman archdeacon who had been martyred during the third century of the Common Era. The legend is that when the Emperor Valerian himself approached the church to confiscate its treasures, he ordered Laurence to point them out to his soldiers. Instead, the archdeacon defiantly pointed to a procession of poor people, saying, "Look! These are the treasures of the church."

Unlike St. Nicholas Church, which witnessed much violence as it made the transition from Catholicism to Protestantism, the transition for St. Laurence Kerk was quite peaceful. The last Catholic mass was conducted there on November 12, 1572, and the first Protestant service was held three days later.

After the bombing in 1940 leveled Rotterdam, the architects charged with rebuilding the city wanted to tear down St. Laurence because it wouldn't fit in with their modern vision, but church officials resisted. Restoration began in 1952 and was completed in 1968, just as Rotterdam's skyline was being reinvented all around it. Today, as with St. Paul's in London, St. Laurence no longer towers over its city. The flock has outgrown the shepherd.

DELFSHAVEN

The next morning I woke up to blue skies and temperatures in the upper fifties. After a quick breakfast I left my hotel and walked the five miles to Delfshaven, a tiny remnant of medieval Rotterdam that miraculously escaped the German bombs during the war. It was at Delf-shaven that the English Pilgrims from Leiden met the ship that would take them to England, and it is entirely possible that my ancestors the

Jenneys and the Woolseys could have stood side by side on the pier there as the ship left port.

By the end of the fourteenth century the village of Delft was known for its beer, and since it did not have a port of its own, the local merchants were forced to pay a heavy toll to exporters in nearby Rotterdam to get their wares to market. That changed in 1389, when they built their own modest seaport, which they dubbed Delfshaven.

In the 1840s, Delfshaven was annexed by Rotterdam and remained largely untouched by modern architecture even as Rotterdam continued to build its world-class trading port all around it. It may have something to do with the fact that Delfshaven was dug out of the inside of the bend of the Maas River. Most successful ports are built on the outside of a bend, where the stronger current assures deeper waters. But here the water pooled at the mouth of Delfshaven's port and deposited layer upon layer of sand that eventually cut it off from the river altogether.

The seventeenth century brought the Dutch Republic a period of prosperity that its people today refer as their Golden Age. In 1602 the Dutch East India Company was formed in what is now Indonesia. It developed lucrative trade relationships with much of the Far East, including an exclusive relationship with Japan. Then, in 1621, the Dutch West India Company was founded. It took control of Brazil as well as the Caribbean islands of Antilles and Aruba, and in 1626 famously purchased Manhattan Island from the local Indians, setting the stage for the New Amsterdam Colony.

Like all of history's great mercantile economies, the Dutch trading empire succeeded because of its free-market attitude and the fiercely independent people it attracted. It was this environment that fostered the world's most famous price bubble, the legendary Tulip Mania (1634–37) during which some rare bulbs sold at the Amsterdam Bourse at prices hundreds of times greater than what the Dutch paid for all of Manhattan Island.

It was this free-market environment that probably enticed my ten-times great-grandparents, George and Frances Woolsey. When they left England for the Dutch Lowlands, they were no doubt able to improve their finances dramatically. For a thirtysomething merchant like George to move to Rotterdam between 1615 and 1620, it was like a bright young computer programmer moving to Silicon Valley early in the 1990s. The timing couldn't have been better.

They were also apparently comfortable with the Calvinist traditions that had been adopted in the Netherlands. After their move to Rotterdam, they joined the Dutch Reformed Church, where two of their children were later married. Daughter Frances married Abraham Brouwer on July 20, 1633, and oldest son John married Maeijke Fransdaughter on March 8, 1637.

It was not very unusual for seventeenth-century English families to migrate to the Netherlands, just as it was not unusual for Dutch families to migrate to England, especially to Norfolk. Since the middle of the 1500s, when Spain began a campaign to crush the Protestant movement in the Netherlands—first under Charles V and then under his son, Philip II—thousands of Dutch citizens had fled their homeland seeking religious freedom wherever they could find it.

In 1565, Queen Elizabeth I allowed roughly three hundred Dutch immigrants to settle in Norwich, just north of Great Yarmouth. By 1620 the number had grown to more than four thousand. The Strangers, as they were known, had a great impact on the local economy. Since the Middle Ages, Norwich had been famous for its fine textiles, but by the sixteenth century that industry had fallen on hard times because of competition from higher-quality and cheaper products coming out of the Lowlands. The Strangers brought their modern weaving techniques with them to English soil and helped to revive Norwich's textile business.

Then, in 1572, the queen encouraged young Englishmen to go to the Netherlands and join the Dutch militias in their battles with Spanish forces. Many of those English military men ended up staying after their service ended, and established English communities. On August 1, 1611, Rotterdam magistrates allowed Protestant church services to be conducted in English.

Delfshaven today is a small district of narrow cobblestone streets, modest apartments, and a handful of shops and cafés. The port area is essentially a narrow canal of water with boats docked on both sides and rows of storefronts. When I entered the district, it really did feel like stepping back into time. I strolled through the area, taking in the sights and enjoying the sun's warmth. Small green buds were beginning to color the branches of the trees that lined the streets, and flocks of seagulls swarmed over the area, scavenging for food.

Was this anything like the Rotterdam the Woolseys had called home? Had they walked these streets? I scanned the cobblestones, wondering if any of them could be four hundred years old. Had they lived in an apartment above their shop, or had George senior prospered enough to afford a home in the country? And did they ever regret moving to Holland? Did they miss England? I know that while Cindy and I were homesick for California for a couple of years after our move east, eventually New Jersey came to feel like home because it was where our children grew up. Rotterdam was where the Woolsey children grew up. Chances are they spoke both English and Dutch.

More than a decade after their move, the Woolseys experienced tragedy when George senior died in the fall of 1629. He would have only been in his mid-forties. Not long after, Frances remarried—she was called "Fransijntije Woolsij" in public records. Eventually, George junior left Holland for the New Amsterdam Colony in America, possibly as an employee of the Dutch West India Company. The date of his departure is unknown.

A church bell sounded off in the distance.

I had almost forgotten about the church I had come to Delfshaven to see. I followed the sound of the carillon as it pealed eleven times, and

came upon a modest-sized storefront church sitting between shops on the waterfront. This was what is now known as Pelgrim Vaders Kerk, or the Pilgrim Fathers Church.

I tried the front doors and found them locked. A small sign, in English, said that the church was open to the public for tours on Saturdays. I was there on a Thursday. My heart sank.

There was a large plaque bolted to the wall next to the front door. It read,

"This is the starting point of the 'Speedwell,' on which the Pilgrim Fathers sailed to England on August 1, 1620. They changed the boat there for the 'Mayflower' bound for the New World. Built in 1417 as St. Antonius Chapel and converted in the sixteenth century into a cruciform church in the late-gothic style with a three-bay nave."

In other words, it was in the same style as St. Nicholas Church in Great Yarmouth, and after coming all this way I wasn't going to be able to see it. I tried the doors again. Still locked. I took several pictures of the front of the church, tried the doors one more time, and then continued my tour of the rest of Delfshaven.

An hour later I returned and found the doors still locked. A café nearby was just opening for business, so I sat on its patio overlooking the water and ate my lunch, all the while keeping an eye on the church, hoping against hope that the doors might suddenly open.

I finished my lunch and lingered at the table reading a booklet called "Pilgrim Trail" that I had picked up in a local shop during my walking tour. It briefly recounted the story of the English Separatists, their time in Leiden, and their journey south here to Delfshaven, where they met the *Speedwell*. It turned out I was sitting maybe 100 yards from the spot where they boarded.

I turned a page and came upon a photo of the Pilgrim Fathers Church. The caption below it mentioned that while it was open to the public on Saturdays, anyone could call the church sexton and have the church opened for impromptu tours. The caption listed a phone number. I checked the copyright of the booklet. It was ten years old. Was it possible the phone number was still valid? I paid my bill and left the café in search of a pay phone.

Just then a car pulled up in front of the church. A man and woman emerged from the car. She opened a back door and lifted a large bouquet of flowers out of the backseat while he unlocked the church's front door.

I hurried toward them.

"Hallo," I called as the man opened the front door. He stopped and looked back at me. "I am an American, and I would dearly love to come inside and look around."

He smiled.

"*Ya*, sure," he said. "Come in." The woman went first with the flowers, and then he gestured for me to follow him in.

"Take your time, please," he called back as he hurried off.

I stood just inside the doors for a moment to allow my eyes to adjust to the dim lighting. Slowly the full church came into view and I saw that it was indeed a miniature version of St. Nicholas Church, where the Woolsey children had been baptized. Rows of wooden pews faced the pulpit and the altar.

The woman came toward me as she headed outside to the car.

"We have a wedding here today," she explained.

"What time?" I asked.

"At half past three."

I looked at my watch. It was 12:45.

"I will be gone by then, I promise."

She pointed to a door at the front of the church.

"The Pilgrim Memorial is back this way, you see."

I thanked her as she headed back out to the car.

I took several pictures of the sanctuary and the front of the altar. I climbed the steps of the small spiral staircase to the elevated pulpit and took a picture of the church as the minister would see it. From there I spotted a scale model of the *Mayflower* sitting on a shelf.

I descended the steps and tried the door to the memorial.

"Is it locked?" the woman asked as she walked back into the sanctuary with more flowers.

"Apparently," I said.

She called to the man, who hurried in with his keys and unlocked the door. He led me in to what looked like a classroom.

There was a handful of folding chairs facing a lectern and several paintings and photos and posters hanging on the walls.

"This is President Roosevelt," he said, pointing to a photo of FDR. "And this," he said, pointing to another photo, "is President Bush." He was referring to the first President Bush.

"They are both descendants of Pilgrim Fathers, you see."

I smiled and nodded, not bothering to explain my own connection.

While the church's name implies that the Separatists worshipped here, perhaps the night before they set sail on the *Speedwell,* it is unlikely. Bradford doesn't mention it in his book. The only thing he writes about that evening was that it "was spent with little sleep by the most, but with friendly entertainment and Christian discourse and other real expressions of true Christian love." They may not have been comfortable worshipping in a Dutch Reformed church. Most likely they spent the night in the homes of other English expatriates, maybe even the Woolseys.

I exited the church through the front door, thanking my hosts once again, and headed toward the end of the canal where the *Speedwell* was said to have been waiting for its passengers.

Bradford wrote that it was a good day for sailing, with a favorable summer breeze kicking up to carry them along.

At the appointed hour, "They went aboard and their friends with them, where truly doleful was the sight of that sad and mournful parting, to see what sights and sobs and prayers did sound amongst them, what tears did gush from every eye, and pithy speeches pierced each heart; that sundry of the Dutch strangers that stood on the quay as spectators could not refrain from tears."

One more time, they hugged and kissed and prayed together, and when it was time to go, John Robinson fell to his knees and with tears streaming down his cheeks he led the group in one last prayer.

"And then with mutual embraces and many tears they took their leaves one of another, which proved to be the last leave to many of them."

I stood at the end of the pier, very near the spot where Robinson and the rest of his flock gathered with the citizens of Rotterdam who had come out to witness the spectacle. It is entirely possible that a Jenney stood here next to a Woolsey as everyone watched the *Speedwell* head north out of the harbor.

Part Two

A M E R I C A

NEW BEGINNINGS

AND SO, TO AMERICA THEY CAME. TENS OF THOUSANDS OF THEM sailed during the 1630s, the period we remember as the Great Migration, when the English monarchy's persecution of the Puritans was at its height, until 1640, when the Puritans gained the upper hand in the English Civil War and it stopped.

It must have been the greatest mass movement of humanity in the history of Western civilization, maybe of the world, to that point. During that ten-year period, more than twenty thousand people left their homeland for a world full of risk and danger.

As they saw it, they were like the ancient Hebrews, a people chosen by their Creator to build a holy kingdom on earth ruled by God's own laws.

"We shall find that the God of Israel is among us," Governor John Winthrop told the passengers on board the *Arabella,* the first shipload of Puritans to arrive in America in the spring of 1630. "For we must consider that we shall be as a city upon a hill. The eyes of all people are upon us. So that if we shall deal falsely with our God in this work we have undertaken . . . we shall open the mouths of enemies to speak evil of the ways of God. . . . We shall shame the faces of many of God's worthy servants, and cause their prayers to be turned into curses upon us."

The Puritans saw themselves as people of destiny who had to set a good example for the rest of the world. In tribute to the ancient

Hebrews, who called their capital *Jeru Salem,* or City of Peace, the Puritans called their first capital Salem.

But what to bring with them? Space was limited on the ships that brought them, but they had to be prepared for the unexpected.

After the Pilgrims arrived in Plymouth in 1620, Edward Winslow sent a letter with a suggested inventory back to other people in England who might be considering the journey.

"Be careful to have a very good bread-room to put your biscuits in," he advised. "Let your cask for beer and water be iron-bound."

He suggested quantities of food to bring: eight bushels of meal, two bushels of peas, two bushels of oatmeal, one gallon of oil, two gallons of vinegar, and so forth.

His apparel recommendations included, among other things, four pairs of shoes per person, three shirts per man, and three pairs of stockings per woman.

For tools, his list included two hoes, two shovels, three kinds of axes, one good hammer, and four kinds of chisels.

As for kitchen utensils, he suggested one iron pot, one frying pan, two skillets, and a kettle.

Finally, weapons would be very important. Among Winslow's recommendations: a complete set of armor, one sword, a long rifle, a pistol, twenty pounds of powder, and sixty pounds of lead to make shot.

The Jenneys were the first of my ancestors to come to America. John and Sarah arrived in Plymouth with their children Abigail, Samuel, and Sarah in the summer of 1623 on board a small merchant ship called the *Little James.* At forty-four tons, it was only a quarter the size of the *Mayflower.*

The ship's captain, Emmanuel Altham, wrote about the voyage in a letter to his brother in England. In it, he made a curious reference to Sarah Jenney:

"One goodwife Jennings was brought abed of a son aboard our ship and was very well."

There is no record of Sarah Jenney having given birth to a child during the voyage. If she had, it would have been reflected in a land redistribution that took place in Plymouth after their arrival. Acreage was awarded based on the number of members in each family, and the record clearly states that the Jenneys were awarded five acres "beyond the brooke to Strawberry Hill," one each for John and Sarah and their children.

A book about the Jenney family written by Jenney descendants speculates that it was actually Sarah, and not a son, who was born on the *Little James,* and the Plimoth Plantation website speculates that if a son was born to the Jenneys en route to Plymouth, he must have died in infancy. It should be noted that four years later, in 1627, when the colonists drew lots to divide a herd of livestock, the public record showed the Jenneys to still be a family of five. So Captain Altham's reference remains a mystery.

As for my other ancestors, I can't be as precise about the date of their arrival. William and Joanna Towne, for example, obviously made the journey sometime after the baptism of their daughter Mary in 1634 and before William's appearance in a Salem Village record in 1640.

Among the hundreds of passenger lists I studied in books and on websites, I found an entry from April of 1637 for a ship from Great Yarmouth called the *Rose.* The Townes's oldest son, Edmund, was listed as an apprentice to a Henry Skerry, who was traveling with his wife and two children. But I never found a listing for the rest of the Towne family.

As for George Woolsey Jr., I don't know what my nine-times great-grandfather did during the eighteen years between 1629, when his father died in Rotterdam, and his first appearance in New Amsterdam Colony records in 1647. I uncovered two distinctly different theories about that period of his life, but frankly I don't believe either of them.

One of the stories says that immediately after George senior's death, George junior returned to England to live with an uncle, Benjamin Woolsey, and together they eventually migrated to the New Amsterdam Colony. It is certainly plausible. George junior would have been roughly thirteen years old when his father died, which would have been an ideal age to begin serving an apprenticeship, if indeed that was why he returned to England. The part I don't believe is their move to New Amsterdam. They don't appear in any of the thousands of ships' records that still exist today; I don't have any evidence that George Woolsey Sr. had a brother named Benjamin; and there is no Benjamin Woolsey in any New Amsterdam records. Years later, George junior's son, George III, had a son named Benjamin who went on to a distinguished career as a Presbyterian minister on Long Island. Was he named for a favorite great-uncle? At this point I have no way of knowing.

The other story is even more fanciful. It says that George junior sailed to Plymouth on a Dutch ship in 1623 as part of an apprenticeship he served under Isaac Allerton. He would have been only seven years old in 1623 (I should point out, though, that this version made him out to be seven years older than he actually was), and the only Dutch ships to arrive in Plymouth in 1623 were the *Ann* and the *Little James*. There was no George Woolsey on either passenger list. As it happens, George did eventually work for Isaac Allerton in New Amsterdam, which is probably what prompted this particular yarn.

My theory is that he remained in Rotterdam, went to work for the Dutch West India Company, and was transferred to New Amsterdam sometime before he and Rebecca Cornell were married there in December of 1647.

What amazes me most about the Great Migration is the degree of risk these people were willing to take. It must have taken a great deal of courage to do what they did. Where did that courage come from? The only answer can be their faith. And it wasn't that they believed God would protect them. They believed that whatever happened to them, whether it was good or bad, was God's will. That was the key.

Would the Townes still have left England for Salem, Massachusetts, if they'd known ahead of time the horrible fate that awaited their daughters Rebecca and Mary in the witch trials of 1692? Or would the Jenneys have uprooted their children from the Netherlands if they had known about the very difficult conditions of the Plymouth Colony?

I think the answer is yes, because they believed that their fate was in God's hands. As a result, the unknown was not something to be greatly feared.

As they saw it, this journey, risks and all, was to be approached with hope. Without hope, there would have been no point.

Chapter Three

PLYMOUTH, MASSACHUSETTS, 1620–1650

The Pilgrims

ISTORIC PLYMOUTH IS not very large. It takes up about six blocks of waterfront property on what is believed to be the site of the original colony. The area where the settlers built their thatch-roofed huts is now a narrow, winding boulevard called Water Street, with motels and inns and souvenir shops overlooking the Town Wharf, where dozens of fishing and pleasure boats are moored. The names of the cross streets are reminders of the *Mayflower* passengers—Carver, Brewster, Winslow, Howland, Chilton—and a few blocks inland there are streets named Alden, Allerton, and Standish.

I spent a few days in Plymouth in April of 2006, familiarizing myself with the area where my nine-times great-grandparents John and Sarah Jenney raised their children, and where their name is still remembered today. Immediately after I checked into my hotel on the northern end of Water Street, I headed south toward Brewster Park, the heart of the historic district where Plymouth Rock and the full-scale replica of the *Mayflower,* called the *Mayflower II,* are located.

There was a buzz of activity along the boulevard: the whining of a power saw slicing through lumber, the rhythmic pounding of nails, dogs barking, seagulls screeching. Surely the Old Colony must have sounded something like this during the spring of 1621 as the hearty survivors of the first winter began to build their new homes in earnest.

I chose a park bench directly in front of the *Mayflower II.* It was almost ten o'clock, and school buses filled with elementary school students were pulling up. A group of fourth-graders lined up near my bench, and I ate my breakfast while their teacher instructed her students not to stray from the group and to be courteous to others on the ship. One young man raised his hand and asked if this was really the ship the Pilgrims had sailed on, and the teacher said no, this was a copy. I heard a few groans of disappointment from the students.

No one knows exactly what the *Mayflower* looked like, only that it was a 160-ton merchant ship typical of its era. Based on descriptions culled from various documents, a replica was built in the mid-1950s, and it replicated the Pilgrims' journey by sailing from Plymouth, England, to Plymouth, Massachusetts, in the spring of 1957.

When I finished eating, I got up and strolled over to the portico that houses Plymouth Rock, where another class of students had gathered at the railing that overlooks the small pit where it sits. They laughed and pointed, and I heard more than one of them say, "It's so small."

I remembered thinking the same thing the first time I saw the Rock in person. It was during the summer of 1987, when Cindy and I were still living in Los Angeles and we spent two weeks touring Boston and Cape Cod with friends. During our drive south on Route 3 toward the Cape, we spotted the sign for Historic Plymouth and decided to stop.

When we looked into the pit where the Rock sits, I remember thinking, *Where's the rest of it?* It was really nothing more than a boulder measuring eight feet by four feet. This was the bedrock on which our nation had been built? And just so there would be no misunderstanding, someone had chiseled "1620" into it.

In 1741, as plans for a new wharf were being made, a longtime citizen of Plymouth named Thomas Faunce, by then ninety-five years old and not in the best of health, was concerned that the Rock would be lost in all the construction, so he insisted on being carried in a chair the three miles from his home down to the water, where, so the story goes, he dramatically identified it. Back in the early 1650s, when he was a small boy, he had listened to stories told by some of the original colonists, and had watched as they'd pointed out the Rock.

In 1774 it was decided that the Rock would be better displayed in the town square. But as it was being lifted from its bed during the move, it broke into two pieces. The top half was moved and the bottom half left behind.

The half-Rock was moved with great fanfare sixty years later, on July 4, 1834, farther inland to the front of the Pilgrim Hall. William Davis, in his *Plymouth Memories of an Octogenerian,* remembered the day:

"A procession . . . preceded by the school children of the town, escorted a decorated truck bearing the Rock, which was followed by a model of the *Mayflower* mounted on a cart drawn by six boys, of whom I was one. . . . The Plymouth Band and the Standish Guard performed escort duty."

But the day was not without incident. The wagon carrying the Rock collapsed under the weight and the Rock crashed to the ground, causing a crack to form and dozens of pieces to break off. Undaunted, the parade resumed and the Rock was placed in front of the Pilgrim Hall.

Alexis de Tocqueville wrote in *Democracy in America* (1835):

"The Rock has become an object of veneration in the United States. I have seen bits of it carefully preserved in several towns in the Union. . . . Here is a stone which the feet of a few outcasts pressed for an instant; and the stone becomes famous; it is treasured by a great nation; its very dust is shared as a relic."

The Rock's own odyssey continued. In 1880 the top and bottom halves were reunited after sixty years apart, and the full Rock was positioned under a concrete canopy at the end of the wharf. Finally, on a rainy day in November of 1921, it was moved one last time to its present location under the majestic portico where it sits today.

And who was the first person to step on it? It depends on whom you ask. One tradition says it was John Alden, while another says it was young Mary Chilton who was said to have jumped in the first landing boat and proclaimed, "I will be the first to step on that rock." But no one knows for sure, and descendants of Alden and Chilton have feuded about it for generations.

The miracle is that Plymouth Colony ever got started at all, given the many hardships and obstacles the settlers had to overcome. After two false starts, the *Speedwell* was finally abandoned in England and most of the Separatists on board had to be crowded onto the *Mayflower*.

The journey across the Atlantic was a difficult one. Because it was getting late in the season, they faced strong headwinds and a number of storms, one of which damaged a support beam in the quarters where the passengers were huddled.

When they arrived at the northern tip of Cape Cod on November 21, 1620, they were two months behind schedule and hundreds of miles off course. Small wonder that upon their arrival, William Bradford wrote that the beleaguered passengers "fell upon their knees and blessed the God of Heaven who had brought them over the vast and furious ocean and delivered them from all the perils and miseries thereof, again to set their feet on the firm and stable earth."

Even Bradford, ever the optimist, writing years after the fact, had to marvel at the grim circumstances they found themselves in:

Being thus passed the vast ocean . . . they had now no friends to welcome them nor inns to entertain or refresh their weather beaten bodies; no houses or much less town to repair to, to seek for succor.

And for the season it was winter, and they that know the winters of that country know them to be sharp and violent, and subject to cruel and fierce storms, dangerous to travel to known places, much more to search an unknown coast. Besides, what could they see but a hideous and desolate wilderness, full of wild beasts and wild men—and what multitudes there might be of them they knew not. . . .

And the whole country, full of woods and thickets, represented a wild and savage hue. If they looked behind them, there was the mighty ocean which they had passed and was now a main bar and gulf to separate them from all the civil parts of the world.

Despite a good omen—the miraculous birth of a child to William and Susannah White, a son they named Peregrine (which means "one who journeys to foreign lands")—things didn't get any easier. James Chilton, the oldest passenger on board, died upon arrival, and William Bradford's wife, Dorothy, fell overboard in Provincetown harbor and drowned. Even today, rumors persist that she committed suicide, unable to face the uncertain future the settlers faced.

Some of the sailors on board, understandably anxious to leave, were threatening to abandon the passengers before a suitable campsite could be found. And there was talk of mutiny among the non-Separatists who argued that the Separatists' land patent didn't cover this territory in New England. So a covenant was drawn up to address governance issues until a new patent could be obtained.

No one knows who actually penned the Mayflower Compact, whether it was one person or a committee. The original document has been lost to history. But whoever it was brilliantly included a simple idea that would become a cornerstone of the nation formed more than 150 years later: the majority rules.

THE MAYFLOWER COMPACT

In the name of God, Amen. We whose names are underwritten, the loyal subjects of our dread sovereign lord, King James, by the grace of God, of Great Britain, France and Ireland, king, defender of the faith, and etc, having undertaken for the glory of God and advancement of the Christian faith and honor of our King and country, a voyage to plant the first colony in northern parts of Virginia, do, by these presents, solemnly and mutually, in the presence of God and of one another, covenant and combine ourselves together into a civil body politic, for our better ordering and preservation, and furtherance of the ends aforesaid; and by virtue hereof, do enact, constitute, and frame such just and equal laws and ordinances, acts, constitutions, and offices, from time to time, as shall be thought most meet and convenient for the general good of the colony, unto whereof, we have hereunto subscribed our names, at Cape Cod, the 11th day of November, in the year of the reign of our sovereign Lord, King James of England, France and Ireland, the eighteenth, and of Scotland the fifth-fourth, Anno Domini, 1620.

Historian Francis Baylies, in his history of Plymouth published in 1866, called it the real miracle of the colony:

> The pilgrims, from their notions of primitive Christianity, force of circumstances, and that pure moral feeling which is the offspring of true religion, discovered a truth in the science of government which had been concealed for ages. On the bleak shore of a barren wilderness, in the midst of desolation, with the blast of winter howling around them, and surrounded with dangers in their most awful and appalling forms, the pilgrims of Leyden laid the foundation of American liberty.

The settlers then elected a governor, and the result was a changing of the guard for the Separatists. Ruling elder William Brewster might have been the obvious choice, but perhaps as a way to appease the non-Separatists, Deacon John Carver was chosen, and then for only a one-year term.

Governor Carver immediately dispatched a group of men to explore the tip of Cape Cod, and they returned with eight badly needed bushels of corn the local natives had hidden in caves for safekeeping. It was a lifesaver for the starving Pilgrims, who had virtually depleted their own supplies. (Months later they would gratefully repay the natives with double the amount.)

Another expedition left on December 7. Ten men boarded the thirty-foot shallop they had brought from England and headed west toward the mainland. They encountered a group of natives who shot arrows at them, and a storm of freezing rain and snow that impeded their progress, but they pressed on and finally came upon the protected sound that is Plymouth Bay, where they went ashore on Clark's Island.

These men then did something extraordinary. On that Saturday evening, December 9, they dropped everything they were doing and prepared to observe the Sabbath. Despite the great perils they faced, between the unfriendly natives and the fierce weather, and the fact that time was of the essence to find a suitable piece of land, everything stopped and on Sunday, December 10, they celebrated the Lord's Day. Certainly they would have been excused just this one time, but they still held to their pious beliefs and traditions.

On Monday they came upon an area directly across the bay from Clark's Island that seemed perfect for their needs. It had already been cleared of trees and brush, it included a tall hill that would afford them a protective lookout, and it was easily accessible from the water. What they didn't know was that only a few years before, it had been the home of a group of natives of the Patuxet tribe. All but one had been wiped out by a disease, probably smallpox, which had been brought to the region by English and French explorers. Because other groups of natives avoided the area as a result, the English settlers had chanced upon a spot ready for settlement where they would be left alone.

By this time it was too late for the *Mayflower* to return to England, so the ship's captain, Christopher Jones, and his men reluctantly hunkered down for the winter and allowed their passengers to sleep on board for the next few months, which was most fortunate for the Pilgrims. The winter of 1620–21 was an especially harsh one, and even with the protection the ship provided, it still took a great toll on the group. Many of the colonists caught colds from wading in the frigid waters as they made their way in and out of the shallop on their way to and from the *Mayflower,* and roughly half died before spring. The fabled first settlement in New England that would be remembered and celebrated for centuries to come was reduced to just fifty-five people, and Robert Cushman later wrote that only six of them were fit enough to care for the others.

When spring arrived, the *Mayflower* returned to England and the survivors began to build their colony and to plant their crops. They got help from the lone survivor of the Patuxets, an English-speaking native called Squanto.

Squanto had led an eventful life. He had been kidnapped by an English merchant ship in 1605 and taken to England, where he learned to speak the language. In 1614 he had returned to North America with Captain John Smith, and helped the legendary English explorer map the coastline of what Smith named New England. Not long after, he was kidnapped again and taken to Spain, where he was sold into slavery. He escaped and returned again, only to find that his entire tribe had been wiped out by disease.

He taught the Plymouth colonists native farming and fishing techniques and he brokered a peace agreement signed by Governor Carver and Massasoit, the leader of another local tribe, the Wampanoags.

According to Bradford's journal, the treaty had six terms:

1. That neither he [Massasoit] nor any of his, should injure or do hurt to any of their [the colony's] people.
2. That if any of his did any hurt to any of theirs, he should send the offender that they might punish him.
3. That if any thing were taken away from any of theirs, he should cause it to be restored; and they should doth like to his.
4. That if any did unjustly war against him, they would aid him; and if any did war against them, he should aid them.
5. That he should send to his neighbours confederates to certify them of this, that they might not wrong them, but might be likewise comprised in the conditions of peace.
6. That when their men came to them, they should leave their bows and arrows behind them.

The treaty remained in effect for forty years until after Massasoit's death in 1660 and the outbreak of hostilities between the New England colonies and the natives, lead by Massasoit's son, who had assumed the English name Philip.

Squanto died during a hunting trip in November of 1622. Bradford deeply mourned the man who had become his best friend, calling him a "special instrument sent of God for their good, beyond their expectation."

Governor Carver died suddenly in late April, of what appeared to be heatstroke, and his grief-stricken widow, Catherine, died a month later.

William Bradford was then elected governor. One of his first official duties was to officiate at the first wedding conducted in New England, a civil ceremony joining Edward Winslow to the newly widowed Susannah White on May 12.

By fall the colony was taking shape. A handful of homes had been built and the first harvest was completed. The colonists held a three-day feast of thanksgiving patterned after the annual celebration they had experienced in Leiden each October 3, commemorating the Dutch victory over the Spanish during the siege of 1577. Winslow wrote a letter to relatives in England rhapsodizing about that time:

"I never in my life remember a more seasonable year than we have here enjoyed. . . . I make no question, but men might live as contented here as in any part of the world."

On November 21 a ship called the *Fortune* arrived with thirty-six more settlers, including Robert Cushman, who brought with him something the colonists had been awaiting anxiously: a new land patent. It was not well received. It still favored the investors, giving them all of the colony's profits during the term of the patent. The only thing it offered the settlers was the promise of a new, and more favorable, agreement in seven years if the colony survived that long.

It fell to Cushman to persuade the colonists to agree to the new patent, and it wasn't going to be easy. When he arrived he found a great deal of tension between the Separatists and Strangers. And because the harvest was barely enough to feed the existing colony for the coming winter, the *Fortune* brought new stresses with the arrival of an additional thirty-six mouths to feed.

So Cushman called everyone together on the morning of Sunday, December 9, and offered what is believed to be the first sermon ever delivered in New England. The colonists had, of course, been without an ordained pastor since they left Leiden the year before, which meant that there would have been no celebration of the two sacraments the Separatists recognized, either communion or baptism. It is possible that one of the deacons, John Carver or Samuel Fuller, could have preached a sermon, but Bradford never mentioned it. Fortunately the text of Cushman's sermon survives.

The scripture he chose to preach about was a line from the Apostle Paul's first letter to the church in Corinth:

> *Let no man seeke his owne, But every man anothers wealth*
> (1 CORINTHIANS 10:24)

Corinth had been an important Mediterranean trading port in the first century of the Common Era. Around the year 50, Paul passed through and converted a small group of important citizens who continued to hold worship services in their homes after he moved on. But after a few years the congregation splintered, with some pledging allegiance to Paul, others to fellow Apostle Peter, and a third to another leading Christian of the time, Apollos.

When Cushman arrived in Plymouth, he found a similar turf war under way between the Separatists and the Strangers, so he used Paul's words of encouragement to the Corinthians to address the disputes.

> As God then did direct this Apostle to lay downe this briefe direction as a remedy for that evill in Corinth, so you may thinke it is by Gods speciall providence that I am now to speake unto you from this text: and say in your hearts surely something is amisse this way, let us know it and amend it.
>
> How many of our deare friends did here die at our first entrance, many of them no doubt for want of good lodging, shelter, and comfortable things, and many more may goe after them quickly, if care not be taken. Is this then a time for men to begin to seeke themselves? Paul sayeth that men in the last dayes shall be lovers of themselves, but it is here yet but the first dayes and the

dawning of this new world. It is now therefore no time for men to looke to get riches, brave clothes, daintie fare, but to look to present necessities; it is now no time to pamper the flesh, live at ease, snatch, catch, scrape and pill, and hoard up, but rather to open the doores, the chests, the vessels, and say, "Brother, neighbor, friend, what want yee, any thing that I have? Make bold with it, it is yours to command, to doe you good, to comfort and cherish you, and glad I am that I have it for you."

Beare ye therefore one anothers burden, and be not a burden one to another, avoide all factions, singularitie, and withdrawings, and cleave fast to the Lord, and one to another continually.

So also shall you bee an encouragement to many of your Christian friendes in your native countrey, to come to you, when they heare of your peace, love, and kindnesse that is amongst you. But above all, it shall goe well with your soules, when that GOD of peace and unity shall come to visite you with death, as he hath done many of your associates, you being found of him, not in murmurings, discontent and jarres, but in brotherly love, and peace, may bee translated from this wandring wildernesse unto that joyfull and heavenly Canaan.

The colonists eventually signed the patent, and the *Fortune* headed back to England with the colony's first offering to its English benefactors, a shipment of beaver pelts with an estimated value of 400 pounds. Before it could reach its destination, French pirates intercepted the ship and the pelts were stolen.

In the summer of 1623 two more ships arrived with members of Robinson's congregation. The *Ann* arrived first in July. Among the passengers on board was a widow named Alice Carpenter Southworth, who almost immediately became Mrs. William Bradford. A few weeks later the *Little James* brought the Jenney family.

Their arrival was bittersweet. As happy as they must have been to be reunited with the other members of the Leiden congregation, they were aghast at the conditions they encountered. The two years of hardship, the difficult winters, and the deaths of so many comrades had obviously taken their toll on the surviving colonists.

Nathaniel Morton, who had been a passenger on the *Ann,* described the scene upon their arrival.

"Those passengers, seeing the low and poor condition of those that were here before them, were much daunted and dismayed. . . . Some wished themselves in England again, others fell on weeping, fancying their own misery in what they saw in others."

Bradford concurred.

"The best dish we could present them with is a lobster or piece of fish, without bread, or anything else but a cup of fair spring water; and the long continuance of this diet, with our labors abroad, has somewhat abated the freshness of our complexions; but God gives us health."

Nathaniel Morton was ten years old when he journeyed to Plymouth on the *Ann* with his father, George. When George died a year later, in 1624, the boy was adopted by Governor Bradford and his wife, Alice, who was young Nathaniel's aunt.

Morton grew up to become the colony's secretary and carefully preserved the day-to-day records of financial transactions, legal judgments, and other colony business that survive today to give historians and descendants a vivid picture of life in Plymouth Colony. His journal, *New England's Memorial* (1669), which rivaled his adopted uncle's own history of Plymouth Colony for its richness of detail, has been hailed as the cornerstone of New England history. In 1637 his wife, Lydia, gave birth to their first child, a daughter the budding historian named Remember.

Morton's meticulous preservation of Pilgrim history is the reason I know as much as I do about the Jenneys. John first showed up in Morton's account of his own arrival at Plymouth in the summer of 1623:

"About ten days after the arrival of the ship called the *Ann,* there came in another small ship of about forty-four tons, named the

James. . . . She was a fine new vessel built to stay in the country. One of the principal passengers that came in her was Mr. John Jenny [*sic*], who was a godly, though otherwise a plain man, yet singular for publicness of spirit, setting himself to seek and promote the common good of the plantation of new Plimouth; who spent not only his part of his ship (being part owner thereof) in the general concernment of the plantation, but also afterwards was always a leading man in promoting the general interest of this colony."

A few miles south of Plymouth's historic district stands the museum complex called Plimoth Plantation, which includes a living reenactment of the Plymouth Colony. It was begun in the 1940s with funding from Boston's wealthy Hornblower family, much the way Colonial Williamsburg in Virginia was begun by John D. Rockefeller Jr. in the 1920s.

I spent an afternoon there during my stay in Plymouth. Just inside the rustic wooden fence that surrounds the village, there is a replica of the two-story fortress/meetinghouse the settlers built in 1622 on the hill overlooking Plymouth Harbor. On its flat roof, Captain Standish positioned

the four cannons from the *Mayflower,* and inside Elder Brewster preached two sermons each week on the Sabbath. Despite the peace treaty signed with the Wampanoag chief Massasoit, the threat of Indian attack was still very real. So each Sunday morning, at the sound of a rhythmic drumbeat, the colonists would climb the hill to attend worship services in their meetinghouse, many of them carrying guns and other weapons.

Beyond the meetinghouse a dirt road, maybe thirty feet wide, extends down the hill toward the beach, with thatch-roofed cottages on either side. This was probably the way the colony looked when Captain John Smith passed through in 1624. It had been ten years since his first trip through the area, when he and Squanto had mapped the coastline, and he had named this place Plymouth.

He recorded his tour of the colony in his journal:

"At New Plimoth, there is about 180 persons, some cattell and goats, but many swine and poultry, 32 dwelling houses, whereof 7 were burnt the last winter, and the value of five hundred pounds in other good; the Towne is impailed about halfe a mile compasse. In the towne upon a high Mount they have a Fort well built with wood, lome, and stone, where is planted their Ordnance: Also a faire Watch-tower, partly framed for the Sentinell."

The year 1627 marked a turning point in the colony's history, when the settlers officially took control of their destiny. In October of 1626, a group of fifty-three men who called themselves the Purchasers pooled their money and bought all of the colony's assets from their English investors for 1,800 pounds. A few months later, in early 1627, eight men who came to be known as the Undertakers agreed to take responsibility for the colony's heavy debt load in exchange for certain privileges, including monopolies on various trades.

The eight Undertakers were Governor Bradford, Captain Standish, Elder Brewster, Edward Winslow, John Howland, John Alden, Thomas Prence, and Isaac Allerton, who by then had become the colony's representative in London. John Jenney was among the fifty-three Purchasers, but he did not join the eight Undertakers, perhaps believing the risk was too great. There is no question, however, that the agreement gave the colony the foundation it needed for future growth.

I walked down the hill from the meetinghouse, past each of the crude structures the settlers called home. There were gardens planted behind each home, and cattle and goats grazed here and there. And there were people in seventeenth-century costume going about their day, tilling the garden, feeding the animals, and generally giving tourists a three-dimensional sense of what life was like in the colony.

Plimoth Plantation is careful to point out that it doesn't hire actors to populate the village. Rather, they are called Interpreters. These are people who are more interested in the colony's history than in the art of acting. The Interpreters' job description says they must "interpret the history of Plymouth Colony . . . to the museum's visitors by initiating personable and informative interactions with particular emphasis on the Plymouth colonists' origins, arrival and presence in New England."

I walked by a small group of tourists who had gathered to talk to a young woman in a long, navy blue skirt and a heavy, cream-colored blouse. A few strands of red hair peeked out from under the modest white bonnet she wore. She was carrying a bucket in one hand and a crude rake in the other while answering questions as people took her picture. Down the road another group was gathered around a tall, weathered-looking man. He was very animated, waving his arms as he regaled them with various stories, and the people around him laughed and applauded.

John Smith had called Plymouth Colony "healthfull":

"The most of them live together as one family or household, yet every man followeth his trade and profession both by sea and land, and all for a generall stocke, out of which they have all their maintenance. . . .

"They have young men and boies for their Apprentises and servants, and some of them speciall families, as Ship-carpenters, Salt-makers, Fish-masters, yet as servants upon great wages."

I ducked into a house that I noticed had smoke coming from its chimney. Inside was a single modest room typical of what the colonists built when they first arrived. A large four-poster bed took up one corner. A bright red spread covered the overstuffed mattress and two large pillows. Two tall storage cabinets stood in another corner. A young woman sat at the table next to the fireplace, cutting slices of bacon.

"Good day, sir," she said.

"Good day," I responded.

"By what river do you come?" she asked as she continued to slice the bacon.

"I come by road, actually," I said, playing along. "The one numbered 95."

"I'm not familiar with that," she said matter-of-factly.

"What are you making?" I asked.

"Fricassee," she explained as she wiped the sweat from her brow. The weather outside was cool, but the heat from the fire made the room very warm.

"What is your name?" I asked.

"Mary Chilton," she said.

"You were the first person to step on Plymouth Rock!" I blurted. She stopped what she was doing and looked up at me.

"Is that a fact," she said. Each Interpreter is given extensive notes about the people they portray to help them develop their interpretation. Apparently the legend about the young Mary Chilton stepping on the Rock didn't make it into her notes because it was obvious that my question had caught her off guard, and we shared an awkward moment of silence as a result.

"Do you seek someone?" She studied my face.

"Yes," I said. "I'm looking for John and Sarah Jenney."

"Do you have business with them?" she asked.

"They are my ancestors."

"Ah, yes." She smiled and went back to her work. We were back on familiar ground for her now.

Just then a family with two small girls walked in. Mary invited the girls to sit at table with her and help prepare the fricassee.

Mary Chilton would have been a teenager in 1627. She was a child when she and her parents, James and Susanna, came to Plymouth on the *Mayflower*. Her father had been a tailor in Leiden. Tragically, he died while the ship was still in Provincetown, and her mother died a few years after that. Years later she married Edward Winslow's brother, John, and they eventually moved to Boston, where she died in the 1670s.

"Do you seek someone?" Mary asked the two little girls, and they shrugged their shoulders.

"Yes," their father said. "We are descendants of John Howland."

"Ah, yes," Mary said.

I excused myself and left the room. Outside I walked past a few more houses, chatted with more Interpreters, and took more pictures.

History witnessed this close is not nearly as big as the history read in a book. But this is exactly what I had come for. While history records the big names and important dates, it tends to forget a lot of people. For every William Bradford that history remembers, there are hundreds of John Jenneys who are forgotten. Here at Plimoth Plantation, the forgotten people were the ones being celebrated. Here we got to see the menial tasks that were performed day after day, and hear about the modest ambitions.

I left the village and drove back to Plymouth to find John and Sarah Jenneys' most visible legacy.

Plymouth's public records and Morton's and Bradford's histories suggest that John Jenney was a smart businessman who cared deeply about the welfare of the colony. For many of the twenty-one years he lived in Plymouth Colony, before his death in 1644, he served as an assistant governor for many of them, and in 1634 he and six other men were appointed by Bradford to lay out Plymouth's system of roads.

The records also reflect the number of business interests he developed, from selling beaver pelts and lumber to setting up a salt works on

Clark's Island. The deal he would be best remembered for occurred on March 7, 1636:

"It is concluded upon by the Court that Mr. John Jenney shall have liberty to erect a Milne for grinding and beating of Corne upon the brooke of Plymouth to be to him & his heires for ever."

The Jenney Grist Mill stands a few blocks south of the historic district on what today is called Jenney Pond. This is the site where the Jenneys lived. John built his mill on the spot where a natural spring that feeds the pond could also power a water wheel. He situated the family home next door.

A sign across the street from the mill reads, JOHN JENNEY GRIST MILL VILLAGE. Below it are smaller signs that mention a museum and a gift shop. I walked past the giant wheel as it churned in the water, and entered the museum's gift shop.

An attractive middle-aged woman with an easy smile greeted me. She stood behind a counter next to the cash register.

"Good afternoon," she said. "We have a tour going on right now. You're welcome to join it, or you can wait for the next one."

I paid for a ticket and joined the tour in progress. A group of ten people were gathered around a man in period costume standing next to the mill's giant grinding stones. He was explaining how the water wheel outside powered the gears that turned the stones. I stood behind the group, next to a scale model of the mill. A sign next to it read,

———————

REVENGE GETS YOU EVEN WITH YOUR ENEMY;

FORGIVENESS PUTS YOU ABOVE HIM.

———————

"This is a reconstruction of the mill built by John Jenney in 1636," he explained. "Mr. Jenney came to America in 1623 with his wife, Sarah, and their children. He started a salt factory on Clarke Island, owned interests in a coastal trading ship, and built and operated this mill until his death in 1644. His wife and their son Samuel continued to run the mill after his death."

He said the mill had continued to run under various owners until 1847, when it burned to the ground. The current mill was built in 1970.

"Any questions?" he asked. When there were none, he thanked everyone for coming, and the group headed back to the gift shop. I stayed behind to chat.

The guide was a barrel-chested fellow with a well-groomed blond beard. He wore a black hat, a white shirt, and khaki knickers. I asked a few questions about the grinding process, and he showed me what the corn looked like before and after it had been ground.

"Are you a teacher?" he asked.

I explained why I was there. He shook my hand enthusiastically and introduced himself. His name was Leo Martin. He and his wife, Nancy, the woman working in the gift shop, had purchased the mill in 2001. They were professional photographers. Nancy had driven through Plymouth looking for a storefront where they could open a studio. Instead, she had found this mill that was for sale. Almost immediately, she'd called her husband to tell him about a crazy idea she had.

When Leo saw the mill, he also fell in love with it. On a whim, they bought it. They upgraded the property, Leo taught himself to grind corn the way John Jenney did, and they opened for business, selling the ground corn and giving tours of the mill.

Leo led me back to the gift shop and introduced me to Nancy. She pointed through a window to the house next door, and told me that was the spot where the Jenney home had been. And she mentioned that a group of Jenney descendants gathered in Plymouth each fall for a small reunion. The Martins had clearly become members of the Jenney family.

When it was time for the next tour, Leo excused himself and I toured the gift shop. It was an odd feeling, seeing all of the items Nancy had stocked with the Jenney name on it. I bought a coffee mug and a beautiful photograph she had taken of the mill. We shook hands, and as I walked out the door we promised to stay in touch.

In Plymouth's old Town Square, two churches stand unusually close to each other. One is a sturdy stone structure built in the ancient Norman tradition in 1897. The other, built in 1830, is a more traditional New England white clapboard style. Both claim to be descendants of the Pilgrim tradition.

The plaque on the stone church reads,

The church of Scrooby — Leiden — and the Mayflower
Gathered on this Hillside in 1620
Has ever since preserved unbroken records
And maintained a continuous ministry
Its first covenant being still the basis of its fellowship
In reverent memory of its Pilgrim Fathers
This Fifth Meeting House was
Erected A.D. MDCCCXCVII

The plaque next to the front door of the white clapboard church reads,

THIS TABLET IS INSCRIBED IN GRATEFUL MEMORY OF
THE PILGRIMS AND
THEIR SUCCESSORS WHO, AT THE TIME OF THE
UNITARIAN CONTROVERSY
IN 1801, ADHERED TO THE BELIEF OF THE FATHERS AND ON THE BASIS
OF THE ORIGINAL CREED AND COVENANT PERPETUATED AT GREAT
SACRIFICE IN THE CHURCH OF THE PILGRIMAGE THE
EVANGELICAL FAITH
AND FELLOWSHIP OF THE CHURCH OF SCROOBY, LEYDEN, AND
THE MAYFLOWER ORGANIZED IN ENGLAND IN 1606

William Bradford would have been deeply saddened to know that the church he loved so dearly split into two parts 150 years after his death, but he probably would not have been surprised. After John Robinson died in Leiden in 1625, the Plymouth church hired a succession of pastors who never measured up to their beloved, charismatic shepherd. As a result, church attendance began to dwindle.

But something bigger was happening in the seventeenth-century Congregationalist movement in America, of which the Pilgrims were a part. Fewer and fewer people were going to the meetinghouse on the Sabbath, and of those who did, more and more of them failed to make public professions of their faith in Christ and what the Puritans called the Conversion Narrative, which mimicked the Apostle Paul's own conversion on the road to Damascus. Such a narrative had long been a requirement before any Protestant in the Calvinist tradition was allowed to take communion. Instead, much to Bradford's horror, more and more Congregationalist churches were beginning to subscribe to the more liberal beliefs of the Arminian movement that John Robinson had so vigorously opposed in Leiden.

Like many of the Congregationalist churches in New England, the church in Plymouth struggled to maintain its Calvinist identity even as the Unitarian movement grew stronger. (The name Unitarian derived from the movement's rejection of the Trinity in favor of a single unified God.) The split finally occurred in 1799 upon the death of a longtime, and very conservative, pastor named Chandler Robbins when the deeply divided congregation voted to install a more liberal Unitarian minister named James Kendall. Almost immediately the members who opposed his election withdrew their membership and built their own meetinghouse next door.

Today the old stone church still maintains its Unitarian ties while the breakaway church, ironically, is now affiliated with an even more liberal denomination, the United Church of Christ.

Behind the stone church is the town's oldest cemetery, known as Old Burial Hill. It was on this hill, roughly 150 feet above sea level, overlooking Plymouth Bay, that the Pilgrims built their first meetinghouse in 1622. And it was here on this eight-acre parcel that the colonists began to bury their dead. The town continued to use it until 1957.

Old Burial Hill is like any other cemetery except for the number of famous Pilgrim names.

There is, for example, John Howland:

HERE ENDED THE PILGRIMAGE OF
JOHN HOWLAND
WHO DIED FEBRUARY 23, 1672
AGED ABOVE 80 YEARS
HE MARRIED ELIZABETH DAUGHTER OF
JOHN TILLEY

WHO CAME WITH HIM IN THE
MAYFLOWER DEC. 1620
FROM THEM ARE DESCENDED A
NUMEROUS POSTERITY

By far the largest monument in the cemetery, an obelisk standing twenty-five feet high, commemorates the lives of Robert Cushman and his son Thomas. It was placed there by the Cushman family in 1858.

The inscription on the monument's west side, dedicated to Robert, reads,

HE DIED, LAMENTED BY THE FOREFATHERS
AS THEIR ANCIENT FRIEND — WHO WAS
AS THEIR RIGHT HAND WITH THEIR FRIENDS
THE ADVENTURERS, AND FOR DIVERS YEARS
HAD DONE AND AGITATED ALL THEIR BUSINESS
WITH THEM TO THEIR GREAT ADVANTAGE.

It also includes a passage from his famous sermon:

AND YOU, MY LOVING FRIENDS, THE ADVENTURERS
TO THIS PLANTATION, AS YOUR CARE HAS BEEN FIRST
TO SETTLE RELIGION HERE BEFORE EITHER PROFIT
OR POPULARITY, SO I PRAY YOU GO ON.
I REJOICE — THAT YOU THUS HONOR GOD
WITH YOUR RICHES, AND I TRUST YOU SHALL BE REPAID
AGAIN DOUBLE AND TREBLE IN THIS WORLD, YEA,
AND THE MEMORY OF THIS ACTION SHALL NEVER DIE.

But the monument that must surely get the most attention commemorates the life of William Bradford. The eight-foot obelisk is off the beaten path, but a sidewalk makes access to it easier. Historians don't believe that Bradford's remains are actually buried there, but fittingly his monument was given the best seat in the house. Its view of Plymouth Bay through the trees is spectacular.

There are two inscriptions on the obelisk's north side. The first, in Hebrew text, reads,

IN JEHOVAH'S NAME I DIE

Below that, in English it says:

<small>UNDER THIS STONE REST THE ASHES OF</small>
WILLIAM BRADFORD, A
ZEALOUS PURITAN & SINCERE CHRISTIAN GOV. OF
PLY. COL. FROM 1621 TO
1657, (THE YEAR HE DIED) AGED 69, EXCEPT 5 YRS,
<small>WHICH HE DECLINED.</small>

There are no monuments to the Jenneys in the cemetery. Chances are they were buried in the shadow of their beloved grist mill. Fortunately, both of their wills are among the documents at Pilgrim Hall. They include some very intriguing passages that shed light on the state of the Jenney family.

John's will was dated Thursday, December 28, 1643:

"I, John Jenney of New Plymouth in New England, being sick and weak in body but through God's special goodness in perfect memory, do settle that estate the Lord in mercy hath bestowed on me according as I conceive he requireth at my hands. And therefore do ordain this my last will and testament."

He named his wife as his executrix, and he bequeathed control of their home and the mill, "My will being that she freely and fully enjoy it together with all other my moveable goods and chattells so long as God shall be pleased to continue her life."

Upon Sarah's death, according to the customs of the time, he bequeathed a double portion of his estate to their oldest son, Samuel, with the rest going in equal portions to the four other children, Abigail, Sarah, John, and Susanna.

Then he made a curious request regarding Abigail, who had apparently been betrothed to a man named Henry Wood. John obviously didn't approve.

"My will is that if she, the said Abigail, will dwell one full year with Mr. Charles Chauncey of Scittuate [sic] before her marriage (provided he be willing to entertain her) then my said daughter Abigail [may] have two of my cows and my full consent to marry with the said Henry Wood. And in case Mr. Chauncey is against it, then I would have her dwell with Mrs. Winslow of Careswell the said term of one year further."

Charles Chauncey had been the pastor of the Plymouth Church for three years before moving north to the neighboring town of Scituate. He later went on to become president of Harvard. John no doubt hoped that a year away from Mr. Wood, whether it was with Reverend Chauncey or Mrs. Winslow, would give Abigail a new perspective and persuade her to change her mind about marrying him. But it is clear John's wishes weren't followed. On Thursday, April 25, 1644, Abigail Jenney married Henry Wood.

> Last of all I do ordain my worthy friends Mr. Wm Bradford, now Governor of Plymouth, and Mr. Thomas Prence, of the same, the overseers of this my last will and testament and do give each of them a pair of gloves of five shillings price.
>
> John Jenney (seal)
>
> Witnesses hereunto : Edward Winslow, Thomas Willett, William Paddy.

TEN YEARS later, on Tuesday, April 4, 1654, Sarah Jenney executed her own last will and testament. Only two weeks before, on March 23, her youngest daughter, Susanna, had died, which no doubt made Sarah mindful of her own mortality.

Much had happened in the Jenney family since John's death: John junior had also passed away, but the date and circumstances of his death are not known.

Samuel had moved to Portsmouth, Rhode Island, where he married

Susanna Wood. They had two sons, John and Job, and a daughter they named Sarah.

By 1654, Abigail and Henry Wood had five children, including four sons named John, Samuel, Jonathan, and David, and a daughter they also named Sarah.

Sarah Jenney married Thomas Pope on May 29, 1646. Thomas helped his mother-in-law run the mill. The Popes had had five children by the time Sarah drew up her will. They included sons Seth, Thomas, and John, and daughters Susanna and Sarah.

In her will, the elder Sarah Jenney bequeathed "to my Daughter Sarah Pope my bed and furniture, being one bolster, two pillows and pillowbeers, three blankets, one old rug, and one pair of sheets. Further, I bequeath to my daughter Sarah Pope all my wearing clothes to dispose of them to my Daughter Abigail Wood and to my grandchild Sarah Wood for their use as they have need, except for two of my petticoats which have not been worn which I give to my daughter Sarah Pope for her pains."

Among the livestock she owned, she mentioned a mare that she wanted divided between Samuel and Abigail. She left all of her cattle to daughter Susanna's widower, Benjamin, and she gave one ewe lamb each to Plymouth church pastor John Rayner, Elder Thomas Cushman, and to Thomas Southworth who witnessed the will.

Finally she mentioned that she wanted Susanna's Bible to go to Elder Cushman.

Circumstances changed dramatically over the ensuing eighteen months. Samuel's wife died and he sent his sons John and Job to live with their grandmother at the mill. For some reason his daughter Sarah was sent to live with neighbor Thomas Clarke and his wife, despite Grandma Sarah's objections.

On August 18, 1655, Sarah drew up a second will, in which she made it clear she was not happy with her son.

She wrote, "My will is that if my son Samuell takes away his children that are now here with me then my will is that none of them shall have anything of my estate."

Sarah Jenney died not longer after. Her will was entered into court records in March of 1656. The mill was sold and the Jenney family scattered.

Abigail and Henry Wood settled nearby in Middleborough. The marriage that John Jenney so vehemently opposed turned out to be the most fruitful. The Woods eventually had twelve children.

Sarah and Thomas Pope moved south, taking advantage of a law enacted in Plymouth in 1633 that offered grants of land to the children of the colony's First Comers. They settled on more than 170 acres with their seven children on the southern coast and what is now the city of Fairhaven, where today you'll find Pope Beach and Popes Island.

As for my eight-times great-grandfather, Samuel Jenney, he eventually remarried and took possession of land that his mother left him in what became known as the town of Dartmouth. He and his second wife, my eight-times great-grandmother Ann Lettice Jenney, raised six children there. On November 2, 1748, their great-granddaughter Anna Jenney married my five-times great-grandfather John Griffeth in nearby Rochester, Massachusetts.

The Separatist movement that had begun more than a century earlier in England had ended. Generation after generation of John and Sarah Jenney's descendants continued to migrate west, farther and farther away from Massachusetts.

Chapter Four

New York, 1645–1700

The Presbyterians

N EW YORK IS unquestionably among the greatest cities in Western civilization, and there are plenty of reasons to believe it is the greatest. But unlike a Rome or a London or a Paris, it hasn't been able to preserve much of its earliest history. In many ways the Protestant Reformation is to blame.

Most of Western Europe's oldest structures are medieval cathedrals. Because the Church was central to their lives, the Europeans built their houses of worship to last, and they took good care of them, even cherished them. The earliest Protestants, though, were content to build their austere meetinghouses of wood that didn't last more than a few generations. It wasn't until after the Puritan generation had passed by the end of the seventeenth century that sturdier, more elaborate churches were built in North America. It's no surprise that one of the oldest buildings in the area that made up the original New Amsterdam Colony is a church—Trinity Church, of course—but this third incarnation was only built in 1846. An infant compared with Notre Dame or, certainly, the Pantheon.

For that reason it is virtually impossible for descendants of New York's earliest settlers to get any sense of their ancestors' lives. My nine-times great-grandparents, George and Rebecca Woolsey, lived for more than fifty years in the New York area, beginning in the 1640s. The first twenty years they lived under Dutch rule, until the English took control in 1664. George lived another thirty-four years, dying in 1698, and Rebecca passed away in 1712.

Today they wouldn't begin to recognize their old neighborhoods. There was the plantation in Flushing on Long Island where they lived in the 1650s and where the first three of their eight children were probably born. There was the house on Pearl Street in lower Manhattan where they lived in the 1660s, next door to Rebecca's sister and her husband, very near the great tavern that became the colony's first City Hall. And finally, in Jamaica, Queens, was their final home where they owned dozens of acres around Beaver Pond and where they are buried today.

The Dutch imported the traditions of the Reformed Church to New Amsterdam while the English brought Presbyterianism, which was founded by John Knox in the 1530s. The two Protestant denominations shared the same root: John Calvin. They believed in the total sovereignty of God and the total depravity of humanity. They differed in how their churches were governed. The Reformers preferred independent congregations while the Presbyterians patterned themselves after the ancient church in the days of the Apostles, using elders or presbyters (from the Greek *presbyteros*) to oversee their churches.

The New Amsterdam Colony was unique among the early North American settlements. It was established for economic—not religious— reasons, and it wasn't populated by people from just one country. It had always attracted people from all over the world. In the spring of 1524, for example, Giovanni Verrazano, an Italian explorer hired by French investors to find a northwestern route to Asia, dropped anchor at Staten Island, but he didn't stay long and nothing came of his visit there. It wasn't until 1609 that another explorer, this one an Englishman named Henry Hudson, who had been hired by Dutch investors to find the same mythical Northwest Passage, steered his ship *Half Moon* past Staten Island and farther up the river that for years was called North River. He got as far as Albany before he realized that he hadn't found the passage, either.

What he found, though, was possibly the world's greatest natural harbor, with upper and lower bays, networks of rivers wide enough for trading ships, and hundreds of miles of shoreline with access to thousands of acres of rich soil and enough wildlife to bring a fortune to trappers.

This was where the English Separatists on the *Mayflower* had originally steered their ship in the fall of 1620 until the jet stream blew them two hundred miles off course to the north. So, after the Dutch established the West India Trading Company in 1621, a contingent of 110 French Walloons was sent to the area in the spring of 1624 to set up camp. Within two years a lucrative fur-trading business had been established.

And then, according to legend, in 1626 the colony's first Director General, Peter Minuit, reportedly purchased all 20,000 acres of the island the local natives called Manna Hatta, or Island of Hills, for a reported sixty Dutch guilders. The prevailing wisdom has long been that the wily Dutch duped the naïve Indians, and indeed, given the critically important role Manhattan Island plays in world commerce, it is easy to say in hindsight that the Dutch made the greatest real estate deal ever. But we shouldn't forget that land was generally being given away to colonists in the seventeenth century, and the Native Americans didn't believe they "owned" the land to begin with. The transaction symbolically foreshadowed the kind of trading activity that eventually established Manhattan's credentials as a center of commerce.

Over the next twenty years the colony became an important, and lucrative, trading post for the West India Company. But by the 1640s the colony's growth had stagnated, and Dutch authorities found it difficult to persuade people to migrate there. The Dutch Republic, after all, was in the midst of its own economic boom. Why would anyone want to leave that and essentially start over again in some remote outpost? Unlike the English colonies north of New Amsterdam, which were regarded as safe havens for the Puritans seeking refuge from persecution and civil war back home, there was no compelling incentive for Dutch citizens to leave the Netherlands.

Then, in 1647, Peter Stuyvesant became the colony's fifth and final Director General. Because of New Amsterdam's economic difficulties, officials of the West India Company (WIC) appointed the iron-willed Dutchman to turn things around. He was both a strict Calvinist and a disciplined military man who had proven himself to be a strong leader. In 1643, Stuyvesant had been appointed governor of the Caribbean islands the WIC controlled. During a battle with Spanish forces there in 1644, a cannonball struck Stuyvesant in the leg and it had to be amputated. He was forced to return to the Netherlands, where he was fitted with the peg leg that would become his signature feature. Two years later Stuyvesant had fully recovered from his injuries and was ready for his next assignment. In July of 1646 he was appointed Director General of New Amsterdam, and he arrived there on Saturday, May 11, 1647.

Right away, he knew he needed to impose discipline on the colony's citizens. He forced the many local taverns to close one hour earlier, at 9:00 P.M. each evening, and he required a stricter observance of the Sabbath, including the prohibition of drinking and other social activities. And to pay for badly needed repairs around the colony, he imposed a tax on all alcohol. Like most agents of change, Stuyvesant was not a popular Director General.

Sixteen forty-seven is also the year when George and Rebecca Woolsey made their first appearance in colony records. That first record, dated July 23, relates a curious incident in which Woolsey testified that he and Thomas Willet, who was married to Sarah, the sister of George's fiancée, offered a bribe to a colony agent to allow the passage of a shipment of goods owned by their employer, Isaac Allerton, without inspection and, presumably, without taxation. The bribe offered was one beaver pelt.

At the request of the Honorable Director General Petrus Stuyvesant and the council of New Netherland, George Wolsey, aged about twenty-six years, from Yarmouth in Old England, attests, testifies and declares in the presence of Captain Lieutenant Nuton [this would be one of Stuyvesant's deputies, Captain Brian Newton; he and his wife, Alice, would later act as godparents to two of the Woolsey children] that on the Saturday last Fiscal van Dyck [the inspector] came on board Mr. Tomas Willit's bark to inspect it and heard the above mentioned Mr. Willit say at Mr. Isaac Allerton's house that because he must be away he had presented the above named Fiscal Van Dyck with a beaver, in order that he would not lose his time by clearing things away and in order that the fiscal would be content to let him sail unhindered; which beaver he, George Wolsey, placed in the hands of the said fiscal himself. The deponent, in the presence of the aforesaid councilors, declares this to be true and offers to confirm the same on oath. Done in Fort Amsterdam in New Netherland, the 23rd of July, 1647.

Woolsey apparently didn't suffer any consequences as a result of his indiscretion. Less than a month later he purchased a grain plantation on the portion of Long Island the Dutch called Vlissingen, or Salt Meadow, which the English pronounced as Flushing, for the princely sum of 130 guilders. Four months later, on December 9, he married eighteen-year-old Rebecca Cornell. She was born in Essex, England, and her parents, Thomas and Rebecca, had settled in Portsmouth, Rhode Island.

Flushing had been founded in 1645 by English farmers, and it remained farmland for another 250 years. George had obviously done well in business if he could afford such a large estate, and I suspect it had something to do with the fact that he worked for Isaac Allerton, who became one of the most prolific businessmen in the seventeenth-century colonies. Ultimately, though, Allerton was not one of the most successful.

After Governor William Bradford banished him from Plymouth Colony in the early 1630s for shady business practices, Allerton moved to Salem, where he built a fishing fleet. Two years later he sold the fleet and moved to New Amsterdam, where he established a thriving trading business that extended to Delaware and Virginia and included interests in furs, agricultural goods, and real estate. In 1646 he moved again, this time to the New Haven colony, and he left a group of men, including

George Woolsey, to tend to his empire. In 1647, Allerton married for a third time and spent the last twelve years of his life in southern Connecticut. He died there in 1659.

Surprisingly, Allerton's will suggests that his debts probably exceeded his assets. The brief document simply listed the creditors to whom he owed money, and his instructions to his widow Joanne and his son Isaac junior to pay each debt and to keep whatever was left. George Woolsey was mentioned four times as the man they should turn to for guidance.

By this time the Woolseys had five of the seven children Rebecca would eventually give birth to. The baptismal records for the Woolsey children reveal a lot about their religious practices. Since they were English living in a Dutch colony, it is clear they were comfortable attending both the Dutch Reformed and English Presbyterian churches in their area.

Their first child, Sarah, no doubt named for Rebecca's sister, was born on August 3, 1650 and baptized four days later. Aunt Sarah acted as her godmother, and her godfather was Captain Brian Newton, who was one of Director General Stuyvesant's most trusted advisers. He had served with Stuyvesant in the Caribbean, had fought by his side when Stuyvesant lost his leg, and had followed him to New Amsterdam.

The man who baptized the infant Sarah was Reverend Richard Denton, possibly the first Presbyterian minister to serve in the American colonies. Reverend Denton was born in Yorkshire, England, in 1603, and like so many prominent English Protestant clergy he graduated from Cambridge University, in 1623. He migrated to New England in the mid-1630s and was among the settlers who founded Stamford, Connecticut, in 1641. Three years later he traveled south across Long Island Sound with some of the members of his congregation. The group purchased land from the local natives and founded the town of Hempstead. That same year, Reverend Denton also founded what is believed to be the first Presbyterian church in America, Christ's First Presbyterian Church, which today is located on Denton Green. It is likely that Sarah Woolsey was baptized there.

Later generations of Woolseys remained active in the Presbyterian Church. In addition to George junior's grandson Benjamin, there was a descendant of Rebecca Woolsey's, Charles Briggs, who taught at the Union Theological Seminary in New York City in the 1800s and who wrote a history of the church titled *American Presbyterianism, Its Origin and Early History,* and perhaps most famously there was Theodore Woolsey, who served as president of Yale University from 1846 to 1871, and who later headed an American commission that revised the New Testament.

On October 10, 1652, George Woolsey III was born. His baptismal record shows that he was baptized two days later in "the Dutch church." Captain Newton's wife, Alice, was his godmother, and his godfather was his uncle Charles Bridges, another of Stuyvesant's inner circle. Bridges had married Sarah Cornell Willet after the death of her first husband, Thomas, the man with whom George Woolsey had been caught offering the bribe five years earlier. The church referred to in young George's baptismal record was no doubt the Dutch Reformed Church on Manhattan Island. There is no way of knowing why the Woolseys did not have him baptized in the Presbyterian Church in Hempstead, and the record does not mention who conducted the baptism.

Child number three was my eight-times great-grandfather Thomas, who was baptized in Hempstead by Reverend Denton on April 10, 1655. After Thomas's birth, the family purchased their home on Pearl Street near Fort Amsterdam, on land that Rebecca's sister Sarah had received when her first husband, Thomas Willet, died.

From its earliest days, Pearl Street was a hub of business activity because it fronted the busy port where goods were sent and received. A number of warehouses were built there to house the goods. Predictably, it saw its share of booms and busts over the next four centuries. Business picked up after the War of 1812, when the British started shipping cheaper goods to the region, and the completion of the Erie Canal opened a huge market for Pearl Street's merchants. But there were also lean years, especially in the late 1800s, after the Civil War devastated the U.S. economy. The area where the Woolseys and the Bridgeses lived is only a few blocks east of the New York Stock Exchange.

After Thomas came daughter Rebecca, who was also probably born on Pearl Street, on February 13, 1659. She was baptized three days later in the Dutch Reformed Church in Fort Amsterdam. Uncle Charles Bridges once again served as godfather, and the woman she was named for, her maternal grandmother Rebecca Cornell Sr., was her godmother.

On January 12, 1661, Rebecca gave birth to child number five, a son they named John. He was baptized four days later in the Dutch Reformed Church, and his godfather was a local businessman named Thomas Hall.

Hall had owned several acres of land on Broadway that abutted the colony's northern border, which was defined by the fabled 2,340-foot-long wall the colonists built as protection against Indian attack. Today the world knows it as Wall Street. Trinity Church is located on a portion of Hall's property. Today the mere mention of Thomas Hall's name probably sends a chill up the spine of the church's proprietors. Here's why:

Back in the 1930s a group of "lawyers" began contacting thousands of people around the country who were believed to be descendants of Thomas Hall's son-in-law, who was variously identified as either Thomas or Robert Edwards. These descendants were told that Trinity Church was illegally occupying land that rightfully belonged to them. The story goes that after Thomas Hall died in 1670, his widow signed a ninety-nine-year lease with the members of the congregation who built Trinity Church. When the lease expired, the land was supposed to revert to Edwards family heirs. But the "lawyers" claimed that Trinity

Church had very quietly, and very illegally, neglected to give the land back. So each heir was asked to pony up a sum of money to cover the legal costs necessary to win back the valuable acreage that was rightfully theirs.

The problem is that the land Trinity Church stands on today was part of a grant given to an Anglican congregation by King William III in 1697. And it turns out Thomas and Anna Hall never had any children, which means they wouldn't have had a son-in-law named Thomas or Robert Edwards.

But that didn't stop other "lawyers" from contacting other Edwards family heirs fifty years later, in 1983, with the same story. More than three thousand people eventually signed up to join that cause, netting their phony legal representatives almost $1.5 million.

It turns out this kind of scam wasn't attached exclusively to the name Thomas Hall. My mother tells the story that near the end of his life, my great-grandfather Charles Woolsey began sending monthly checks to "lawyers" in New York City who claimed they could help him take possession of land on Manhattan Island that rightfully belonged to the Woolsey family. After he died in August of 1935, one of his daughters, my grandmother Mabell, continued sending checks until— according to Mom—Granddad Griffeth put his foot down and insisted she stop "the nonsense."

The year 1664 was an eventful one for the people of New Amsterdam in general, and for the Woolseys in particular. On March 19 a daughter, Mary, was born and baptized in the Dutch Reformed Church in Fort Amsterdam.

That same month, King Charles II boldly assigned ownership of all land from Maine to Delaware to his brother James, the Duke of York. Ever since the Stuarts had been restored to power in 1660 following the death of Oliver Cromwell and the fall of the Commonwealth, the English and Dutch had engaged in a series of trade wars, and one of their battlegrounds was the New Netherland territory, which extended from Albany south to the New Amsterdam Colony. In the spring of 1664,

James I dispatched a fleet of ships to New Amsterdam to seize control of the area. They formed a blockade around the port and positioned hundreds of troops in Brooklyn and east of Hempstead.

Stuyvesant's first instinct was to fight, but he knew he was outnumbered. A petition signed by ninety-three men in the colony urged him to surrender. On August 27 he did, and by September 8 the colony had officially been renamed New York.

Why did the Dutch give up so easily? As always, they were simply being practical. The New Amsterdam Colony had never been the profitable boomtown for them that they hoped it would be; the terms of the surrender allowed the Dutch people in the area to remain, and the West India Company was free to continue trade relations there. In their eyes, the English could assume the risk of ownership and they were content to be customers.

The change of leadership probably did not greatly affect the Woolseys. They had obviously become accustomed to life under Dutch rule, and, given the lenient terms of the surrender, there was no reason to believe their lives would change all that dramatically except for one thing: English would now become the language of record and George, who had long signed his name "Joris," became "George" again.

The Woolseys kept their home on Manhattan until 1669. By then they had already moved their family to the area where they would spend the rest of their lives.

The town of Jamaica was established in 1655 by a group of English settlers from Hempstead. While the Dutch had originally referred to that region as Rustdorp, or Rest Town, because of the respite it offered between existing settlements, the English initially called it Jameco after the Algonquin Indians who called themselves the Yamecahs, the Indian word for "beaver."

Jamaica became the seat of Queens County. By the ninteenth century its main thoroughfare, Jamaica Avenue, had become the county's center of commerce, and in the early twentieth century its central location made it a transportation hub for train routes, bus lines, subways, and highways. New York International Airport opened on Jamaica Bay in 1948. It was renamed John F. Kennedy International in December of 1963.

George and Rebecca Woolsey lived for the final thirty years of their lives very near where York College is located today. They had owned a number of acres on the banks of Beaver Pond, which was the area's most notable feature before it either dried up or was filled in to make way for real estate development. And it was here that most of the Woolsey children grew to adulthood, married, and settled on land of their own.

During their years in Jamaica, the Woolseys endured the greatest crisis of their lives, in 1673. The year had been an eventful one anyway. A Dutch militia had briefly seized and then lost control of New York. George began a new career as town clerk of Jamaica, and forty-four-year-old Rebecca was no doubt surprised to learn that, eight years after she had last given birth, she was pregnant again. But the event that overshadowed all of it was the bizarre death of Rebecca's mother, Rebecca Cornell.

My ten-times great-grandparents Thomas and Rebecca Cornell were Puritans who left England in 1638 with eight children and settled first in the Boston area of the Massachusetts Bay Colony. Two years later they joined Rebecca's brother John Briggs in the new settlement called Portsmouth on Aquidneck Island, which later became part of Rhode Island.

Portsmouth had been founded by William and Ann Hutchinson and sixty people (including Briggs) who followed them from Boston in 1638. Ann Hutchinson had been banished from the Massachusetts Bay Colony by Governor John Winthrop for, among other things, holding meetings for the women of Boston where she audaciously preached women's equality.

It would appear that the Cornells became friendly with the Hutchinsons. After Will Hutchinson died in 1642, Thomas and

Rebecca were among a group of people who followed Ann to southern Westchester County in the New Amsterdam Colony. But the Cornells didn't stay long.

The colonists in the area had been battling with the local natives. During the summer of 1643, a band of Mahicans attacked a number of settlers. In August, Ann Hutchinson and five of her children were massacred and their home was burned to the ground. The Cornells escaped a separate attack, fleeing by boat with only the clothes on their backs. They returned to Portsmouth, where they were granted more acreage, and where they remained the rest of their lives.

Thomas died in 1656 at the age of sixty-three, and Rebecca eventually moved in with her oldest son, Thomas junior, his wife, Elizabeth, and their four young sons. Elizabeth died around 1664, and Thomas married Sarah Earle three years later. They had two daughters.

On Saturday afternoon, February 8, 1673, Thomas returned home after completing his chores and spent some time with his mother in her bedroom, maybe as long as an hour and a half. Rebecca had not been feeling well, so she did not join the family for supper that evening.

After everyone had eaten, Sarah sent her youngest stepson, Edward, to his grandmother's room to see if she wanted some boiled milk. He returned immediately and frantically asked for a candle, explaining that he had seen something smoldering on the floor in the darkened room and he couldn't make out what it was.

The Cornells' handyman, Henry Straite, was first to rush into the room, where he came upon the charred remains of what he thought was a "drunken Indian" lying in front of the fireplace. As the Cornell boys stood over him, Straite shook one of the body's arms and spoke a few words in the local native dialect. By this time, Thomas had entered the room. He immediately recognized the shoes on the body's feet, and he cried out, "Oh Lord it is my mother!"

Indeed it was the body of Rebecca Cornell. Somehow her dress had caught fire, caused either by a burning ember from the fireplace or the pipe she loved to smoke. She was buried on Monday, February 10, on the Cornell homestead.

But that was by no means the end of the story. Two days after the funeral, during the early morning hours of February 12, Rebecca's brother John Briggs had a dream about his sister. It greatly troubled him, and he approached local authorities to tell them about what he had experienced.

On Thursday, February 20, the Portsmouth Town Council convened and heard Briggs's sworn testimony. Council secretary John Sanford recorded the proceedings:

> John Brigs [*sic*] of the Towne of Portsmouth, Aged sixty foure yeares or thereabouts, being According to Law Sworne and Ingaged before the Councell, Testifieth that on the Twelfth Day of this instant month February in the night, as the Deponent lay in his bed, he being in a Dream of Mrs. Rebecca Cornell deceased, and being between Sleeping and Wakeing, he thought he felt something heave up the Bedclothes twice, and thought some body had been coming to . . . him, whereupon he awaked, and turned himself about in his bed.
>
> And being turned, he perceived a light in the room, like to the dawning of ye day, and plainly saw the shape and appearance of a woman standing by his bed side whereat he was much affrighted.
>
> [He] cried out, In the name of God what art thou?
>
> The Aperition answered, I am your sister Cornell, and twice said, See how I was burnt with fire.
>
> And she plainely appeared unto him to be very much burnt about the shoulders, face, and head.

The members of the council agreed with Briggs that the dream suggested there was something suspicious about Rebecca Cornell's death. Later that same day, they exhumed her body and an autopsy found a puncture wound in her stomach.

Had someone murdered this ailing seventy-three-year-old woman by stabbing her and then burning the body to cover up the crime? If so, who would do such a thing? A full investigation was begun.

During the next several weeks, more sworn testimony was taken from neighbors and family members, and two possible scenarios emerged: Rebecca had either been murdered by her son Thomas, or she had committed suicide.

The murder theory was supported by testimony from a number of neighbors who suggested that Thomas had been unkind to his mother and that they had fought about money.

One of the neighbors, sixty-one-year-old Sarah Wilde, recounted a conversation she had once had with Rebecca:

"Mrs. Rebecca Cornell told his deponent that her son Thomas, one time being angry with her, looked very fierce upon her & nasht or sett his teeth at her and said she had beene a cruell mother to him. She [Rebecca] told him shee had not been cruell . . . and sayd his carriage and expressions therein was a great trouble or terror to her."

Another neighbor, thirty-three-year-old Mary Almy, testified that Rebecca complained about being neglected by her oldest son's family:

"Mrs. Rebecca Cornell told this deponent . . . she was forced in ye winter season in ye cold weather to goe to her bed unmade and unwarmed and was therefore forced to procure some woollin cloth to wrap her selfe in before shee went to her cold bedd.

"And also ye said Mrs. Rebecca Cornell told this deponent that if shee could not eate [with] all ye foalkes of ye house . . . shee must fast, for there was nothing brought in for her to eate."

Sarah Wilde's seventy-three-year-old husband, Nicholas, shed light on the family's conflict over money.

"Mrs. Rebecca Cornell came to this deponent's house, & there complained of her son Thomas Cornell. He was to pay her yearly [rent] of six pounds and [provide] for a maid servant, which shee sayd he refused to pay and did withhold."

Thomas Cornell Sr.'s will had stipulated that Thomas junior would be allowed to set up housekeeping in the Cornell home—which he did—but only after he paid ten pounds to each of his ten siblings—which he did not. According to Nicholas Wilde's testimony, this had also been a source of conflict between mother and son.

So money had been established as a motive if, in fact, Thomas had killed his mother. But what about access? His wife, Sarah (who was pregnant with her third child), and each of his four sons testified that he had been the last person to see Rebecca alive during the ninety minutes he had spent with his mother in her room. And Thomas himself had been caught in a potentially damaging lie. A man from Newport named Joseph Torrey, who had served on the jury during the coroner's inquest, testified that when he visited the Cornell home he asked Thomas about the second door to his mother's room, which provided direct access to the outside, and whether it had been locked on the night of his mother's death. Theoretically, whoever killed Rebecca could have slipped in and out through this door without being noticed. According to Torrey's testimony, Thomas Cornell told him there was no lock on the door, but when Torrey examined the door himself, there was in fact a bar on the latch.

As for the theory that Rebecca Cornell had somehow committed suicide, her twenty-eight-year-old daughter-in-law, Mary, recalled a conversation she had once had with her mother-in-law in which Rebecca in a moment of despair had "thought to have stabbed a pen knife in her [own] heart . . . and then shee should be ridd of her trouble."

More troubling was the testimony of Rebecca Woolsey, who was four months pregnant when she journeyed to Portsmouth to speak with authorities on April 10. She told them that the last time she had visited Rhode Island, her mother remarked that she didn't look well. The daughter explained that she was recovering from a recent bout with smallpox. But there was more to it.

Shee [Rebecca Woolsey] was very much afflicted and troubled in mind, and she was sometimes perswaded to drowne her selfe, and sometimes to stab her selfe. Soe the deponent's mother told her daughter that shee must pray to God, and he would helpe her. The deponent told her mother, shee did often call upon God, and he did hear her.

When the deponent had done with this discourse, the deponent's mother told her daughter that shee had beene . . . possessed with an evill spirit, and that she was divers times perswaded to make away with her selfe, and yet the Lord was pleased from time to time to preserve her.

The deponent told her mother that shee would tell her brother Thomas of it, and her mother charged he not to tell him, soe shee did not tell him.

After weighing the testimony and the evidence, prosecutor John Easton presented his case to the jury on May 12:

I present and indict Thomas Cornell of Portsmouth . . . That against the feare of God, the Honour of our Soveraigne Lord the Kinge, and the Law and peace of this Colony, on the evening of the 8th day of February in the 25th yeare of the Reigne of his Majesty Charles the Second . . . the sayd Thomas Cornell did violently kill his Mother, Rebecca Cornell, Widdow, or was ayding or abetting thereto, in the Dwelling House of his sayd Mother in the foresaid towne of Portsmouth, which act of his is Murder, and is against the honored Crowne and dignity of his Majesty the laws and peace of this colony.

Despite the fact that no murder weapon was ever identified, the jury found Thomas Cornell guilty of the charge, and he was hanged on the afternoon of May 23.

Four months later, on September 8, Rebecca Woolsey gave birth to her last child, a daughter she and George named Mary, perhaps to honor the memory of the daughter they had lost some years before.

And a short time before that in Portsmouth, the newly widowed Sarah Cornell also gave birth to a daughter. As an obvious protest of the verdict against her husband, she named the little girl Innocent.

ON NOVEMBER 2, 1691, seventy-five-year-old George Woolsey drew up his last will and testament. In it, as was the custom of the time, he left the family home and the land it stood on to his beloved widow. The rest of his land holdings he divided among his three surviving sons:

> 1st. item—I give and bequeath unto my well beloved and eldest Son, GEORGE WOLSEY all my lott of land being at ye Beaver Pond within ye town of Jamaica aforesaid.
>
> 2nd. item—I give and bequeath unto my well beloved Son, THOMAS WOLSEY all ye fifteen acre lott of land lying to ye westward of Anthony Walters home lott in Jamaica.
>
> 3rd. item—I give and bequeath unto my well beloved Son, JOHN WOLSEY all ye my thirty acre lott of land lying to ye eastward by ye Little Plains runing within ye bounds of Jamaica a for said to have and to hold the said thirty acre lott of land with its appurtenances.

To his youngest child, eighteen-year-old Mary, he left "one feather bed and bolster, two pillows, a pair of sheets and two coverlids to be delivered her at her day of marriage or when she attains ye age of eighteen years, also one cow to be delivered her at ye same time."

His final instructions were that when Rebecca passed away, the house and land were to be divided equally among the three boys and all of the home's fixtures and furnishings were to go to daughters Sarah, Rebecca, and Mary.

George Woolsey died sometime during 1698 when he would have been either eighty-one or eighty-two years old. Rebecca lived another fifteen years. She died in 1712 at the age of eighty-four. They are both said to be buried in the Old Prospect Cemetery, which is tucked in the northwest corner of York College in Jamaica, next to the Long Island Rail Road track that runs through town.

I drove past the cemetery with Cindy and Carlee one summer afternoon. It is obscured by a tall iron rail fence with barbed wire running along the top. Grass and weeds have grown up around the few headstones still standing, and the tiny chapel on the grounds is badly in need of repair. We drove around the block twice, looking for a place to park and an entrance to the cemetery. We found neither. A uniformed guard posted at the entrance to one of the college parking lots told us very politely that there really was no way of getting into the cemetery. We thanked him and left. I was disappointed that I wasn't able to walk the grounds of George and Rebecca Woolsey's final resting place. I had to be content just driving by.

My journey with George was complete. I had taken communion in the church in Great Yarmouth, England, where he had been baptized almost four hundred years earlier. I had walked the narrow cobblestone streets of the Delfshaven district of Rotterdam, Holland, where he had come of age and learned about the rigors of business from his father and their Dutch neighbors. And now I found myself living not far from where he and Rebecca had raised their family, where Cindy and I raised our own children three hundred years and nine generations later.

Chapter Five

TOPSFIELD, MASSACHUSETTS, 1650–1691

The Congregationalists

C OME ON, I want to show you something."

We were at what I thought was the end of a personal tour of the Congregational Church in Topsfield, Massachusetts, one Tuesday afternoon, standing in the balcony of the beautiful 170-year-old meetinghouse, when Pastor Norm Bendroth asked me if I was up for an adventure. I was.

He opened a door just off the balcony, shoved some Christmas decorations out of the way, and invited me to follow him up the vertical steel ladder just inside the doorway. We slowly made our way up through the narrow steeple, past all the pipes and wires and insulation.

Two days before, on Palm Sunday, I had worshipped with this congregation. The service had begun across the town's Common in front of the church offices where we gathered with the choir, a parishioner dressed as Jesus, and the smallest donkey I have ever seen. Palm fronds and bulletins were passed out to everyone. The front of the bulletin said, "The Congregational Church of Topsfield, Gathered for prayer, scattered for service."

Promptly at nine-thirty, Jesus and the donkey led us in a procession across the Common back toward the church. We passed by a small boulder resting against a tree. The inscription carved into it read:

IN MEMORY OF THREE
WOMEN OF TOPSFIELD PARISH
MARY ESTY
ELIZABETH HOW
SARAH WILDES
VICTIMS OF
THE WITCHCRAFT DELUSION
OF 1692
TOPSFIELD HISTORICAL SOCIETY
MAY 25, 1992

"Watch your head," Pastor Bendroth warned as we continued our ascent to the top of the steeple, passing by what appeared to be large air-conditioning ducts. "We're almost there."

Before our tour, we had spent time in his office getting acquainted and comparing notes about our respective Puritan ancestors. He proudly declared that he was a descendant of Samuel Sewall, who had been a highly respected judge throughout the Massachusetts Bay Colony in the late 1600s and early 1700s. We shared an awkward chuckle when I pointed out that Justice Sewall had been one of the three judges who presided over the Salem witch trials, and that my ancestors Mary Towne Estey and Rebecca Towne Nurse had been two of the nineteen people hanged. (I should point out that in January of 1697, Justice Sewall publicly repented and asked forgiveness for his role in the trials.)

Hosanna, hosanna, hosanna in the highest
Lord we lift up your Name, With our hearts full of praise.

the choir sang as we continued our procession across the Common and up the steps into the church where we filed down the two side aisles and took our seats in the old wooden pews. I looked around the sanctuary at the large stained-glass windows. Up front in the chancel area, the choir members took their seats behind the altar and Pastor Bendroth sat behind the pulpit on the left side. Jesus and the donkey stood front and center with two more parishioners who held baby lambs in their arms.

The congregation stood and we were led in a responsive reading:

LEADER: He comes! He comes to Jerusalem!
PEOPLE: We see him as he draws near.
LEADER: God's salvation is upon us!
PEOPLE: God's Christ is bringing us the kingdom.

These people were the spiritual descendants of the first congregation formed in Topsfield in 1641 under Reverend William Knight. They were Congregationalists, the Protestant denomination with roots that go back to the English village of Scrooby, the home of the earliest Separatists, and the theologians William Ames and Henry Jacob, who were mentors of the Pilgrims' spiritual leader, John Robinson.

Reverend Knight stayed only two years in Topsfield, until 1643, and there is no record of another minister serving the community until 1655 with the arrival of William Perkins, who served eight years. A plaque on the front of the Topsfield Congregational Church pegs its formal organization to November 4, 1663, when the Reverend Thomas Gilbert took over.

The Topsfield Church's website says, "In those early days it was not possible to separate the governance of the Town from the governance of the Church because Church and Town were one and the same. The

Meetinghouse was both the place of worship and the place of conduct-ing the business of the community.

"Records of the earliest town meetings are devoted to such matters as the cost of building a pulpit, orders to the selectmen to repair the Meetinghouse, and a matter of great contention—how to organize the seating arrangements for the people of the community in the Meeting-house."

Reverend Gilbert stayed until 1671, when he was dismissed by the congregation for "intemperance." According to the historian George Francis Dow, who wrote the definitive *History of Topsfield, Massachu-setts,* "The charge was not on account of his use of wine, but, because of his coming intoxicated to the Lord's Table."

There are conflicting accounts about the role my nine-times great-grandmother Joanna Towne may have played in Gilbert's dismissal. One private Towne family genealogical website I discovered claimed that it was Goody Towne herself who brought the charges against the minister.

But there is also this account in a book about the Salem witch trials titled *Currents of Malice*:

"Relations between the Gould family and the Townes and Estys had been strained ever since the quarrel over their minister, the Reverend Mr. Gilbert, when Mary Esty's mother, old Joanna Towne, had supported him against the Goulds' faction."

The congregation stood once again and we sang a Palm Sunday hymn:

> *Praise to our God, wave high the palm*
> *Praise to Christ Jesus, God's own Son.*
> *Praise to the Spirit we now sing,*
> *For in our hearts hosannas ring. Amen.*

"Here we are," Pastor Bendroth said, as he lifted himself up onto a platform that served as the floor in the bell tower section of the steeple.

I pulled myself up and stood next to him in the cramped space. A ray of sunlight came through the dusty window that faced to the west.

"There it is," he said, pointing down.

"It" was a large bell the town had purchased for $400 in 1817 for its meetinghouse. It had been placed in this church building when it was built in 1842.

"Take a closer look," Pastor Bendroth said.

Along the upper band was the inscription REVERE & COMPANY, BOSTON, 1817.

"Paul Revere cast this bell."

Now I understood why he had dragged me up here. Norm Bendroth and his wife, Peggy, had lived all over the country: in Chicago where they met in seminary; in Baltimore, where Peggy got her doctorate at Johns Hopkins University; in Washington, D.C., where Norm worked on Capitol Hill for a couple of nonprofit Christian ministries; and in Michigan and Massachusetts where Norm had served a number of local congregations. But at this moment, high up in the bell tower of this old New England church standing before this historic relic, I sensed that Norm was reaching back to his Puritan roots. And he brought a fellow Puritan descendant to this place, perhaps for a specific reason. Judge Sewall's great-grandson was standing peacefully with Mary Towne Estey's great-grandson and, as a result, an old score that went back three hundred years was being laid to rest.

I took a few pictures of the bell, and we lingered for a while discussing the view out each of the tower's four windows. Then we made our way back down the ladder.

Before my meeting with Pastor Bendroth, I had driven around Topsfield. Its downtown area is only a few square blocks surrounded by hundreds of tract homes that extend for a few miles in all directions.

Topsfield is roughly twenty-five miles north of Boston. Its most distinctive features are its hills, which are among the highest in the region, its many fertile meadows, and a river the natives called Agawam and that the English settlers renamed Ipswich. During his mapping tour of New England in 1614, Captain John Smith remembered the area as "an excellent habitation" with "many rising hills: and on their tops and descents, many corne fields and delightful groves."

When word spread in January of 1633 that the French were setting up camp north of Boston with the intention of bringing in more settlers, Governor Winthrop immediately dispatched his son, John junior, and a group of twelve men to begin preparations for what turned out to be some very successful English settlements. The Great Puritan Migration of the 1630s had just begun. It would eventually bring twenty thousand people to the area, and they spread out from Boston, fueling the Massachusetts Bay Colony's rapid growth. As an example of that growth, John Winthrop Jr., in 1638, bought three hundred acres from a local native sagamore for twenty pounds. Four years later he sold the land for 250 pounds.

The earliest land grants in the area north of the Ipswich River went to men with names that were later very important to New England's history: Endicott, Bradstreet, Symonds, and Paine, just to name a few. Informally, the area was referred to as the New Meadows, and in October of 1648 it was officially named Topsfield after a small parish north of London in Essex County, England.

I headed south a couple of miles to the corner of Main Street and Salem Road where the town's agricultural co-op is located. On the south side of the road were several acres of farmland that looked as if they were ready for planting. A farmhouse sat on the southern portion of the land, and behind it was the Ipswich River.

This was part of the forty acres William Towne had purchased from William Paine in February of 1651 for twenty-nine pounds, and it was here that the Townes had built a home and finished raising their children. By then, their oldest daughter, Rebecca, would have been about thirty years old and already married to Francis Nurse; Edmund would have been about twenty-two years old (and perhaps already married to his wife, Mary Browning); Jacob would have been nineteen; Mary seventeen (in a few years she would marry Isaac Estey); Sarah fourteen; and Joseph twelve.

The first time the Townes show up in New England public records is in late 1640, when William was granted a ten-acre plot of land in the Northfields section of Salem, now known as Danversport. That is virtually all that is known about them until their move to Topsfield ten years later.

In 1663, when young Joseph married the Reverend Thomas Perkins's daughter, Phoebe, the Townes deeded two-thirds of their property to him. By then, Jacob lived on land east of there, and Edmund owned property to the north.

Isaac and Mary Estey lived to the west with the three children they had had at that point: four-year-old Joseph, two-year-old Sarah, and the infant John.

Rebecca and Francis Nurse and their children lived closer to Salem, and records don't indicate where Sarah lived at that time.

Given the number of acres he owned, it is a safe bet that William was a farmer, which many men in Topsfield were, and chances are he grew either corn, which he would have sold to the local grist mill, or flaxseed for the area's cattle and sheep, or both.

Public records show that Isaac Estey was Topsfield's first cooper, a trade he taught to at least two of his nephews: Edmund's oldest son, Thomas, and Jacob's youngest son, Edmund.

William died in 1672 or '73 without leaving a will. Joanna died ten years later. A petition for settlement of her estate dated January 17, 1683, showed that the three sons received equal portions of their parents' property and the three daughters divided the so-called movables, in other words all of the furniture and other effects. The petition was signed by Edmund's widow, Mary, and by Jacob, Joseph, Francis Nurse, Mary Estey, and Sarah Bridges.

After our tour of the Congregational Church, Pastor Bendroth walked me across the Common toward the Parson Capen House, where we met the president of the Topsfield Historical Society, Norman Isler. He looked to be in his late sixties, dressed casually in a bright blue plaid shirt and a beige sportcoat with an American flag on the lapel. He had the earnest demeanor that you would expect of a Puritan, but he smiled easily and it was clear that history was his passion. We stood in the middle of the Common and chatted, and then we began our tour of what is considered one of the oldest and best-preserved homes in all of New England, the Parson Capen House.

The young Topsfield church found stability with the arrival in 1684 of the Reverend Joseph Capen, who stayed forty years and came to be known affectionately by all as Parson Capen. The people had heard about the young preacher, then living in Dorchester, in 1681. They dispatched Reverend Perkins's son, Thomas junior, and another man to persuade Capen to come to Topsfield. By then they were in competition for his services with a church in New Haven, Connecticut.

Capen agreed to come to Topsfield, perhaps to be near his in-laws who lived in the area. But even then the people of the town feared they

would lose this dynamic young man of God, so whenever he ventured out to visit friends and family, he was accompanied by Jacob Towne and John Howe to make sure he returned.

On June 11, 1684, Capen was ordained as minister of the Topsfield Congregational Church. He was paid sixty-five pounds a year, twenty of that in silver and the rest in what was called "country pay," or corn, pork, and beef. The town also granted him twelve acres of land on which he built his own parsonage. In his *History of Topsfield, Massachusetts*, George Francis Dow explained why:

"The tradition is still preserved that the young bride of the Parson did not look with favor on the parsonage owned by the town and as she came from the well-to-do Appleton family of Ipswich, the frame of a new house was erected on a small knoll beside the training field."

Dow wrote that the Capen home was an example of the sturdy construction typical of second-generation colonists:

The houses that were built by the earliest settlers along the New England coast usually were small, rude affairs that in a few years were replaced by more permanent structures. The large number of those erected in Salem to accommodate the first immigration had disappeared before 1661.

With more leisure and additional man power came the more substantial house. . . . At first, the structure generally was a one-room house, that is, a huge chimney with one room on the ground floor and a loft above. Frequently, however, it was of two stories. As the family grew in number or became more prosperous, a room was built on the other side of the chimney and often times at a still later day, a one-story lean-to was added along the back of the house.

The Parson Capen House was a good example. It was a two-story structure built around a centrally located chimney, with two rooms on each floor, each room with its own fireplace.

As we walked up the hill toward the house, Norm Isler pointed out its most unusual feature. The second floor extended beyond the first by several inches, giving the front of the house a top-heavy look. Local lore said that it would make it more difficult for invading Indians to climb to the top floor during an attack. But since there is no overhang in the back of the house, it's likely the style was more aesthetic than functional.

Isler unlocked the front door and we stepped into the small entryway that included the stairwell to the second floor. He pointed us to the right and we walked into a rustic-looking room with creaky, uneven floorboards and a very long dining room table with place settings for ten or twelve. There was a faint odor of old wood and smoke.

I tried to picture the Towne family gathered around a table like this for a meal. If they followed the customs of the time, father William would have sat at the head, eating off a pewter plate and drinking from a pewter stein while everyone else used wooden plates and cups. Everyone would have used knives and spoons to eat with. Forks were introduced in the late seventeenth century.

Another feature typical of homes from that era were the low ceilings, which made the rooms easier to keep warm, and the exposed wooden girders the colonists called summer beams. Mr. Isler had me walk to a corner of the room and look up at one particular beam, in which someone had carved, "July Ye 8ᵗʰ 1683."

"That tells us the exact date this home was framed," he explained.

We walked to the other side of the house to the more formal parlor. This was a much cheerier room since the walls were covered with white plaster and the beams in the ceiling were painted white. A small oval-shaped table sat in the middle of the room with four upright chairs around it.

"This is where Parson Capen would have received members of his congregation," Isler said. He pointed to the chair on the south side of the table.

"Take a look," he said.

On the back of the chair was carved "P. Capen 1708."

"That was, indeed, Parson Capen's own chair," he said.

The two Norms talked about some of the pieces in the room while I circled the perimeter of the room, pretending to look at the bed in one corner and the spinning wheel in another. But I didn't really see or hear anything, because I was thinking that my eight-times great-grandmother Mary Estey had been in this room, had seen these walls, had walked on this floor. And it was entirely possible that members of the Towne and Estey families had come here looking for solace during the witch trials of 1692. In 1703, Parson Capen was among the group of ministers who petitioned the courts to clear the names of the nineteen people who had been hanged because "there was not as is supposed sufficient evidence to prove the guilt of such a crime." When that finally happened in 1711, maybe family members gathered here once again to celebrate or simply to pray.

During the forty-two years that he served the Topsfield church, until his death in 1725, Parson Capen kept books of records. The first entry in the first volume was a list of the names of the original forty-nine people in his flock. There were twenty-two men listed in a left-hand column and twenty-seven women listed on the right.

1684.

*A List of ye members in full communion at
Topsfield when I was first ordained.*
— JOSEPH CAPEN

Francis Peabody	*Deacon Perkins wife*
John Reddington	*Lieftenant Goulds wife*
Abraham Reddington Senr	*Tho Dormans wife*
Joseph Bixby Senr	*Isaak Esties wife*
John Gould Senr	*Jacob Towns wife*
Thomas Baker	*Joseph Towns wife*
Thomas Perkins Deacon	*Widdow Mary Towne*
Died May 7th 86	*Ephraim Dormans wife*

John Pabody	John Wilds his wife
Thomas Dorman	James How Sen. Wife
Ephraim Dorman	Michael Dunnels wife
Samuel Howlett	John Nichols wife
William Howlett	Daniell Bormans wife
Isaak Cumins	Isaak Cummins wife
John French	William Howletts wife
Isaak Estie	Abraham Reddingtons wife
James How Senr	Joseph Bixbys wife
Samuell Perley	John Pabodys wife
Nehemiah Abbott	Samuell Simons his wife
John Cummins, Decem 7 85	Robart Smiths wife
Was dismissed to ye	William Smiths wife
church at Dunstable	Widdow Andrews
Robert Stiles dead	Nehemiah Abbots wife
Thomas Perkins Jnr	Widdow Perley
Daniel Hovey	William Watson his wife
John French, his wife	John Cummins his wife
drowned herself	
May 13, 1701	

Of course, the woman listed as "Isaak Esties wife" was my ancestor Mary. Edmund Towne is thought to have died in 1678, hence his wife Mary's designation as a "Widdow." I have no idea why neither Jacob nor Joseph Towne was listed, even though their wives were.

Unfortunately, the reason for Parson Capen's most interesting notation on the list—about John French's wife drowning herself—remains a mystery. But there is at least one story of great historical significance from this document to tell. It concerns the Robert Smith family.

Three of Smith's daughters married Towne men. Jacob's oldest son, John, married Mary Smith in 1680. They moved to Oxford, Massachusetts, where they had ten children. Jacob junior married Phoebe Smith in 1683. They remained in Topsfield, where they also had ten children. Finally, Edmund's son Joseph married Amy Smith in 1687. They had eight children.

But here's the reason history remembers the Smith family: Robert's great-great-great-grandson was Joseph Smith Jr., the founder of the Mormon Church.

There is a plaque sitting in the open grassy area west of the Congregational Church that was dedicated in the spring of 2005. It tells the whole story:

TOPSFIELD CONGREGATIONAL CHURCH
Situated on Topsfield's Common, three Congregational
meetinghouses have provided a place for spiritual
communion and worship for over three hundred years.
The first church was built in 1703, the second in 1759,
and the present one in 1842.
Five generations of the Robert Smith family of Topsfield
were Congregationalists including
Robert (1626–1693), Samuel I (1666–1748),
Samuel II (1714–1785), Asael (1744–1830), and
Joseph I (1771–1840).
Both Asael and Joseph Smith I were baptized in the
second meetinghouse. Like many families in the area,
the Smiths were noted for their Revolutionary
patriotism and religious devotion. Joseph Smith Jr.
(1805–1844), prophet and founder of the Church of Jesus
Christ of Latter-day Saints, is a descendant of the
Topsfield Smiths.
Erected by the Topsfield Historical Society
And the Mormon Historic Sites Foundation
2005

After the Revolution, Asael moved his family north to the Green Mountains of Vermont. It was there, in 1795, that Joseph Sr. married Lucy Mack. Joseph Jr, the fourth of their surviving children, was born in December of 1805. The family later moved west to Palmyra, New York, and for a time, during the period of Christian revival known as the Second Great Awakening, the Smiths flirted with Methodism. But all of that changed in 1820 when young Joseph junior saw what Mormons refer to as his First Vision, the seminal event in the history of the Mormon Church. Today, Topsfield is an important destination for Mormon pilgrimages.

Most of the forty-nine people on Parson Capen's list were second-generation New Englanders. By this time in 1684, as the seventeenth century was drawing to a close, the great Puritan zeal had begun to wane. Much had happened to cause this.

When civil war broke out in England in 1642 and King Charles I was captured and executed in 1649, the monarchy was replaced by a commonwealth under the charismatic Puritan Oliver Cromwell. The flow of Puritans from England to New England came to a virtual halt, and in fact a number of them returned to England to help take up the cause. The New England economy suffered as a result, and that in turn led to a decline of the religious fervor the first-generation Puritans had brought to the area. It was replaced by a more pragmatic attitude that emphasized economic well-being more than spiritual discipline. Cromwell's death in 1658 and the restoration of the monarchy two years later did nothing to change that.

In 1648 a group of theologians gathered in Cambridge, Massachusetts, to develop a constitution for the Congregational movement in New England. The document, written by Richard Mather, was called the Cambridge Platform. It was a lengthy treatise that encouraged groups of Saints to covenant together, "each one a distinct society of itself, having officers of their own, which had not the charge of others; virtues of their own, for which others are not praised; corruptions of their own, for which others are not blamed."

When we had finished touring the Parson Capen House, I shook hands with Norm Bendroth and Norm Isler, thanked them for their hospitality, and promised to stay in touch.

On my way out of town, I drove through the Pine Grove Cemetery, which is less than a mile north of the town Common. Inside, on the thirty-plus acres of rolling hills, are a number of Towne family headstones dating from the early 1800s to the late 1900s. The oldest decipherable headstone in the cemetery belongs to Ebeneezer Averill, who died December 22, 1717.

At the south end of the cemetery is an open space where Topsfield's first two meetinghouses were built. Parson Capen and his wife are buried nearby, as are Reverend William Perkins and a few other pastors who served the Topsfield church through the years.

On the western edge of the cemetery stand a handful of small headstones scattered about in no particular order. They are meant to portray the graves of the town's earliest settlers, who were buried under wooden headstones that long ago decayed in the elements. William and Joanna Towne and their children were probably buried here, but the locations of their graves have been lost to history.

I had been through this cemetery a couple of times already. During previous visits I had taken the time to study each Towne family headstone, recording names and dates. But this time I passed through without stopping, thinking about the generations of my family buried there and about an epitaph on one of the headstones:

> *Behold and see as you pass by,*
> *As you are now so once was I,*
> *As I am now so you must be,*
> *Prepare for death & follow me.*

I continued south on Main Street back through town toward the site of the original Towne homestead. Norman Isler had given me a map of the area from 1872. When I got to the corner of Main and Salem Road, I pulled over, got out of the car, and laid the map out on the hood of my car. The names of landowners were printed within the boundaries of the lots they owned. Towne and Estey showed up here and there, most often along the Ipswich River.

Border disputes were common in the early days of the colonies, mostly because the process of determining where one lot began and another ended was far from precise. Disputes in the area where I stood looking at my map began in the 1640s, after people in adjacent villages of Ipswich and Salem expressed interest in the territory that became Topsfield.

The formal establishment of Topsfield in 1651 didn't end the disputes, so in 1659 a committee of men from Topsfield and Salem was formed to establish formal boundaries between the two villages.

The disputes persisted. In June of 1682, Salem Village resident John Putnam filed suit against the people of Topsfield, claiming the town illegally encroached on his property. The Salem court that heard the suit ruled in his favor. The people of Topsfield appealed to a higher court, which ruled in Topsfield's favor, and the ill will among neighbors only got worse.

Several members of the Putnam family owned land along the Salem/Topsfield border, and they were often party to disputes. In his *History of Topsfield, Massachusetts*, George Francis Dow described the Putnams as "strong-willed men, of high temper, eager for controversy and even personal conflict."

Indeed, when members of the Towne and Estey families filed suit against the Putnams in 1687, their petition quoted in Dow's book showed the acrimony that existed:

[The Townes and Esteys] testified that they were in the woods within Topsfield bounds on the south side of the [Ipswich] river and "saw Capt. John Putnam of Salem Farms or Village & his sons

& som of his cozins cutting down tymber within Topsfield bounds
& on Topsfield mens properties and several of Topsfield men fore-
warned Capt. John Putnam from cutting tymber on their land."

The said Captain replied, "I have felled the tymber that is here
cutt down on my orders & I will keep cutting and carrying away
from this land till next March . . . and further you may sue me, you
know where I dwell," and his company [continued] on.

The court decided against the Putnams, which only served to
increase the acrimony.

George Francis Dow is among the historians who believed that the
land disputes between the Putnams and the people of Topsfield were a
cause of the Salem witch trials of 1692.

For example, he wrote, after the Putnams lost their case in 1687,
"They entered a complaint at the next Ipswich Court that Isaac Estey
had told a lie in open Court during the trial of their land case. The Court
summarily referred their complaint to the next quarter session and
nothing more came of it.

"Five years later Anne Putnam accused Mary Estey, the wife of
Isaac, of afflicting her and the accusation led to her ignominious death
on Gallows Hill, Salem."

The teenaged Anne Putnam was certainly a central figure in the
witch trials, and it is possible that she accused Mary Estey of being a
witch at the behest of her relatives, who could have been out for
revenge. But in the end, the Salem witch trials were a highly complex
series of events that defy a single explanation. Unfortunately, my ancestors were key players in what is still among the most bizarre episodes in
American history.

I rolled up my map, got back in the car, and drove south along the
Ipswich River toward Salem.

Chapter Six

SALEM, MASSACHUSETTS, 1692

The Witch Trials

M ARY TOWNE ESTEY *was executed September 22, 1692 in Salem,
MA, for witchcraft."*

The first time I came across that sentence on page 29 of my cousin's
family tree, I had to read it a few times to understand exactly what it was
saying. Someone in my family had been executed for witchcraft. There
was a witch in my family.

I backtracked a few pages to figure out how I was related to her. I
found Mary and Isaac Estey and their children. The youngest, a son
named Joshua, was born July 2, 1678. Joshua went on to marry Abigail
Stanley, and on March 5, 1704, they had a daughter, Eleanor. On
September 24, 1723, Eleanor married Samuell Griffeth eighty miles
south in Rochester, Massachusetts. After riffling through a few more
pages, I determined that Samuell Griffeth had been my six-times great-
grandfather, which meant that Mary Towne Estey was my eight-times
great-grandmother.

My great-great-great-great-great-great-great-great-grandmother had
been a witch—not just any witch, but one of the legendary Salem
witches. I wasn't sure how to react. Was I supposed to be embarrassed
or proud?

I went to the Internet and typed "Mary Estey" into a search engine,
and I was amazed at the number of websites dedicated not only to the
witch trials but also to Mary herself. And most of them devoted consid-
erable space to a petition she had written while she was in jail. There
were debates about whether she was literate enough to have composed
it, but there was no question that the petition had been one of the most
important documents—maybe even *the* most important—to emerge
from the trials.

My birthday is in August. The year I turned forty-eight, it fell on a

Saturday. A few weeks before, Cindy had asked what I wanted to do to celebrate, and I said, "I want to go to Salem." By this time she didn't have to ask why. She and the kids had already been dragged to enough cemeteries and libraries to know what I had in mind. But at least this one would have an attractive hook: witches. And while I can't say that Chad and Carlee agreed eagerly to the trip, they didn't put up much of a fight when they realized this would have something to do with our "cool" ancestor.

I'm not sure what I expected of Salem. I guess I had pictured quaint and historic cobblestone streets and homes with gables, anything that would suggest its Puritan heritage. Instead we found a town with identity issues.

Salem reminds me of Hollywood, which is near where Cindy and I grew up. (I was born in North Hollywood.) During the 1960s, 1970s, and 1980s tourists who visited Tinseltown were confused and dismayed by what they did, and didn't, find. There were no stars walking the boulevards, no more Brown Derby restaurant, and only a few studios hidden behind brick walls. A long time ago, Hollywood became a series of strip malls and parking lots; it had moved beyond the reputation the public still embraced.

Salem has the same problem. Let's face it: most tourists flock there each year for one reason. But unlike, say, Boston, where you can still retrace Paul Revere's ride or see where the boxes of tea were dumped in the harbor, in Salem there is scant tangible evidence that the witch trials ever happened. The jail where many of the accused were held was torn down decades ago, and no one can pinpoint the exact location of Gallows Hill, where the convicted were hanged.

Salem's real problem is that most of the witch hysteria of 1692 didn't actually occur there. It happened a few miles to the north and west in what were then a collection of remote farms loosely organized as Salem Village, which long ago changed its name to Danvers. No one has ever heard of the Danvers witch trials, which is exactly what the chamber of commerce had in mind.

So today there are two Salems for tourists to visit: the one it never really was, and the one it is desperate to become.

I'll start with the second one first. The reputation Salem is most anxious to develop is best represented by its Peabody Essex Museum, which bills itself as the oldest continuously operating museum in the country. It opened in 1799, but after a $150-million-dollar makeover, it began life again in 2003 in a dramatic, ultrafuturistic glass building that sits in the middle of downtown. (Think I. M. Pei's pyramid at the entrance of the Louvre.)

The library's mission statement reads:

"The Peabody Essex will be one of the nation's major museums for Asian art, including Japanese, Chinese, Korean, and Indian art, along with the finest collection of Asian Export art extant, and nineteenth-century Asian photography. It will present the earliest collections of Native American, African, and Oceanic art in the nation—all collections of exceptional standing. The historic houses and gardens, and American decorative art, and maritime art collections will provide an unrivaled spectrum of New England's heritage over 300 years."

Not a word about you-know-what. And, in fact, there isn't a single exhibit devoted to the witch trials. And while the museum's Phillips Library houses all of the original court records and transcripts from the trials, its own mission statement—"a major resource for maritime history and art, New England life and culture, American decorative arts, Asian art and culture, Native American history and art, the art and culture of Oceania, natural history and genealogy"—still doesn't mention the trials. Instead, there is this one line tucked in a random corner of its website:

"The library's best known holdings are undoubtedly the records of the special 1692 Court of Oyer and Terminer, better known as the 1692 Salem Witchcraft Trials."

In journalism, we call that burying the lead.

We looked into a tour of some of the city's historic homes offered by the museum, and as luck would have it we were told that one of the museum's best guides had just returned from vacation and was on hand to give us a private tour.

Our guide looked to be in his late sixties. He dressed the way I imagined a retired Ivy League professor would: white shirt with button-down collar, khakis and worn chinos. Before we began our tour, he gathered the four of us in front of the museum entrance.

"So tell me," he asked, "why are you taking this tour? What can I show you that will make it more enjoyable for you?"

"I'm glad you asked," I said. "I'm descended from one of the Salem witches."

Looking back, I'm not sure what kind of response I expected. Maybe an offer to veer off the normal tour in order to see some of the juicier landmarks? Or the name of another person who could do that for us? Or, at the very least, a smile of recognition? A warm handshake? We got none of that.

"You'll need to go to Danvers for that," he said without a hint of enthusiasm.

There was an awkward moment when it seemed the tour was over before it started, but Cindy smoothed things over, assuring him that we were still interested in seeing whatever he had to offer. As it turned out, we enjoyed the tour very much, but I never again brought up the witch trials, and our guide never asked.

One of the attractions that brings tourists to Salem is its wax museum. Its brochure boasts of "eerily lifelike London-made wax figures that depict Salem's vivid history from its founding in 1626 through the terrifying Hysteria of 1692."

We aren't exactly talking about the scope and grandeur of Madame Tussaud's in London, though. It was more like a small-town carnival exhibit. We paid our money and made our way through the two rooms, both darkened for effect, with spotlights trained on each of the tableaux of wax figures posed in dramatic fashion. We were in and out in fifteen minutes. The souvenir shop where we spent considerably more time sold hats and T-shirts and mugs and shot glasses, all decorated with the same silhouette logo of a witch on a broomstick.

Next door to the wax museum was the Witch Museum, which promised to reveal the truth about real witches. By this time, though, I'd had enough museums. While Cindy and the kids headed there, I walked to the cemetery in the middle of town.

The sign on the wrought-iron gate at the entrance reads:

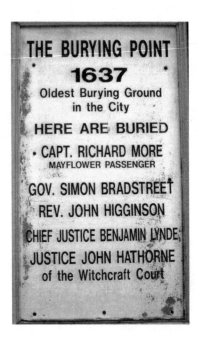

Captain More had sailed on the *Mayflower* as a child with his brother and two sisters only after their father discovered that they were not his real children. Richard was the only one of the four children to survive the first brutal winter the Pilgrims endured in Plymouth. He grew up to become a sea captain who, historians discovered many years later, had two wives: one in Salem and the other in England. He died in 1696.

Governor Bradstreet was governor of the Massachusetts Bay Colony from 1679 to 1686. He had sailed to America with John Winthrop and the other original Puritans on the *Arabella* in 1630.

The Reverend John Higginson had, for a time, been the pastor of the fabled First Church of Salem.

Benjamin Lynde was chief justice of the Massachusetts Bay Colony from 1729 to 1737.

And John Hathorne, one of the magistrates who presided over the witch trials of 1692, was the great-grandfather of author Nathaniel Hawthorne, who added the *w* to the family name in order to conceal their shameful relationship. It was Colonel Hathorne, I learned, who called for—and witnessed—the execution of Mary Estey.

Next to the cemetery I found a memorial dedicated to the people executed during the witch trials. Full-grown ash trees hover over nineteen stone benches arranged in two rows facing each other. Carved on each bench is the name and execution date of the people convicted during the trials.

I fell in behind a middle-aged couple holding hands as they made their way past each of the benches, stopping briefly to read each name and date:

Bridget Bishop	June 10
Sarah Good	July 19
Elizabeth Howe	July 19
Susannah Martin	July 19
Rebecca Nurse	July 19
Sarah Wildes	July 19
George Burroughs	August 19
Martha Carrier	August 19
George Jacobs	August 19
John Proctor	August 19
John Willard	August 19
Martha Corey	September 22
Mary Estey	September 22

Alice Parker	September 22
Mary Parker	September 22
Ann Pudeator	September 22
Margaret Scott	September 22
Wilmot Redd	September 22
Samuel Wardwell	September 22

I sat down on Mary's bench. More people filed by, including a group of women and children, the smallest—a girl probably a year old—barely able to navigate the uneven cobblestones.

Carlee showed up. She had lost interest in the Witch Museum, so she joined me on the bench, being careful not to cover Mary's name. While we chatted about nothing in particular and watched more people go by, I tried to picture Mary Estey. Had any of her features or mannerisms survived eight generations? I wondered. When I looked at my daughter, was I looking at Mary's eyes or nose, or something as subtle as the shape of her ear?

I took a picture of Carlee sitting on the bench. She smiled, out of habit I suppose. This was a photo I knew she would be showing her friends at school. Then she took my picture, but I didn't smile. Somehow it didn't seem appropriate.

THE EARLIEST settlers in the Cape Ann area of northern Massachusetts called their settlement Naumkeag, a word from the local native language that meant "comfort haven." Later these people who identified themselves as God's chosen, just as the ancient Israelites had, renamed their growing seaport Salem, employing the same Hebrew word for "peace" used in Jerusalem.

During the early part of the great Puritan migration of the 1630s, Salem was the center of New England commerce, until that distinction slowly moved south to Boston.

Gradually it developed two distinct identities: Salem Town, the more progressive trading port on the east side that was liberal both politically and theologically, and Salem Village, the more conservative farming community to the west.

In 1670 the people of Salem Village petitioned the church in Salem Town to have their own minister. They no longer appreciated the distance they had to travel in order to attend services, nor did they approve of the progressive message they heard from the pulpit when they got there. In October of that year, permission was granted and the Reverend James Bayley was hired to tend the village flock. It was a troubled flock. There were constant disputes over land, fear of Indian attacks, and concerns about the impact that weather—driven by God's judgmental hand—would have on their crops.

Given Salem Village's theocratic nature, it often fell to the Reverend Bayley to mediate the land disputes and to interpret the meaning of failed crops or the deaths of infants. Apparently not everyone was happy with his abilities. By 1679, angry letters were being exchanged between minister and various constituents, then lawsuits alleging slander were filed and finally the Reverend Bayley had had enough, and he left in 1680. He was replaced by the Reverend George Burroughs, whose tenure was just as tumultuous as, and even shorter than, Bayley's.

Soon after moving to Salem Village, Burroughs's wife, Hannah, died, leaving him to care for their two children. He even had to borrow money from his new parishioners to pay for her funeral.

And then the same old disputes came up: Should the minister be allowed to assume ownership of the parsonage? How much should the minister be paid? Should his firewood be provided for free or not? Was this the minister who should be ordained so that Salem Village could finally have its own chartered church? And on and on. And, as had been the case with Reverend Bayley, some in the village questioned Burroughs's abilities as a preacher.

Finally, after an especially embarrassing incident in which Burroughs was almost jailed for failing to repay the debt on his wife's funeral, he took his children and a new wife and left Salem Village mid-year in 1683, not knowing that he would return one final time in 1692.

It took the people of Salem Village several months to find another minister. In January of 1684 they offered a contract to Deodat Lawson, a second-generation Puritan minister from Boston. The offer was a generous sixty pounds a year with no free firewood. Lawson apparently accepted, but even as he served the community, negotiations continued on and off for another three years.

In 1687 the village sought the advice of a board of laymen from Salem Town. After a careful inspection and analysis, the members of the board, which included Colonel Hathorne, bluntly advised the village to pay their minister and not to bother them again. Ironically, Lawson—whose wife and daughter had recently died—soon took another job elsewhere, forcing the people of the village to begin yet another search.

By June of 1688 they had their man: Samuel Parris, the son of a modestly successful English merchant, who had to leave Harvard College after two years to take over his father's estate in Barbados when the elder Parris died in 1673. The younger Parris tried to continue his father's work, but found business not to his liking, so he sold the island property and returned to Boston, where, in 1680, he married Elizabeth Eldredge. They began a family and he pursued a career in the ministry.

By June of 1688 they were ready to take up housekeeping in the Salem Village parsonage with their five-year-old daughter, Betty, their nine-year-old niece, Abigail Williams, and two slaves of Indian descent from Barbados, a man called John Indian and a woman called Tituba.

The Reverend Parris was doubtless hopeful he could engineer a more peaceful climate than his predecessors had. He had no way of knowing, of course, that he would preside over perhaps the strangest episode in American history. And it would begin in his own home.

Sɪɴ ʜᴀs been defined, in simple terms, as the act of breaking one of God's rules. In a more profound sense it is the chief corrupting influence in the universe. But the underlying theme, the common denominator, of sin is humanity's attempt to be like God. It is ultimately a kind of idolatry, which the first of the Ten Commandment prohibits. When Adam and Eve knowingly defied God's edict regarding the fruit from the tree of the knowledge of good and evil in Genesis 3, they were essentially flouting God's rules and creating their own.

Even though it wasn't specifically mentioned in the Decalogue, the sin of all sins for the Puritans, and for generations of their ancestors before them, was witchcraft. The classic definition of a witch was a human who made a pact with Satan. For the Puritans, Satan was as real as God. According to Puritan theology, God had ultimate control over the physical world, and Satan had the ability to control a human's spirit.

There is no question that the Puritans sought out, and killed, witches because the Bible told them to do so. The first reference to a witch occurs in Exodus 22:18. The Hebrew word used in the original text to describe the heretic in question is *m'khashepah*. The closest thing to a literal translation in English, I am told, would be "woman who does evil magic." It's important to note that not all biblical translators have used the word *witch*. The New Revised Standard Version, for example, reads, "You shall not permit a female sorcerer to live." But the Geneva Bible, the only translation that counted with the Puritans, made it clear: "Thou shalt not suffre a witche to live."

Witchcraft per se wasn't exactly a high priority for the Roman Church's earliest organizers. While they worked hard to identify the various forms of heresy against Christianity, witches were rarely pursued, in part because there was no clear definition of what constituted the heretical "witch" mentioned in Exodus.

That changed dramatically in the late fifteenth century. The Inquisition had been under way for more than two centuries (the Spanish

Inquisition had only just begun) and witches had become a favorite target of inquisitors. And the question of what exactly constituted a witch was settled once and for all with the publication in 1486 of a book called *Malleus Maleficarum* (Latin for "The Witch's Hammer"), written by two German witch hunters, both Dominican friars, named Heinrich Kramer and James Sprenger. Kramer and Sprenger were either highly aggressive inquisitors or brilliant marketers, because when they asked the pope himself for permission to pursue their hunts in southwestern Germany, and when Innocent VIII gave that permission via a papal bull in 1484, they placed this obvious and incredibly important sign of Church approval at the front of their book, fashioning it as a kind of foreword.

Over the next 180 years the *Malleus* enjoyed enormous popularity. Roughly thirty separate editions were printed, in at least four languages. In its time it was considered one of the most famous and influential books in all of Western Europe, second only to the Bible. Today the range of opinions about its legacy is wide. Scholars and others view it variously as an important historical text, a quaint misogynist oddity, and outright pornography. It is all of those.

The *Malleus* is divided into three parts. Part one identifies all of the ingredients necessary for witchcraft (the short answer: the devil, one human willing to work with the devil, and—most important—God's permission that this should occur).

Part two explores the many devious ways that witches work, either by promising to protect crops and livestock, or to inflict harm on human enemies, or through good old-fashioned seduction.

Part three outlines in great detail the eleven steps necessary to prosecute a witch in court successfully, which run the gamut from coddling to outright torture. It also contains several prurient passages that involve detailed descriptions of relations between the devil and humans.

The *Malleus* was a highly influential book. As one of its modern translators wrote, "The *Malleus* lay on the bench of every judge, on the desk of every magistrate. It was the ultimate, irrefutable, unarguable authority. It was implicitly accepted not only by Catholic but by Protestant legislature." And even though, by 1692, it was not as widely read as it had been, it is clear from how the Salem witch trials were conducted that its teachings were very much a part of American Puritan society.

DROPPING AN egg white into a clear glass of water produces the most interesting visual effects. Because it is denser than water, the egg white sinks to the bottom of the glass, but given its viscous consistency, it takes its sweet time getting there. When I sacrificed an egg one afternoon in the name of research, its white looked to me like thin, filmy strands of cigarette smoke wafting through the air in super slow motion.

But what would a teenage girl of the seventeenth-century Salem Village have seen? The answer was important, because the egg white dropped in a clear beer mug of water and held up to the sunlight was called a Venus Glass, and it was used to tell the girls' fortunes. The images they saw would somehow tell them what their future husband would do for a living, maybe even show his face.

Making Venus Glasses became a popular pastime for the girls who gathered in the kitchen of the Parris household during the winter of 1691–92. The winter that year had been especially nasty, restricting unnecessary outside activities, keeping people indoors for long spells. By January of '92, six or seven of the village girls gathered regularly in the Parris kitchen, drawn there by the highly entertaining antics of the Parrises' slave woman, Tituba.

The Carib Indian woman spent hours teaching the girls about the mysteries and exciting customs of her native Barbados. Tricks like the Venus Glass would most certainly have been frowned upon by the citizens of this Puritan village, most especially since they were taught in the home of the minister. The hours spent with Tituba may or may not have had a direct connection to the witch trials that were to take place that year. Ultimately there is no way of knowing for certain. What we do know, though, is that the trials were the result of the accusations made by these very girls against many of the citizens of Salem Village.

In January, young Betty Parris and Abigail Williams were the first of the girls to begin exhibiting odd behavior, described at the time as "fits." One witness described Abigail running through the Parris household screaming "Whish! Whish!" and stopping to point at unseen specters lurking in dark corners.

An entire library of books about the witch trials has been written over the past three centuries. One online search I did turned up 170 titles devoted specifically to them, and another 7,500 that included references to them. Theories abound about the cause of the girls' behavior.

Was it physical? some wondered. Could they have eaten something? One theory has it that they could have ingested rye meal contaminated with a fungus called ergot, which contains alkaloids chemically related to the components of LSD. Was it psychological? Had the discovery of the girls' clandestine activities with Tituba so shamed them that they developed psychological trauma? Was it political? Plenty of scholars point out that all of the accusing girls lived in the more theologically conservative western portion of the village, while the vast majority of the people they accused lived in the more liberal eastern side. Had they been pressured by their parents in order to settle scores? the scholars wondered. Or, in the end, was it merely an extreme juvenile prank by young girls bent on getting attention or expressing their independence? No one knows for sure, and, barring the discovery of some form of irrefutable evidence, we may never know.

Reverend Parris asked the village doctor, William Griggs, whose niece Elizabeth Hubbard had also spent time with Tituba, to examine young Betty and Abigail. After hitting a number of medical dead ends, Dr. Griggs finally declared the girls to be "under an evil hand," a hand that, of course, belonged to Satan.

The diagnosis would no doubt have been chilling news to the people of Salem Village. It had only been a few years since a strange episode in Boston, in 1688, when thirteen-year-old Martha Goodwin exhibited similarly strange behavior, blaming it on the invading spirit of an elderly neighbor, Mary Glover.

One of New England's most celebrated ministers, Cotton Mather, had taken an interest in the Goodwin case, twice meeting with Goody Glover in jail, encouraging her to repent, but to no avail. In short order she was tried, convicted, and hanged. Reverend Mather and his wife took young Martha into their home to live with them. He then added an account of the whole affair into a book he was writing titled *Memorable Providences, Relating to Witchcrafts and Possessions*. It was published in 1689 and became a widely read best-seller.

The Mary Glover trial was probably fresh in the minds of the Salem villagers when Dr. Griggs declared Betty Parris and Abigail Williams bewitched. The girls were pressed to identify their own malefic attackers. After some time, they named three people: Sarah Good, Sarah Osborne, and their own beloved Tituba.

On February 29, arrest warrants were issued for the three women. On March 1, they were examined physically for evidence of witch "teats," any kind of blemish as described in the *Malleus Maleficarum* that would mark their covenant with the devil (none were found), and they were questioned by two local magistrates from Salem Town, Jonathan Corwin and Colonel John Hathorne. To accommodate the large crowd of villagers who had come to see what this was all about, the examination was moved from the small inn where the magistrates were staying to the larger village meetinghouse.

Each woman was brought in separately for questioning. The first was Sarah Good. Few people in the village were surprised when the girls accused this pipe-smoking vagrant who had a ne'er-do-well husband and two small children. The blackest mark against her was that she never attended services at the meetinghouse. And she made people uncomfortable when they met her. Inevitably she would beg them for food, and then mutter that whatever had been offered was not enough.

Col. Hathorne conducted the examination:

Q: Sarah Good, what evil spirit have you familiarity with?
A: None.

Q: Have you made no contract with the devil?
A: No.

Q: Why do you hurt these children?
A: I do not hurt them. I scorn it.

Q: Who do you employ then to do it?
A: I employ nobody.

Q: What creature do you employ then?
A: No creature, but I am falsely accused.

Sarah Osborne's testimony was largely the same. Like Sarah Good, Osborne had not been to meetinghouse services in quite a while, but her husband and neighbors confirmed that she had been in ill health for more than a year. Under questioning, she denied ever having seen the devil or hurt the children.

Finally it was Tituba's turn. It is entirely possible that if her testimony had mirrored that of the first two women, with more denials of collusion with the devil, the investigation into the charges brought by the young girls might have ended with these three women. But Tituba's dramatic testimony gave the investigation new life; it brought up more questions and took it into new directions.

Q: Did you never see the devil?
A: The devil came to me and bid me serve him.

Q: *Who have you seen?*
A: Four women. [Tituba also testified to seeing what she described as a tall man from Boston.]

Q: *Who were they?*
A: Goody Osborne and Sarah Good, and I do not know who the others were.

Q: *What did they say to you?*
A: They said "Hurt the children."

Q: *And did you hurt them?*
A: No. There is four women and one man. They hurt the children and then lay all upon me, and they tell me if I will not hurt the children they will hurt me.

Q: *And did you not hurt them?*
A: Yes, but I will hurt them no more.

Q: *Are you not sorry you did hurt them?*
A: Yes.

Tituba was questioned again a day later in the Salem Town jail, where she and Sarah Osborne had been taken. Sarah Good was sent to the jail in nearby Ipswich. Tituba's testimony was even more damaging. She said that a mysterious tall man from Boston had come to her, revealed to her that he was God, that she must serve him for six years, and in return he would give her "many fine things." Then she testified about a book he had brought with him.

Q: *What did he say you must do in that book?*
A: He said write and set my name to it.

Q: *Did you write?*
A: Yes. Once I made a mark in the book and made it with red blood.

Q: Did you see any other marks in his book?
A: Yes, a great many. Some marks were red, some yellow.

Q: Did he tell you the names of them?
A: Yes . . . Good and Osborne, and he say they make them marks
   in that book and he showed them me.

Q: How many marks do you think there was?
A: Nine.

Q: Did he tell you who they were?
A: No, he not let me see.

There it was. Other members of the community had also made pacts with the devil. Salem Village was infested.

The girls began to identify more spectral tormentors. Surprising names: There was Martha Corey, an outspoken but godly woman in her sixties whose headstrong husband, Giles, had only been allowed to take communion in the meetinghouse the year before, at the age of eighty. Even more surprising were the charges leveled against Rebecca Nurse, the seventy-one-year-old grandmother, whom many suspected of being one of God's Elect, who with her husband Francis and three of their eight children and their spouses ran one of the largest and most prosperous farms in the area.

Meanwhile, Tituba continued to be examined in jail. She volunteered the tantalizing tidbit that the wife and child of the village's previous pastor, the Reverend Deodat Lawson, had in fact died at the hands of an evil spirit.

The Reverend Lawson (whose rather unusual first name in Latin means "God-given") was by this time living in Boston. After hearing of the slave woman's assertion, he returned to the village to see for himself what was happening in his former parish. He saw plenty—enough to fill a ten-page pamphlet he wrote about his witch-trial experiences, published late in 1692 and titled "A Brief and True Narrative."

Lawson wrote that he arrived in the village on the evening of March 19. Soon after he had taken a room at the inn run by village deacon Na-thanial Ingersoll, Ingersoll's nephew Captain Jonathan Walcott, who headed the village militia, showed up with his sixteen-year-old daughter Mary in tow. According to Lawson's account, the girl, who had also been tormented recently by unseen specters, had something she wanted to tell him, but he doesn't say what. After the conversation, as they were preparing to leave, Mary suddenly cried out that she had just been bitten on the wrist. Lawson writes that he and Captain Walcott examined her wrist by candlelight, and they did indeed see upper and lower tooth marks on each side of her wrist.

After that, Lawson accompanied Mr. and Mrs. Ingersoll to the parsonage to visit Reverend Parris.

He wrote of his troubling visit:

When I was there, his Kins-woman, Abigail Williams, (about 12 years of age,) had a grievous fit; she was at first hurryed with Violence to and fro in the room; (though Mrs. Ingersol endeav-oured to hold her,) sometimes makeing as if she would fly, stretch-ing up her arms as high as she could, and crying "Whish, Whish, Whish!" several times; Presently after, she said there was Goodw N[urse]. and said, "Do you not see her? Why, there she stands!" And then said Goodw. N. offered her The Book, but she was resolved she would not take it, saying Often, "I wont, I wont, I wont take it, I do not know what Book it is: I am sure it is none of Gods Book, it is the Divels Book, for ought I know." After that, she run to the Fire, and begun to throw Fire Brands about the house; and run against the Back, as if she would run up Chimney, and, as they said, she had attempted to go into the Fire in other Fits.

The next day, Sunday the twentieth, Lawson was the guest preacher during services at the meetinghouse. Before he could begin his sermon, he was heckled by Abigail Williams, who at first demanded to know the biblical text he would be preaching about. Then she pointed to the rafters and cried out that she could see the specter of Martha Corey sitting on a beam holding a yellow bird similar to the one Tituba had mentioned in her testimony.

On Monday, Lawson sat in and observed the magistrates as they questioned Goodwife Corey. It became a highly contentious session, with her adamantly denying that she was guilty of anything. She declared herself to be a "Gospel woman."

By Thursday the twenty-fourth, it is clear that Lawson was deeply disturbed by what he had seen during the week. That evening he delivered the weekly lecture, and he used the opportunity to give his assessment of what was going on in Salem Village. Reverend Lawson called his lecture "Christ's Fidelity: The Only Shield against Satan's Malignity." It is not clear what he hoped to accomplish with the fiery sermon he hurled at those in attendance that evening, but it is entirely possible that this open and frank discussion of the troubles plaguing the village was enough to push an already tense populace over the edge into full-blown hysteria.

Lawson based the sermon on a line of text from book 3, verse 2 of Zechariah in the Old Testament: "And the Lord said unto Satan, 'The Lord rebuke you, O Satan! The Lord who has chosen Jerusalem rebuke you! Is not this man a brand plucked from the fire?' "

The book of Zechariah was written in 519 B.C., a critical moment in the history of the Hebrew people, with whom the Puritans identified so closely. At the end of their seventy-year exile in Babylon, they returned to Judea in 538 B.C. to find their homeland ravaged by years of neglect. Their efforts to rebuild were frustrated by years of bad crops and the inevitable inflation that resulted. To make matters worse, an aggressive new Persian King, Darius I, who reigned from 522 to 486 B.C., had been intimidating the Judeans to keep them in line. So the prophets Haggai and Zechariah encouraged the people to rebuild Solomon's great temple in order to curry favor with God.

The book of Zechariah begins with a description of eight inspiring visions he experienced over a two-month period, visions that, so Zechariah wrote, proved that the Hebrew people, despite the trauma and devastation of their exile, were still worthy of God's love and protection.

The passage Reverend Lawson chose to base his sermon on was from the fourth of the prophet's visions. It depicted a trial before God in which the angel in the heavenly court known as Satan (whose name in Hebrew means "the accuser") accuses the high priest Joshua of being unfit to serve the Lord in the new temple. In verse 2 of chapter 3, God renders a verdict, rebuking Satan and asking, "Is not this man a brand plucked from the fire?" (Joshua had come from a long line of priests dating back to the time of King David.) The vision continues with God removing the "filthy clothes" of sin and guilt from Joshua and dressing him in ritually pure apparel.

Lawson's point, obviously, was that the members of his congregation were just like Joshua, caught between God and Satan, "the Fountain of Malice, the Instigator of all Contrariety, Malignity and Enmity."

"The Covenant People of God," he wrote, "and those that would Devote themselves Intirely to his Service, are the special Objects of SATAN's Rage and Fury."

And just as Eve turned away from God and chose to heed the serpent's counsel, Lawson warned that there were those in Salem, "Witches and Wizzards," who had put their stock in the devil, making them "instruments by whom he may more secretly affect and afflict the bodies and minds of others."

But there was hope. He reminded those in attendance that despite "Satan's Malicious Designs and Operations, he is absolutely Bounded and Limited, by the Power and Pleasure of the Great and Everlasting GOD, the LORD JEHOVAH." It was classic Puritan theology: nothing—*nothing*—happens without God's knowledge and approval.

And then, whether he intended it or not, Lawson echoed one of Martin Luther's fundamental arguments: that all temptation is God's way of testing his people, and that all crises lead to an even stronger faith, because—as Lawson wrote—"Whensoever God hath declared a Person or People to be in Covenant with Him, as the Objects of his Special mercy and Favour, he will assuredly and shortly Suppress the malice of Satan, however violently engaged against them."

The message was clear: God's chosen people must choose God.

Looking back, that would have been the perfect point to end on. It would have been a subtle reminder to shun the temptations of Satan and remain in God's good graces. But Lawson was only warming up. After flattering his listeners with the notion that Satan's growing interest in them only proved how much God favored their community, he turned his attention to those who had so obviously succumbed to the devilish temptation.

"For it is a most dreadful thing to consider, that any should change the Service of God for the service of the Devil, the worship of the Blessed God for the worship of the Cursed Enemy of God and Man. But Oh! How shall I name it? If any that are in the Visible Covenant of God, should break that Covenant, and make a League with Satan, if any that have set down and eat at Christ's Table should so lift up their Heel against him, as to have Fellowship at the Table of Devils; and Eat of the Bread and Drink of the Wine that Satan hath mingled . . . [then] we must cry out in Scripture Language: 'Be astonished O ye Heavens at this, and be Horribly afraid; be ye very Desolate, saith the Lord.'"

Before he had finished, Deodat Lawson was undoubtedly pounding the pulpit and angrily pointing fingers, calling the people of Salem Village to take up arms against Satan ("What, therefore I say unto one, I say unto all in this important case: PRAY PRAY PRAY"), to identify the people who had abandoned God's favors and to deal with them accordingly, in one passage urging them to "make tryal of witches."

Lawson ended his sermon where he had started it:

"And the Lord said unto Satan, the Lord Rebuke thee O Satan, even the Lord that hath chosen Jerusalem, Rebuke thee: Is not this a brand pluckt out of the fire?" When he was finished, the fire that had been simmering in Salem Village suddenly burned white hot.

WE ARRIVED at the Nurse Homestead on Sunday afternoon. This was the final stop of my birthday weekend in Salem and Danvers, and almost immediately I realized that it should have been our first. There were no wrought-iron silhouettes of witches on broomsticks here, as there had been in Salem. No wax figures or souvenir shops. Instead we found a modest red farmhouse nestled quietly at the end of a long dirt drive, set back a few hundred yards from the highway. The acres of green grass surrounding the house had been freshly mown, and the trees that towered over it rustled in the breeze. It was peaceful here.

We parked in what we could only assume was the parking lot. There were no signs, no paved areas; our only clue was a car sitting idly in front of a split rail fence. I parked next to it, and we got out.

The Nurse Homestead has three buildings on its grounds. In addition to the farmhouse there is an old barn that has been converted into a modest gift shop, and next to it is an exact replica of the old Salem Village meetinghouse, built by a motion picture production company for a movie about the Salem witch trials made in the mid-1980s.

Inside the barn, we were greeted by a young woman, probably in her late twenties, dressed in a period costume: a white billowy blouse, black floor-length pleated skirt, and a soft white linen bonnet. She asked if we were interested in listening to an audio presentation in the meetinghouse before we toured the farmhouse. We were, and we did.

The meetinghouse was essentially one large room, maybe thirty by thirty feet, and like all Protestant houses of worship of the time, it lacked any religious symbols: no crosses, no altar, no stained-glass windows. Instead, the focal point of the room was the pulpit that had been raised a few feet above the floor with a hexagonal wooden canopy attached to the ceiling directly overhead, a kind of acoustic sounding board designed to improve the audibility of the minister's sermon.

On Sunday mornings the preacher would climb the three or four steps to the pulpit, allowing him a good view of the members of the congregation who were seated according to strict rules: old people and deacons up front, military officers and village officials behind them, the greatest contributors to the church next, and everyone else behind them. Children and servants sat in the crude "balconies" on either side of the room, allowing them to be at eye level with the minister.

We sat in the front row, the only people in attendance, and the young woman cheerfully welcomed us. She explained that she would eventually be taking us on a tour of the home where Francis and Rebecca Nurse had lived, but first we were to listen to a brief audio presentation about the Salem witch trials. She turned the tape on and left.

The tape began with a brief history of Salem and of the meetinghouse, which came to symbolize the independence of the village people from Salem Town. It was completed in the 1680s, and on

November 19, 1689, the Church of Christ at Salem Village was formally dedicated by its brand-new minister, the Reverend Samuel Parris.

I drifted in and out as the tape played, trying to picture the people of the day sitting where we now sat, listening to sermons that would last three hours during the morning Sabbath service, followed by lunch and then another three hours during the afternoon service. Historians suggest that people welcomed these marathon services as a break from the hard work they endured the other six days of the week, but—skeptic that I am—I couldn't help picturing members of the congregation drifting in and out, planning the week's chores, worrying about the weather, and counting the minutes to lunch. Or was I not giving them enough credit? Were these brave, hardy souls engaged enough to be able to focus on the business at hand for such long periods? We view these people mainly through the prism of their strong religious beliefs. Was that, in fact, the focal point of their lives each and every day? Did they view their mundane chores as service to their God? And if so, when did we begin to lose that focus?

The tape began its description of the witch trials, and of the important role the meetinghouse played. It was here on March 24 that Rebecca Nurse was questioned by Colonel John Hathorne, with Reverend Parris acting as recording secretary. A group of actors played out the drama:

A woman's voice, acting as Ann Putnam Sr., yelled at Rebecca Nurse, "Did you not bring the black man with you, did you not bid tempt God and dye? How oft have you eat and drunk y'r own damnation?"

The voice of Colonel Hathorne asked, "What do you say to them?"

Rebecca Nurse cried, "Oh Lord help me!"

Q: Do you not see these afflicted persons, and hear them accuse you?
A: The Lord knows I have not hurt them. I am an innocent person.

Q: It is very awful to all to see these agonies and you, an old professor, thus charged with contracting with the devil. . . . Yet to

see you stand with dry eyes when there are so many wet.
[The Malleus Maleficarum *said witches were unable to cry.]*
A: You do not know my heart.

Q: *You would do well if you are guilty to confess and give glory*
to God.
A: I am as clear as the child unborn.

Q: *When this witchcraft came upon the stage there was no suspicion*
of Tituba. She professed much love to that child Betty Parris, but it
was her apparition did the mischief, and why should not you also
be guilty, for your apparition doth hurt also.
A: Would you have me belie my self?

Reverend Parris recorded that Goody Nurse held her neck to one side, and the young girls in the congregation immediately did the same thing, showing how they were under her influence.

Q: *What do you think of this?*
A: I cannot help it. The Devil may appear in my shape.

When the tape ended, the girl reappeared and invited us to follow her outside and across the clearing to the Nurse farmhouse. Even though it was August, it was not an especially warm day, and a late-afternoon breeze had begun to blow. She stopped us at the gate in front of the house just as four more people joined our party, two women and two children.

Our tour guide told us that the Nurse family had moved to the homestead in 1678. A wealthy Boston merchant had inherited the three-hundred-acre farm, and since he had no use for it he was willing to allow the Nurses to purchase it by way of a twenty-year lease. Three of Francis and Rebecca's grown children and their spouses also lived and worked on the farm, and it was a great success, much to the envy of some of the villagers who resented the Nurses' prosperity. It has been suggested that this envy might have motivated the charges against Rebecca Nurse.

We were led into the house. The first stop was the kitchen, which was now cluttered with artifacts and utensils from the period. Our guide described how food was cooked and consumed here, and the new people in our party asked plenty of questions. Was it true, they wanted to know, that the man of the house ate his meals off the more expensive pewter dinnerware while the wife and children ate out of wooden bowls? And what about the iron on the hearth, was it authentic to the time period and how often did women accidentally burn clothing? I caught Cindy's eye and signaled that I was headed upstairs by myself to the bedroom. She smiled and nodded.

A small bed sat in the opposite corner of the room, a lumpy down mattress resting on a web of roping that required periodic tightening in order to ensure some degree of comfort. Each of our guides during the weekend had been quick to point out that this was where the expression "sleep tight" had come from.

I stood in the middle of the room and took it all in. This, I realized, was what I had been looking for all weekend. This made up for the traffic jams and the wax figures and the tacky souvenirs. These very walls had been there the day in March of 1692 when four people stood on this very floor and informed my eight-times great-aunt as she lay sick in bed that she had been charged with witchcraft.

The four included Peter Cloyce, her brother-in-law, married to her youngest sister Sarah (who would also be accused in coming months), Israel and Elizabeth Porter (Israel's father, Joseph, and Rebecca's father, William Towne, had been friends and neighbors years before in Topsfield, and Elizabeth was the sister of—of all people—Colonel John Hathorne), and Israel's brother-in-law Daniel Andrews. The four of them later signed a statement describing their visit with Goody Nurse. It said that they found her sick in bed but in relatively good spirits.

"And then of her own accord," it continued, "she began to speak of the affliction that was amongst them and in particular of Mr. Parris, his family, and how she was grieved for them, though she had not been to see them by reason of fits that she formerly used to have, for people said it was awful to behold. But she pitied them with all her heart and went to God for them."

It was at this point, they wrote, that they informed her that some of the villagers had charged her with witchcraft.

"Well," they quoted her as saying, "if it be so, the will of the Lord be done."

And then, in one of the most heart-wrenching moments in the entire witch trial saga, after the four of them had sat with Goody Nurse for several minutes in silence, she finally said, "Well, as to this thing, I am innocent as the child unborn, but surely what sin has God found out in me unrepented of that he should lay such an affliction upon me in my old age?"

Even as she professed her obvious innocence, this gentle woman of faith was still willing to concede the possibility that something from her own past, a sin long forgotten and left unrepented, may have come back to haunt her.

The rest of our tour group caught up with me, and the young woman pointed to the bed in the corner and launched into an explanation of the expression "sleep tight."

THE PUBLIC executions of those convicted of witchcraft in Salem Village in 1692 were conducted on four separate dates, the first being Friday, June 10, when Bridget Bishop was hanged. She was a middle-aged mother of three children, by three separate husbands, who had long been suspected of witchcraft. Hers had been the first trial conducted, and the jury wasted no time convicting her.

On July 19, five more people were hanged, including Rebecca Nurse. Rebecca's death was especially heartbreaking to her family and friends, since there had been so many missed opportunities to clear her. She had been tried on Wednesday, June 29, and the jury had acquitted her, much to the great distress of her accusers.

According to the eyewitness account of one Robert Calef, a clothing merchant who took it upon himself to keep an unofficial record of the trials and hangings, the chief judge overseeing the trials, Massachusetts Lieutenant Governor William Stoughton, asked the members of the jury to reconsider their verdict, citing something Goody Nurse had said when Abigail Hobbs was led into the courtroom to testify for the prosecution.

Rebecca was heard to say something like "What, do you bring her? She is one of us." Was she, Lieutenant Governor Stoughton wondered, referring to a fellow witch?

The jury went back out to deliberate some more, but they were unable to agree on exactly what Rebecca had meant, so everyone returned to the courtroom and jury foreman Thomas Fisk asked her to explain what she had meant by her "one of us" reference to Goody Hobbs.

According to Calef's written account—and also according to foreman Fisk's own sworn testimony taken a week later—Rebecca Nurse failed to answer the question, remaining silent and staring into space. The jury found her guilty.

A petition later filed on her behalf explained that her silence had been grievously misunderstood:

"I being hard of hearing, and full of grace, none informing me how the Court took up my words, and therefore had no opportunity to declare what I intended."

She had simply not heard the jury foreman's question. But if she had, the petition continued, she would have explained that she referred to Abigail Hobbs as "one of us" simply because she had been a fellow prisoner in the Salem Town jail.

Soon after her conviction, Governor William Phips himself granted her a reprieve, but Calef writes that a group of "Salem gentlemen" whom he did not name lobbied successfully to have the reprieve recalled.

Rebecca Nurse was hanged three weeks later with Susanna Martin, Sarah Good, Sarah Wildes, and Elizabeth How, who, like Mary Estey, had been a member of Parson Capen's congregation in Topsfield.

Five more people, including the Reverend Burroughs, were hanged on Friday, August 19. Calef's account of the proceedings is especially dramatic:

"Mr. Burroughs was carried in a cart with the others through the streets of Salem to execution," he wrote. "When he was upon the ladder, he made a speech for the clearing of his innocency, with such solemn and serious expressions, as were to the admiration of all present; his prayer [which he concluded by repeating the Lord's Prayer—a prayer the *Malleus Maleficarum* had said real witches would be unable to recite without stumbling] was so well worded, and uttered with such composedness and such . . . fervency of spirit . . . it drew tears from many."

In addition to the Reverend Burroughs, the other four people hanged that day included Martha Carrier, John Willard, George Jacobs Sr., and John Proctor.

By September, Mary Estey must have known that if a governor's reprieve couldn't save her beloved oldest sister, and if a flawlessly recited Lord's Prayer couldn't save George Burroughs, she was truly doomed.

She had been arrested on April 21 on charges that her spirit had attacked three of the girls in the village: Mary Walcott, Abigail Williams, and Ann Putnam Jr. The next day she was hauled into court and questioned by John Hathorne and Jonathan Corwin. Reverend Parris, who recorded the proceedings, wrote that the moment Mary Estey appeared in the courtroom, the girls "fell into fits."

Q: *What do you say, are you guilty?*
A: I can say before Christ Jesus, I am free.

Q: *What have you done to these children?*
A: I know nothing.

Q: *How can you say you know nothing, when you see these tormented*
   [girls] that accuse you?
A: Would you have me accuse myself?

Q: *Yes, if you be guilty.*
A: I will say it, if it is my last time, I am clear of this sin.

Q: *Of what sin?*
A: Of witchcraft.

The questioner then turned to the girls and asked, "Are you certain this is the woman?" Reverend Parris wrote that "never a one could speak for fits."

Mary Estey was released on May 18 for lack of evidence. But the next day another girl, Mercy Lewis, experienced a series of severe fits that she blamed on Mary's specter. Just before midnight, village sheriff George Herrick returned to the Estey home, dragged Mary out of bed, and took her to jail, where she was placed in irons. During her trial that summer, a number of villagers testified against her, describing in detail the horrible fits the girls experienced that they witnessed firsthand.

On September 9, Mary Estey and five other defendants were convicted and sentenced to hang in two weeks.

Ten days later, wealthy farmer Giles Corey, who had refused to enter any kind of plea before the court, was subjected to an Old English form of punishment for petty treason, rarely used in New England, known as "pressing." He was made to lie down in an open field on his back with a few flat wooden boards covering him and large rocks piled on top. As time passed, more rocks were added, which Corey stubbornly endured without giving in. He is said to have uttered only two words during the whole ordeal: "More weight." Eventually he died of suffocation.

Sometime before Mary's execution, a petition was filed on her behalf. There are questions about who actually penned it—no one can say for sure whether she was literate enough to write—but there is no question that it is a remarkable and very personal document:

> Your poor and humble petitioner, being condemned to die, do humbly beg of you to take it into your judicious and pious considerations that your poor and humble petitioner, knowing my own innocency, blessed be the Lord for it, and seeing plainly the wiles and subtleties of my accusers . . . cannot but judge charitably of others that are going the same way [as] myself . . . I petition to your honours not for my own life for I know I must die and my appointed time is set. . . .
>
> I question not but your honours would not be guilty of innocent blood for the world but by my own innocency I know that you are in the wrong way. The Lord in his infinite mercy direct you in this great work if it be his blessed will that no more innocent blood be shed. I would humbly beg of you that your honours would be pleased to examine these afflicted persons strictly and keep them apart some time and likewise to try some of these confessing witches, I being confident there is several of them that has belied themselves and others as will appear if not in this world I am sure in the world to come whither I am going. . . . The Lord above who is the searcher of all hearts knows that as I shall answer it at the tribunal seat that I know not the least thing of witchcraft, therefore I cannot, I dare not, bely my own soul. I beg your honours not to deny this my humble petition from a poor dying innocent person and I question not but The Lord will give a blessing to your endeavors.

Mary Estey knew she was innocent, but she also knew that there was nothing she could say or do to save her own life, and she accepted that. She chose instead to plead the case for those who would come after her, humbly beseeching the officers of the court not to shed any more innocent blood.

When I think about all of the many ancestors I discovered while writing this book—the courage they showed and the tremendous risks they took—I have to place Mary at the top of the list for the graceful way she faced such an unjust and violent death, and most especially for the Christian love she showed in pleading unselfishly for the lives of others.

On Thursday, September 22, Mary and seven others were placed in an oxcart at the Salem Town jail, and together they made the journey to Gallows Hill. On the way, Robert Calef wrote, the cart became stuck for a time, no doubt the work of the devil.

According to Calef's account, Martha Corey was defiant to the end, just as her husband, Giles, had been a few days earlier. She loudly proclaimed her innocence and recited a prayer aloud to prove it. Another defendant, Samuel Wardwell, who had at one point confessed to being a witch and then recanted, tried one more time to proclaim his own innocence, but he was stopped short by a coughing fit caused by the smoke of the executioner's pipe. Once again, witnesses believed, the devil was still at work.

Finally it was Mary's turn. Calef wrote that her farewells to her husband, children, and friends were as "Serious, Religious, Distinct &

Affectionate as could well be expresst, drawing tears from the eyes of almost all present."

After the task at hand was completed, the minister of the church in Salem Town, Reverend Nicholas Noyes, was quoted as saying, "What a sad thing it is to see eight Firebrands of Hell hanging there."

As it turned out, Mary's wish was granted: there were no more executions after hers.

THE SALEM witch trials have been portrayed as a battle of Good and Evil, which they were. They were also a test of the delicate, and still evolving, relationship between church and state in late-seventeenth-century American Puritan society, especially when it came to the curious but critical issue of spectral evidence. By 1692, Massachusetts law had at least acknowledged what Christians had known for centuries: that witches did indeed exist. The first law, written in 1641, declared witchcraft a capital crime, and the second, in 1655, made "consulting" with a witch punishable by "death, banishment, or other suitable punishment." There was nothing on the books that allowed for the pressing of charges against people when spirits that resembled them—and visible only to a select few—wreaked havoc. So while the notion of an unruly spirit being egged on by Satan himself had the church's blessing, its acceptance as evidence in a court of law was tenuous at best.

This was the issue church and political leaders wrestled with throughout the summer of 1692 while the witch scare raged on. Eventually it would be resolved by two men, one the most influential and respected church leader in New England, and the other its most powerful political figure. They arrived together in Boston on the frigate *Nonesuch* on Saturday, May 14, 1692.

The Reverend Increase Mather, the president of Harvard College, was returning from England after negotiating a new charter for the Massachusetts Bay Colony, and he brought with him the brand-new royal governor, William Phips.

Before the month had ended, Governor Phips appointed a special Court of Oyer and Terminer (Latin for "hear and determine"), comprising five judges and presided over by Lieutenant Governor William Stoughton, to try the witchcraft cases. As for the issue of spectral evidence, Governor Phips sought the opinion of a group of twelve area ministers.

On June 15, five days after Bridget Bishop was hanged, the clergy panel submitted a list of recommendations written by Increase Mather's son, Cotton. Under the unwieldy title "The Return of Several Ministers Consulted by his Excellency and the Honorable Council upon the Present Witchcrafts in Salem Village," the ministers concluded that tales of spectral visitations were not in themselves sufficient to convict anyone of witchcraft. They also asked the jurists trying the cases to proceed with "very critical & exquisite caution" and to treat each of the accused with "exceeding tenderness."

In the end, the members of the Court agreed with the ministers on only one point: the need for "speedy & vigorous prosecutions of such as have revealed themselves obnoxious." Otherwise the recommendations in "The Return of Several Ministers" were largely ignored and the trials proceeded apace.

All of that changed on Monday, October 3, when a group of ministers gathered at Harvard College to hear the first public reading of an essay written by the Reverend Increase Mather, titled

Cases of Conscience
concerning evil
SPIRITS
Personating Men,
Witchcrafts, infallible Proofs of
Guilt in such as are accused
with that Crime.
All Considered according to the Scriptures,
History, Experience, and the Judgment
of many Learned men.

The "many Learned men" were the members of an association of ministers in Boston who had been loosely organized in 1633 in order "to form a centre at which the Boston ministers may periodically meet each other for friendly acquaintance and consultation about their common work, and other matters of religious interest."

Since 1690 they had been meeting at Harvard under the direction of Congregationalist minister Charles Morton. The association had closely followed the progress of the witch trials in Salem, and after Cotton Mather's essay had failed to dissuade the courts from the further use of spectral evidence, they asked his father to write a more forceful argument against it.

Increase Mather's "Cases of Conscience," which was eventually published in book form in 1693, is a remarkable document, given that it reads like both a sermon and a legal brief.

"The First Case that I am desired to express my Judgment in," Mather wrote, "is Whether it is not possible for the Devil to impose on the imaginations of persons bewitched, and to cause them to believe that an innocent, yea, that a pious person does torment them, when the devil himself doth it; or whether Satan may not appear in the shape of an innocent and pious, as well as of a nocent and wicked person, to afflict such as suffer by diabolical molestations?"

The answer, he decided, was that it was indeed possible for the devil to impersonate an innocent person, and he spent the rest of the thirty-five-page essay proving it.

His most persuasive argument came from the twenty-eighth chapter of the book of 1 Samuel, which told the story of Israel's first king, Saul, and the woman the Puritans' Geneva Bible called the Witch of Endor. (Modern translations refer to her as a medium.) The night before a decisive battle with Israel's archenemies the Philistines, the troubled king turned to God for guidance and comfort, but he did not receive a reply. Horrified, he asked the witch to conjure up the spirit of Samuel, the great prophet who had himself once led the people of Israel and who had anointed Saul king.

Then Samuel said to Saul, "Why have you disturbed me by bringing me up?" Saul answered, "I am in great distress, for the Philistines are warring against me, and God has turned away from me and answers me no more, either by prophets or by dreams; so I have summoned you to tell me what I should do."

Samuel informed Saul that God's silence was a signal that Saul had lost favor with the Lord. Therefore, Samuel said, the Philistines were destined to win the battle, Saul would lose his life, and David would become the next king, which of course is what happened.

Reverend Mather's argument was that this could not have been the spirit of the real Samuel speaking, because he failed to rebuke Saul for turning to a pagan witch for help when God ignored him. That proved, he concluded, that the image Saul saw was merely the devil disguised as Samuel.

After many more examples of genuine witchcraft, Mather anticipated his audience's next question:

"But then the Enquiry is, What is sufficient Proof?"

He outlined two criteria. First, "a free and voluntary confession" by the person accused, and second, "If two credible Persons shall affirm upon oath that they have seen the party accused . . . doing things which none but such as have familiarity with the devil ever did or can do. That's a sufficient ground for conviction."

The line most often quoted from "Cases of Conscience" may have spoken most clearly to the people of Salem Village: "It were better that ten suspected witches should escape, than that one innocent person should be condemned."

Little more than a week later, Governor Phips disbanded the court of Oyer and Terminer, and by the following spring all of the people in the Salem area who had been accused of witchcraft, including those who had been convicted but not yet executed, had been released from jail. The Salem witch hysteria was over.

Chapter Seven

STILLWATER, NEW JERSEY, 1793–1850

The Methodists

W<small>OULD YOU LIKE</small> to come preach to our congregation?"

That was the first sentence of an e-mail I received from Kem Monk, the pastor of the Harmony Hill United Methodist Church in Stillwater, New Jersey. I had contacted her a few weeks before because I had read on the church's website that it was founded in 1802 by my five-times great-uncle Elijah Woolsey. I had asked if I could bring my family to services some Sunday and ask some of the longtime parishioners about the church's history. After a few more exchanges we had become fast friends, and now I was receiving this generous invitation.

The answer was a resounding yes. The Sunday we chose in July turned out to be one of those scorchers when the heat and humidity combined to push the temperature well past a hundred degrees.

Stillwater is not far from the Pennsylvania border, in a heavily wooded area of northwestern New Jersey. Just past the WELCOME TO STILLWATER sign, I turned onto Fairview Lake Road and headed up the hill where I spotted the church through a cluster of trees. Next to it was a small cemetery surrounded by a low stone wall.

I had discovered Elijah Woolsey one Sunday afternoon when I dragged Cindy and the kids to the public library in Marlborough, New York, which had a copy of a history book about that area written by a distant cousin named C. M. Woolsey.

I identified myself at the front desk and one of the librarians ducked into the back room and returned with a beaten-up old volume that smelled of dust and age. I turned to the title page and read the long, unruly title: *History of the Town of Marlborough, Ulster County, New York, From Its Earliest Discovery.* The copyright said 1908.

In the preface, Woolsey wrote,

It has been said by a great writer that local history was the greatest
of all history; it brings us in touch with the place and its inhabitants
of former times. We see why certain habits and customs have been
handed down to us—connects the past with the present—shows
the character and services of our fathers—and, as far as may be,
produces the familiar scenes of by-gone years. But what little care
has been taken to preserve ancient papers and records and memo-
randa of past events. . . .

I well remember, when a little child of a few years my grandfather, Richard I. Woolsey, died, and his large trunk, filled with
valuable records of the past, which had been the pride of his life to
gather and save, was removed to the room over the wagon shed and
it was a pastime for other little children and myself to examine and
scatter this data all about the building in the search for a stray
picture. No one appeared to know its value. How safely we would
treasure those records if we had them now! The works of the dead
are soon forgotten, but in after years we realize our mistakes.

And so he had written his piece of local history, perhaps to make
amends for what happened to his grandfather's trunk, and as he might
have predicted, the copy I held appeared to have sat on a library shelf
unmolested for years and years.

I turned to the index and looked for more Woolseys. There were
many, but one in particular caught my attention—"Elijah, experiences of:
379–397." I turned to page 379 and saw that it was part of a chapter titled
"Methodism in the Town of Marlborough." At the top of the page, it read,

"Elijah, who was a native of this town and resided here a greater part
of his life, has left the following narrative of some of his experiences,
which will show some of the hardships that the early preachers had to
encounter."

The narrative began, "I now began to exhort sinners to turn to God;
and it was not long before I felt an impression on my mind that it was
my duty to preach," and ran for the next eighteen pages.

I looked up at Cindy.

"We may have an ancestor who was a Methodist circuit rider," I said.

Circuit riders were an invention of the American Methodist Church in the late 1700s. Because there were so many towns and so few preachers, the American colonies were divided into districts and each year one or two preachers were assigned to each district. They rode on horseback through the countryside preaching, baptizing, and establishing new churches the way Methodism's founder, John Wesley, had done in England in the early 1700s.

When we got home, I went immediately to my cousin's family tree and found Elijah. He was born in 1771 in Ulster County, New York. I knew that Methodism had been in my father's family for generations, especially among the Woolseys on his mother's side. And now I had discovered the very first one.

My line of Woolseys left New York City after my nine-times great-grandmother Rebecca Cornell Woolsey died in 1712. Her son, my eight-times great-grandfather Thomas Woolsey, moved forty miles north with his wife, Ruth, and their six children to the town of Bedford in Westchester County. Their youngest son, Richard, my seven-times great-grandfather, and his wife, Sarah, remained in the area and raised their own family of twelve children there. My six-times great-grandfather John moved even farther north along the Hudson River into Ulster County, to the town of New Paltz. It was there that he and his wife, Chlorene, raised their seven children. My five-times great-grandfather John junior was the oldest and Elijah was number six.

I looked Elijah up on the Internet and found Methodist churches in the area that mentioned him on their websites. That was how I discovered the Harmony Hill church. I had no idea where Stillwater was, so I looked it up online. The map showed it tucked in the northwest corner of the state, on the border between Warren and Sussex counties. I zoomed out to get my bearings, and instantly I knew where this was. The church was five or ten minutes away from the Boy Scout camp my son Chad had been going to every summer since the fifth grade. NoBeBoSco, as it's called, was famous for being the location of the slasher movie *Friday the 13th* (1980). The fictional Camp Crystal Lake was actually good old NoBe, and the dreaded cabin on the banks of the lake is still there. I know. I slept there one frigid winter weekend with Chad's troop.

After all these years, we had been taking him to camp and we didn't have a clue that one of our ancestors had also passed through this area each year two hundred years ago.

When I accepted Pastor Monk's invitation to speak to her congregation, I told her about Elijah Woolsey's journal. After months of combing the Internet, I discovered that it had been published as a book with a very catchy title: *Supernumerary, or the Lights and Shadows of Itinerancy, Compiled from Papers of Rev. Elijah Woolsey.* I went to a website that lists the inventories of rare-book shops around the country, and carefully entered the title. Miraculously, up came a single copy offered by a shop in Massachusetts. I bought it immediately.

A few weeks later I returned home from a road trip. My flight touched down in Newark close to midnight, and I arrived home just after 1:00 A.M. Cindy had left a package with a Massachusetts postmark on the desk in the study. Inside was a tiny, fragile book measuring just four by six inches. Its cover was worn and frayed, and its pages yellowed and brittle. I opened it carefully, and there on the first page was that title. The date at the bottom of the page was 1845.

I poured myself a glass of wine, sat down in my easy chair, and turned to page one.

"I was born in the same year that the venerable Bishop Asbury came to this country, 1771," he began. "My morals . . . were such that many of my friends thought me to be religious."

For more than an hour I rode the circuit with Elijah, experiencing the hardships the itinerant preachers endured: the rain and snow, the lonely nights spent by a campfire eating boiled potatoes, and the many, many miles of dusty roads.

A Methodist circuit rider's job was nearly impossible. He was expected to cover hundreds of miles each month, often preaching twice a day during the week and more frequently on Sundays.

The goal was to reach out to the people who lived in the remote villages that were so prevalent after the Revolution. As John Wigger pointed out in his *Taking Heaven by Storm: Methodism and the Rise of Popular Christianity in America,* "In 1795, 95 percent of Americans lived in places with fewer than 2,500 inhabitants; by 1830 this proportion was still 91 percent."

As difficult as it all sounded, there was still a precious joy to Elijah Woolsey's tone as he described the people he encountered. It was like reading a letter from a long-lost relative eager to tell his stories again. And there were indeed some wonderful stories.

At the Harmony Hill church, I parked next to the only other car in a field next to the cemetery. I got out and spent a moment studying the building. It was a small white stucco design with a bell tower above the entrance and a room attached on the side. I took a quick picture and walked inside.

The church was more the size of a chapel. It had only eight rows of pews, which were divided by a narrow center aisle and framed by two side aisles. Above it a balcony wrapped around three quarters of the sanctuary. And at the front there was a simple altar with a pulpit on one side and a lectern on the other. The organ stood off to the right side.

"You must be Bill."

Kem Monk emerged from a side door and we shook hands like old friends meeting for the first time. She looked to be in her mid-fifties. Her brown hair was cut stylishly and she wore a light summer dress. I was immediately taken by her highly contagious smile.

Kem was born Karen Marlene Eisinger, the free-spirited daughter of a military man. Very much a child of the sixties, she announced at the age of thirteen that henceforth she wanted to be called Kem, a name she took from her personal monogram, k-E-m. By the fall of 2000 she was a middle-aged mother of two grown sons, divorced after almost thirty years of marriage, and she began a new chapter in her life by entering seminary. She was appointed to Harmony Hill in the summer of 2004.

After a quick tour, we stood near the church entrance and began to greet the parishioners as they arrived. There was the elderly woman who had been married in the church many years ago, and the spry eighty-five-year-old man who served as both official greeter and usher. He told me how his grandfather had crafted the railing around the balcony when the church was renovated in 1907. More people arrived with more stories. And there were a few visitors, too, who had seen an announcement Kem had placed in the local newspaper about this "special" service. Cindy, Chad, and Carlee arrived and took seats near the front.

Just before ten o'clock, when almost everyone had been seated, I spotted a yellow rope hanging in the entry hall.

"Is that how you ring the bell in the tower?" I asked.

"As a matter of fact, it is," said Kem. "Would you like to ring it this morning?"

I gave the rope a tentative tug and felt the bell's pull on the other end. Its rich baritone rang from above, and I wondered if they could hear it at the Boy Scout camp. I counted out loud each time I pulled, to make sure I stopped at ten.

Then Kem lit a candle and she and I walked slowly down the center aisle toward the front of the church while the organ played quietly. I took my place in the chair behind the lectern while she lit the candles on the altar. There were no more than thirty people in the congregation, but the church looked full. I gazed up at the empty balcony. I love balconies. We used to have one in my home church in Los Angeles, and I loved sitting up there during services, listening to the sound of the organ echoing in the rafters during the hymns.

The music stopped and Kem stepped up to the pulpit.

"Good morning," she said, and the congregation returned her greeting. "We welcome you to Harmony Hill United Methodist

Church on what we believe will be a historic service." She told the story of how she had "roped" me into preaching, and everyone chuckled.

Then the congregation stood and we were under way.

KEM: Eternal God, you have called us to be members of one body.
CONGREGATION: Join us with those who in all times and places have praised your name;
KEM: that with one heart and mind, we may show the unity of your church,
CONGREGATION: and bring honor to our Lord and Savior, Jesus Christ.
KEM: Almighty God, you have raised up servants to proclaim the gift of redemption and a life of holiness.
CONGREGATION: For our spiritual forebears, Susanna, John, and Charles Wesley, Elijah and Thomas Woolsey, inspired by your Spirit, we give thanks.

Kem had asked if I wanted to include any particular hymns in the service, and I chose one that I thought would fit the morning's theme. "Faith of Our Fathers" was written by the British theologian Frederick W. Faber (1814–1863). Faber had experienced a kind of reverse reformation in his lifetime. He was raised a Calvinist, but because of a personal crisis of faith he converted to Roman Catholicism at the age of thirty-one in 1845. Four years after that he wrote what is probably his most famous hymn, a simple, nondenominational homage to Christian martyrs of the past:

> *Faith of our fathers, living still*
> *In spite of dungeon, fire, and sword;*
> *O how our hearts beat high with joy*
> *Whene'er we hear that glorious word!*
> *Faith of our fathers, holy faith!*
> *We will be true to thee till death.*

Each Methodist Hymnal devotes a page to John Wesley's "Directions for Singing."

"Sing lustily," he directed, "and with a good courage. Beware of singing as if you were half dead, or half asleep; but lift up your voice with strength.

"Above all sing spiritually. Have an eye to God in every word you sing. Aim at pleasing Him more than yourself, or any other creature. In order to do this attend strictly to the sense of what you sing, and see that your heart is not carried away with the sound, but offered to God continually; so shall your singing be such as the Lord will approve here, and reward you when he cometh in the clouds of heaven."

Kem and I took turns reading the morning's scripture lessons. The United Methodist Church publishes suggested Bible passages to read each Sunday of the year. Pastors are free to use others if they choose to, but the idea is that theoretically all members of the United Methodist Church around the world, no matter where they are, can hear the same Bible verses on the same day. It unites us as one congregation.

On this particular Sunday the suggested passages were from the fourteenth chapter of the Gospel of John. Jesus and the disciples were seated in the upper room of a home in Jerusalem, sharing their last supper on the night before the events that led to the crucifixion, and Jesus launched into his final sermon.

"Do not let your hearts be troubled. Believe in God, believe also in me. In my Father's house there are many dwelling places. If it were not so, would I have told you that I go to prepare a place for you? And if I go and prepare a place for you, I will come again and will take you to myself, so that where I am there you may be also. And you know the way to the place where I am going."

Thomas said to him, "Lord, we do not know where you are going. How can we know the way?"

Jesus said to him, "I am the way, and the truth and the life. No one comes to the Father except through me. If you know me, you will know my Father also. From now on you do know him and have seen him." (John 14:1–7)

Then it was time for the sermon. I stepped up to the lectern feeling a little awestruck by what I was about to do. I opened the manila folder in front of me and prepared to read aloud words written by my ancestor in a church he had founded more than two centuries ago.

ELIJAH WOOLSEY and his fellow Methodist circuit riders were products of what has come to be called the Great Awakening, a period in the 1730s and 1740s when the American colonies experienced a kind of spiritual rebirth. After the last of the Puritans died in the late 1600s, the colonies went through a time of religious stagnation when preachers droned on through their long intellectual discourses the way their predecessors had, only now their words fell on deaf ears. The passion the earliest Protestants had brought to the New World was gone, replaced by a nationalist sentiment that united the people ahead of the Revolution.

The Old Testament is full of stories like this, when the people of Israel turned away from God usually in times of prosperity. And each time a prophet stepped up to reacquaint them with their Maker, perhaps none more strikingly than the charismatic prophet Ezekiel, who prophesied during the agonizing early days of the Babylonian exile. Ezekiel's vivid visions foretold the day when the Judeans would be released from their captivity and returned to their homeland. His mission was to gird the people's spirits (In Hebrew, *Ezekiel* means "God strengthens"), and give them hope.

The people of the American colonies were awakened from their spiritual stupor by a handful of charismatic preachers, most notably Jonathan Edwards (1703–1758) and George Whitefield (1714–1770).

Born in East Windsor, Connecticut, Edwards was the son of a Congregationalist minister. He was a staunch Calvinist with a gift for public

speaking, and he used that gift to great effect with his passionate dia-
tribes that warned his congregations of impending doom if they didn't
wake up to God. His most famous sermon, the legendary "Sinners
in the Hands of an Angry God," first delivered to a congregation
in Enfield, Connecticut, in 1741, came to symbolize that era with its
"hellfire and brimstone" style that preachers mimicked for centuries
afterward.

"O sinner!" he wailed. "Consider the fearful danger you are in: it is
a great furnace of wrath, a wide bottomless pit, full of the fire of wrath,
that you are held over in the hand of that God, whose wrath is provoked
and incensed as much against you, as against many of the damned in
hell. You hang by a slender thread, with the flames of divine wrath flash-
ing about it, and ready every moment to singe it, and burn it asunder;
and you have no interest in any Mediator, and nothing to lay hold of to
save yourself, nothing to keep off the flames of wrath, nothing of your
own, nothing that you ever have done, nothing that you can do, to
induce God to spare you one moment."

In 1758, Edwards became president of the Presbyterian College of
New Jersey (which was later renamed Princeton University), where
he died as a result of a smallpox vaccination after only a few months on
the job. One of his daughters went on to marry Aaron Burr Sr., father of
the future vice president of the United States.

George Whitefield was born in Gloucester, England, the son of
a poor widow. He attended Oxford as a servitor, which meant he
earned his tuition by serving his fellow students, polishing their shoes,
carrying their books, and so forth. During his time there, he fell in
with the brothers John and Charles Wesley, who were sons of an
Anglican priest, and they formed a Holy Club that fellow students
referred to derisively as the Methodists, because of the members' odd
methodical ways.

John Wesley was the highly disciplined deep thinker of the group,
always studying scripture and writing scholarly tracts. Charles Wesley
was the creative one, musically talented and adept at a clever turn of

phrase. Whitefield was the gregarious one who brought a spiritual fervor to the pulpit. And while it was not their original intention to form a new Protestant denomination, eventually the spiritual revival their preaching sparked among the English working class of the early eighteenth century became the Methodist Episcopal Church, which took its structure from its parent Anglican Church and much of its doctrine from the Arminian movement of the previous century, which had replaced Calvin's predestination with a more flexible grace from God. John Wesley also believed all humans should strive for a life free of sin, which he called Christian Perfection. He agreed with Luther that salvation was the result of faith in Jesus Christ alone, and he disagreed with Calvin by believing that even the most devout Christians—the Calvinist Elect—could lose their salvation by succumbing to temptation.

Whitefield had a falling out with John Wesley over the issue of predestination (Whitefield had sided with Calvin), and he eventually moved to America, where his passionate style of preaching ignited a number of revival meetings that lasted for days, attracting thousands of people, some of whom went into convulsive fits. By the time of his death in 1770, he was the most famous preacher in America, and had, by his own estimate, delivered as many as eighteen thousand sermons.

Elijah Woolsey was born a year later in New Paltz, New York. In his journal he portrayed himself as a highly sensitive child, given to fits of weeping.

"Like Joseph," he wrote, "I could not refrain myself, but had to seek a place to weep in," which he said often brought peace to his soul.

I frequently attended public worship, both among the Presbyterians and Baptists, and also among the Quakers, without prejudice or respect of persons. But I cannot say that I ever heard any preaching that reached my heart until I heard the Methodists.

My father was a trustee of the Presbyterian meeting-house, and having returned from meeting one day, said to my mother that the trustees were out of humour, because they could not keep the minister any longer. He said that he had told them there were sixty or seventy Methodist preachers in New Jersey, and that they were great preachers, too.

I was then a small lad, and stood by and heard the conversation, and shall always remember the thoughts that passed through my mind at that time. Having read in the Scriptures that the gospel of the kingdom must be preached in all the world for a witness, and then shall the end come, I thought that those preachers were great and good men, and that they had begun at the southern extremity of the world and were making their way to the north, and when they had gained the northern extremity, the world would come to an end.

Elijah developed a fascination with these itinerant preachers. But he was also severely conflicted about how to relate to them. On the one hand he longed for the knowledge and insights these men obviously had of the scriptures, and the close relationship with God they enjoyed, but on the other hand he quietly suffered from a suffocating shyness that had him diving for cover each time one of them came to town.

On one particular occasion, for example, as a preacher was getting ready to leave, he made his way around the room and took each person by the hand, beseeching them to seek the Lord, which completely unnerved Elijah.

"This affected me much; and though I believed he was a man of God, yet through fear, and pride, and shame, I would not always give him an opportunity to speak to me, but used to hide myself among the trees of the garden until he went away. I would then creep out of my hiding place, and look after him as long as I could see him. Such love had I for a true minister of the gospel, as I believed him to be."

The year Elijah turned sixteen, a young preacher came through who changed the shy young man's life and set him on his course toward a career in the ministry.

The preacher's name was Ezekiel Cooper. He was born in Maryland, where he was baptized in the Anglican tradition, but he did not consider his parents or their neighbors to be devout Christians.

"Religion in those days, in our parts, appeared to be universally neglected," Cooper later wrote in his own journal. When he turned eighteen, he left home, moved in with his sister and her husband, and began a period of deep soul-searching.

"By night I walked the fields in meditation, and brokenness of heart; or, when all were sleeping, would frequently pour out my soul in supplication. In the spring and summer seasons I made the woods my constant resort, walking and meditating, or reading and praying, sometimes prostrate on my face."

This went on for several months until finally Cooper experienced his spiritual breakthrough:

"One day, as I was walking alone in the woods, I felt great encouragement. I knelt down and prayed fervently. Presently I had an opening to my mind of the infinite fullness of Christ, and of the willingness of the Father, through his Son, to receive me into his favor. I had such confidence in the merits of Christ and the mercy of God that I laid hold of the promise, felt my burden remove, and a flood of peace, love, and joy break forth in my soul."

Such episodes of spiritual conversion were typical of that era, and virtually a requirement for any young man who wanted to pursue the ministry, because they proved he was one of God's chosen in the tradition of the Apostle Paul's experience on the road to Damascus and—in the case of budding Methodists—John Wesley's own conversion.

John's brother, Charles, had experienced his own moment of clarity, and John had pretty much given up when his own experience occurred only a few days later. His brief account of it is the most famous paragraph in all of Methodist literature:

"In the evening, I went very unwillingly to a society in Aldersgate Street, where one was reading Luther's preface to St. Paul's Epistle to the Romans. At about a quarter before nine, while he was describing the change which God works in the heart through faith in Christ, I felt my heart strangely warmed. I felt I did trust in Christ, Christ alone for salvation; and an assurance was given to me that He had taken away my sins, even mine."

Ezekiel Cooper went on to a long, distinguished career in the Methodist Church, riding the circuit for a number of years in the New York/New Jersey area. Early in his career, only two weeks after his twenty-fourth birthday, in March of 1787, he passed through the New Paltz/Marlborough area of upstate New York and spoke to a gathering of Presbyterians in the Woolsey home, where he unknowingly had such an impact on the young Elijah Woolsey.

Elijah later wrote in his journal that he couldn't recall exactly when Ezekiel Cooper's visit occurred, but Ezekiel's own journal set the date as Friday, March 9. Of that day, Cooper wrote, "Captain Woolsey took me in his sleigh up to the New Paltz, where I preached at two o'clock. The house was full of people."

The text on which he based his sermon that afternoon was Mark 13:37: "What I say unto you, I say unto all: Watch."

It was the last verse of the chapter that biblical scholars have come to call the Little Apocalypse (the book of Revelation being the Big Apocalypse). Jesus had been sitting on the Mount of Olives overlooking the Great Temple with his four closest disciples, Peter, James, John, and Andrew, as darkness fell on the Tuesday of Holy Week. Jesus pointed to the temple and predicted that it would be destroyed in the not-too-distant future. Andrew asked him how they would know it was about to happen, and Jesus laid out an Apocalyptic vision, a period of great suffering when "brother will betray brother to death, and a father his child, and children will rise against parents and have them put to death." (Mark 3:12.)

"But about that day or hour no one knows," Jesus said, and so he advised them to be mindful at all times and to "watch."

A story like that in the hands of a skilled preacher would no doubt have had a profound impact on an impressionable young man like Elijah Woolsey. And apparently it did.

> His preaching was like a dagger to my heart; but my pride was such that for fear I should be seen weeping, I went into another room, and placed my ear against the door, that I might hear every word, for it seemed that he knew my whole heart.
>
> I could in part adopt the language of the woman of Samaria, who said, "Come, see a man that told me all that ever I did." This was the preaching that was blessed of God to my soul; and I for one shall have cause, I trust, to bless God to all eternity for that truly apostolic plan of carrying the gospel to every creature, by means of itinerant ministers. How many parts of our country would have remained destitute of the gospel and gospel ordinances to this day, if they could not have had them until they were able to have a minister settled among them!

In due course he decided to devote his life to God. But, shy young man that he was, he couldn't bring himself to pursue such a course alone, so he resolved to ask a friend to join him on his quest.

> Accordingly I fixed on a day and plan to speak to him on the subject. I went to his father's house and said to him, "Will you go to meeting with me to-day?" He at first said he could not. I told him he must go, for I had particular business with him that day. (He has since told me that he then suspected what I wanted to say to him.)
>
> He complied with my desire, and our conversation was on religious subjects; but I was not satisfied. I wanted him to say that he would go with me to the heavenly Canaan. So when we left the meeting I made a covenant with God in my own mind that I would speak to him on that point particularly, that I might know his mind; and when we came in sight of the house I trembled, but dared not go in until I had freed my mind.

I at length said to him, "My dear friend, I have often times thought I would set out in the service of God with all my heart, if I could get one of my companions to go with me." To which he replied, "I will go as far as God will enable me." The satisfaction I then felt I cannot express. It was better to me than if I had found thousands of gold and silver.

We then turned aside into the field, and sat down on a rock, and bathed it with our tears, while we covenanted together to be for God.

Elijah's youngest brother, Thomas, joined them and they formed their own Holy Club just as the Wesley brothers had done with George Whitefield in England.

My brother and my friend soon found peace, but I was left comfortless. Satan now set in with his horrid temptations, and strove hard to make me believe that God had consigned a part of his creatures to eternal misery.

O! horrible decree, thought I. I cannot believe it, and yet the enemy of God and man would crowd on my mind such passages of Scripture as these:

> "Jacob have I loved, and Esau have I hated;"
> "One shall be taken, and the other left;"
> "Many are called, but few chosen;"
> "The first shall be last, and the last first."

And never having heard these scriptures properly explained, but often quoted in support of the doctrines of "election and reprobation," I was almost driven to despair. I thought I should be willing to exchange my condition with the worst man on earth, for I thought he might be within the reach of mercy and I was not.

Finally, mercifully, Elijah experienced his own personal epiphany as he stood alone in the middle of a vacant field. In a moment of despair, he remembered crying out, "God be merciful to me, a sinner.

"It was while I was thus crying to God for help that his Holy Spirit brought comfort to my poor soul by applying these words, 'Whom the Lord loveth he chasteneth.' I was enabled to believe, and all was joy and peace."

By this time, following the Revolutionary War, American Methodism had separated from the English church and appointed its own presiding bishop, the thirty-nine-year-old Englishman Francis Asbury (1745–1816).

Asbury was a second-generation Methodist who came to America the year Elijah was born, in 1771. Following John Wesley's example, he climbed on a horse and road the circuit, covering an average six thousand miles a year, preaching virtually every day for the next forty-five years. In the process, he inspired hundreds of other itinerant preachers, who in America were called "circuit riders," to do the same. All of the preachers met with the bishop annually, where they were assigned to their next territory.

The annual conference of 1793 was held in Lynn, Massachusetts. It was an opportunity for the Methodists to show their unity in a region where they were locked in battle with the local Calvinists over the thorny issue of predestination. As it happened, Lynn was part of Ezekiel Cooper's circuit that year, and it fell to him to defend the Methodist view, which he did with an editorial he wrote for the local newspaper.

"In it," Cooper later remembered in his journal, "I undertook to show that if all things were decreed then there can be no sin, for sin is opposed to the law of God, and consequently contrary to the will of God.

"I also undertook to show that if all things were unavoidably fixed by an unalterable decree, then man had no freedom of choice, but was obliged to choose what was decreed, consequently was not a free agent but only a machine; and in such a case, how can he be held accountable?"

It was during this annual conference that twenty-two-year-old Elijah Woolsey received his first assignment as a circuit rider. But a surprise awaited him. When he arrived in Lynn on Wednesday evening, July 31, the night before the conference was to begin, he was told that he had been chosen to preach to the whole conference the next day. The thought terrified him.

> The cross of having to preach before the preachers was so great, that I slept none that night, but prayed and wept continually.
>
> As I went to the meeting-house my knees smote one against the other, and when I was in the pulpit, I trembled so much that I could not hold the hymn-book steady enough to see to read the hymn, without laying it on the pulpit and placing my hand on it. I then thought I should not live long, if such were to be my trials. After prayer, however, I gave out my text, and my fears were soon gone, and by the help of the Lord I preached for once, if I ever preached in my life.

Bishop Asbury obviously liked what he heard. Elijah was given his first assignment, north into Canada, where he soon discovered how hard life could be on the circuit.

"Sometimes," he wrote, "I had no bed to lie on, nor blanket to cover me in the coldest weather. My saddle-bags were my pillow, and my great coat my 'comfortable.'" The consequence was repeated and violent colds.

> Some part of the circuit I had to travel on foot, being unable to get my horse across the bays and rivers. Sometimes I had to travel fifteen miles a day, preach twice, and have never sat down from the rising to the setting of the sun.
>
> My knees and ankles pained me very much: and when I was preaching I used to stand sometimes on one foot, and then on the

other, to get rest. But rest was not easily obtained, even in bed, my knees and ankles were so swelled and full of pain.

My soul, however, was happy in the Lord, and my spirit rejoiced in God my Saviour. The flesh was often weak, but the spirit was willing to endure hardness as a good soldier for Christ's sake.

Indeed, it is clear that this highly sensitive young man who had been prone to fits of weeping did not exactly have the strongest of constitutions, and he sometimes became a burden to his fellow preachers.

When we came to Oneida lake, being in the month of August, the weather was very hot, and having the fever, and lying in the heat of the sun, I was almost overcome. My companions at length concluded to take me to the shore, where I could be in the shade, and accordingly they did, which, when I had fairly gained, I fainted, and the first thing I knew, one had hold of my hand and was calling to the rest to come and assist him. It seemed to me as if I had just waked out of sleep.

At one time I laid all night by the side of a fence, with a burning fever raging in every vein, without any covering but my clothes, or canopy but the vaulted heavens, with not so much as Jonah's gourd to shelter me from the chilling dews, or downy pillow on which to recline my weary head.

But life on the circuit could also be a great adventure, as he found during his time in Canada. Sometimes the most efficient way to travel was by boat on local rivers. And one time as he and his traveling companions made their way toward the Canadian border, they made arrangements in Albany to have professional sailors take them through the treacherous rapids in the area, only to find that their guides had abandoned them.

We were then left alone, and had to work our own passage. When we came to the first rapids, which by the Dutch people are called "knock 'em stiff," we had our difficulties. I had never used a setting pole in my life, and my colleague was not a very good waterman. When we had almost ascended the rapids, the boat turned round, and down the stream she went, much more rapidly than she went up.

We tried again, and when we had almost conquered the difficulty, the boat turned again. I then jumped overboard, thinking to save the boat from going down stream; but the water was over my head. So away went the boat, with my companions in it, and I swam to shore.

The next time we "doubled the cape," and that day made a voyage of ten miles. At night we brought up the boat, and made her fast to a tree. We then kindled a fire, put on the tea-kettle and the cooking-pot, boiled our potatoes, made our tea, and ate our supper with a good appetite and a clear conscience, and after smoking our pipes and chatting a while, we sung and prayed, and then laid ourselves down among the sand and pebbles on the bank of the river to rest; but I was so wearied with the toils of the day that I could not sleep much that night."

[Another time] on our way to Canada, we were met at Schenectady by some of our Canadian friends, who helped us on our way. We ascended the Mohawk in company with Captain Parrott, who . . . was very friendly, and we got along without any difficulty until we came to the Oneida Lake.

When we arrived at the lake, the wind was very high, and the lake was all in a foam, which continued all that day, and until about midnight. The wind then ceased, and the troubled waters became calm. About 1 o'clock, A.M., we embarked and after we had rowed about six miles down the lake, the wind began to roar tremendously, and the streaks of light broke through the clouds in a manner I had not seen before.

Our captain seemed to understand it as foreboding a heavy storm. We therefore made what preparation we could to encounter it. We spread our little sail, expecting the wind aft. We lashed two oars to the stern. The wind soon struck us, but we received no particular damage. The clouds were dense and dismal, and the waves broke over us with fury. Our friend, the captain, though an old sailor, was frightened, and cried out, "We are all dead men!"

I said, "The Lord will provide," and yet, notwithstanding my firm confidence in the power and mercy of the Lord, I sometimes feared for a moment that the lake would be my grave. These fears, however, were salutary: they caused me to examine myself, and the motives which induced me to undertake the work in which I was engaged.

At length the good providence of God brought us safe through. When we reached the shore we all rejoiced. The captain said he did not much expect, at one time, ever to set foot on dry land again, and that all his hopes were founded on this consideration, namely, he did not know but that the Lord might spare his life for the preachers' sakes.

As difficult as conditions could be, Elijah still found that he could help people who had it worse than he did.

We had rain and snow fifteen days out of nineteen during that journey. When we were going down the Oswego River, two men hailed us from the shore, and desired to work their passage about twenty miles. It was very stormy. I was very weary and glad to rest a little; so we took them in, and I took the helm; but being warm with work, and then sitting still in the boat, I took a violent cold.

Toward evening we saw a small log house and went to it. We found the woman sick in bed, and the man in poor health. They had three children, and but very little to eat. Here we lodged all night. I laid me down on the stones of the floor, which were very hard and uneven, but we kept a good fire all night, and got into a perspiration which relieved me of my cold a little, so that in the morning I felt much better than on the preceding night.

Brother D., being a physician, administered some medicine to the woman, which greatly relieved her. She appeared to be a pious woman, and had been a member of the Baptist Church at Ridge-field, in Connecticut, but said she had never seen a Methodist before. We had a very pleasant and edifying interview with the family that evening in religious conversation, singing, and prayer.

When we discovered that they were so destitute of provisions, we divided our little stock, and shared with them of all that we had. They appeared equally surprised and thankful—surprised that Methodists (of whom they had heard strange things in their own country) could be both religious and kind, and thankful for the timely relief. They wished that we would tell any of our Methodist friends who might have to travel that way to be sure and call on them. They desired us also, if ever we came within forty miles of them, to be sure and go that distance at least out of our way to see them—telling us that we should be welcome to any thing that the house or farm afforded.

The house, however, was not likely to afford much, and there was scarcely anything on the farm but forest trees. This was the only time, during our journey of nineteen days that we found a house to shelter us; and it was good for that family that they entertained the strangers, for we were in truth as angels of mercy to them. They must have suffered greatly had we not called on them.

The young preacher also found creative ways to reach people when they least expected it, such as the time he and two companions—one of whom he referred to as his cousin—came upon a local tavern one evening.

We traveled one day until nearly dark, when we came to a tavern which stood a little way off from the road. There appeared to be a number of noisy people within, and I thought if we had to stay there we should have an unpleasant night of it; so I sent on my companions first, to inquire if they could stay all night, and then rode up myself, and inquired if I could stay. We were all answered with the affirmative, and while the landlord took my horse to the stable, and the brethren took theirs, I walked into the house, and a very noisy place it was.

This being the case, I took my seat by the fire; and when the brethren came in, my cousin sat down by my side, as though he were a stranger, and asked me where I was from. I took the hint, and replied, "From Newburgh."

He said, "What, from that place of Deism?"

I said, "Yes," and by this time we had the attention of all in the house. He then asked me if there were any Presbyterians there.

I answered, "Yes."

"Any Baptist?"

"No."

"Any other religious denomination?"

I replied, "There are a few Methodists."

He asked what sort of people they were. I told him they appeared to be pious. He asked me what they believed. I answered him, that they believed in the depravity of the human heart; that penitents were saved by faith in Jesus Christ; and that believers might be made perfect in love in this life.

He asked me if I had ever heard them preach. I said I had. He then asked me if they undertook to prove their doctrines from the Scriptures. I told him they did. He asked me if I could recollect any of those scriptures which they quoted in favour of their doctrine. I told him I could; and quoted all I could then recollect on those points. He then asked me what other doctrine they believed. I said they believed a man might fall from grace.

He said, "Mercy on me! Do they undertake to prove that also from the Scriptures?" I replied they did.

He asked me for the Scripture proofs; and I gave him all I could recollect. He then asked me if they believed that there was a hell— what kind of place it was—was it a place of fire and brimstone, &c. I answered, "If it is not a place of fire and brimstone, as 'fire and brimstone' are so often mentioned in Scripture, they must be used as types of the miseries of hell, and that an antitype is greater than the type, and therefore hell must be worse than fire and brimstone."

He then asked what kind of people would go to hell. I told him, "swearers, drunkards, Sabbath-breakers, and all unbelievers, if they did not repent."

I then walked out of the doors, and he said to the landlord, "What did you think of that man?" He said, "He talked very reasonable." My cousin said he thought so too.

The man then said, "I guess he is a preacher—you must ask him to pray when he comes in." So when I returned to the house I was requested to attend prayers, and I did so, and the rest of the evening was spent in a very agreeable manner; and thus, as it were by stratagem, we took those captive who had long been "led captive by the devil as his will," and, by a little management, preached Christ, even in a tavern.

In the morning I started before my companions, and when they were about to start in the same direction, the tavern keeper desired them to tell me, that if I ever came that way again, I must call at his house and preach.

When he returned from Canada, he was appointed to a circuit in Connecticut, and his weak constitution continued to plague him.

On this circuit I was taken ill again with the fever and ague, which lasted for some time and was very severe. At one time I fainted while preaching, and was carried to bed. But at length I concluded that I would go to all my appointments, whether I could preach or not.

As I was going to one of them, I called at several houses and told them there would be no preaching for my ague fit would come on about the time of meeting. But the people came notwithstanding this.

As I lay on the bed in the back room shaking with the ague, the man of the house came to me and said there were more people than usual in the house and he asked me if I could not come and preach to them. I told him that I did not feel as if I could stand without fainting. He said he wished I would go and sing and pray, if nothing more.

I thought I would try; but I shook so with the ague that it was with difficulty I could read the hymn; but when I prayed I felt better and concluded I would try to preach. And so it was that when I got into the work the good Spirit of the Lord came down and so warmed my heart with the Redeemer's love that I rose above my bodily weaknesses and preached until the fever gave way and left me. I have had no more of it from that day to this.

It was while he was in Connecticut that he met his first wife. Sometime in either 1796 or 1797 he officiated at the funeral of the passionately devout matriarch of a large family in the Fairfield area by the name of Rockwell.

"She died in the triumphs of faith," he wrote, "clapping her hands until the last, in token of victory over all her spiritual enemies."

Six months later he married one of her daughters, Electa.

The good news for Elijah was that he now had a companion with whom he could share his joys and concerns about life. The bad news was that he sorely missed her while he was on the road.

The district was nearly eight hundred miles round, and I was between eight and nine weeks absent from my dear wife. The thoughts of home would often crowd upon my mind, and the distance of time and place, instead of weaning my affections from that dear spot, only drew them nearer and nearer to it. As a cord, when stretched to its utmost degree of tension, draws harder and harder and flies with greater force when it is let loose at one end back to the point from which it was extended, so my affections, the further and longer I was removed from home, drew me with greater force toward the place of my abode.

In 1799, Elijah was appointed to the large Flanders circuit in northern New Jersey. His Presiding Elder (a position the United Methodist Church today calls District Superintendent) warned him that it was in "poor condition," but Elijah felt he was up to the challenge.

The night before I started for conference, I dreamed that I went to seek for springs of living water and took a crow-bar on my shoulder. I soon found some springs that were filled with mud, and I began to clear the mud out. The water then ran as clear as crystal and the barren places became pools of water. In my dream I was very much delighted with my success; for the springs were full and running over.

In the morning I told my dream to brother Fowler (lately deceased), who said he could interpret it. Said he, "You will go to Flanders circuit, and find it in a very bad case, and you will ultimately see the greatest work of God there that you ever saw in your life."

That turned out to be an understatement. It was while he worked the Flanders circuit that Elijah participated in the largest revival meeting of his career, one that lasted a number of days.

Electa apparently accompanied her husband on this particular trip. The day before the meeting was to begin, as they approached the area, Elijah remembered saying to his wife, "The Lord will be with us at this quarterly meeting."

She said, "I know it, for I have never prayed for it but the Lord has so filled my soul with his love that I could scarcely keep from shouting."

The next day, Elijah's Presiding Elder began the meeting with a sermon based on Psalm 23. Something in it greatly stirred the people, and as the day wore on, the size of the gathering continued to grow.

Elijah was deeply affected. "I never had such feelings in my life, for it was as if a fire was shut up in my bones," he wrote.

When he and Electa left the meeting at 11:00 P.M. at the end of the first day, it was still going strong. He returned the next morning to prepare for Sunday services, and was startled to find a crowd estimated to be six thousand.

"There was preaching from the pulpit, exhorting from the windows, and sinners crying for mercy in the house and out of it. From this meeting the work spread all around the circuit, and many were added unto the Lord that year."

Elijah worked the Flanders circuit for three years. During his final year, in 1802, he was paired with a preacher named Gamaliel Bailey. The region that had been in such poor spiritual condition a few years earlier was now sprouting new congregations everywhere.

> At one place, called "the Log Jail," we had a good time, and the work of the Lord went on prosperously. We preached at the house of one Amos Mann, a spiritual son of Benjamin Abbott, and a very good one he was. For a time we had but few hearers, but at length some cried out for mercy and at the next meeting our congregation was much increased and the cries of the people made it somewhat noisy. Sister Mann was troubled at this and said that the people had now begun to attend meetings and the noise would drive them away. I said to her, "Be not troubled. There will be no lack of hearers, for they will come to see what is going on." The event proved the truth of my words.
>
> Our congregations soon became so large that the house would not contain them. I then said to Brother Mann, "You must enlarge

your house." He said, "I will have another house enclosed by the time you come here again."

And so it was. We had now two houses, and they were both filled. Still Sister Mann could not believe but that the noise would soon drive the people away. At the next meeting, however, we had to take the open air for our temple, though the weather was very cold.

To accommodate the preacher as well as they could, they fixed up a blanket to keep off the cold north-west wind, and under these circumstances I preached to the people while they sat on the ground. They heard the word with attention and some were deeply affected.

At night two souls were converted in a place called the "Shades of Death." It was in a valley of shady trees, and so called on account of its gloominess. They had gone thither to pray, and while there divine light visited their benighted souls. By this time our doubting sister dismissed her fears, and enjoyed her mind well all through the revival which continued, with but little abatement, throughout the year.

It was probably this revival that spawned the Harmony Hill church. A few miles north of the "Log Jail" area, a group of twelve people gathered in the home of Jacob and Catherine Mains and formed a Methodist Episcopal class under the supervision of the Reverends Woolsey and Bailey. They continued to meet in private homes in the area until the size of the group forced them to begin meeting outside in a local apple orchard. Incredibly, the Harmony Hill congregation met in that orchard for the next thirty years, until the church was built in 1832. The bell tower and fellowship hall were then added during a major renovation in 1907.

In 1807, Elijah's beloved Electa died.

It was during my last tour round the district that my dear wife was taken sick, with what proved to be her last sickness. I was more than three hundred miles from her, and knew not of it until I was within six miles of home. But O the distress and affliction I felt when I first beheld her pale face and feeble frame! My heart almost sunk within me. She lived, however, almost eleven months after I returned home, during which period her state of mind was such as afforded me the greatest satisfaction of anything below the sun.

I now wished to have my next appointment on Newburgh circuit, where she lived, and I sent my request to Bishop Asbury at the conference accordingly. He did not see fit, however, to grant it. . . . He appointed me to Brooklyn, where I could fill my sabbath appointments, and be with my suffering companion most of the time. The friends at Brooklyn were exceedingly kind; indeed, a kinder people I never saw.

One day I saw my beloved companion weeping, and said to her, "What makes you weep?" She said, "I want to live." I said to her, "What makes you want to live?" She said, "To compensate you for your kindness to me." This made me weep, and I felt unhappy for a time. A few days after I asked her if she was willing to give me up. She said she was. I felt thankful to God for it. She then asked me if I could give her up. I told her I could. She appeared to be glad. I continued to watch with her night and day as long as she lived.

Father Garrettson came to see her just one week before she died. He asked how she felt in her mind. She told him it was a sweet time to her soul; her views of God, Christ, and eternity were almost too much for the tabernacle of clay. He asked her if she had known what religion was before her sickness. She told him that the Lord had sanctified her soul more than two years before, and that she had not seen one moment since that time in which she doubted it any more than she doubted her own existence. He asked if she had given up her husband and all in the world besides. She said she had. He inquired whether the thoughts of death, judgment, and eternity were terrifying to her or not. She replied, "These are the happiest contemplations."

He said, "Well sister, you must suffer patiently." She replied, "Not one murmuring thought has entered my mind all through my sickness."

After this she asked me if she had said any thing in all her life that had hurt my feelings. I assured her she had not. Just as she was departing, she said to me, "Do you see any alteration in me?" I said, "No."

She then said, "I feel an alteration, and want you to pray for me, that I may have a quick passage to the kingdom of glory."

She then folded her hands together, and said, "Now, Lord Jesus, take me to thyself speedily." These were her last words. She immediately fell asleep in Jesus, without a struggle or a groan. This was on the 14th of February, 1807.

> *Farewell, bright soul, short farewell,*
> *Till we shall meet again above,*
> *In the sweet groves where pleasures dwell,*
> *And trees of life bear fruits of love.*
> *There glory sits on every face,*
> *There friendship smiles in every eye;*
> *There shall our tongues relate the grace*
> *That led us homeward to the sky.*

Ezekiel Cooper presided over Electa's funeral.

Brother Cooper asked me but a few minutes before he preached if I had any choice of a text: I said, "No"; but, while the people were singing, I wished I had given him the text that I had preached at her mother's funeral twelve years earlier, "O death, where is thy sting? O grave, where is thy victory?"

Lo, to my surprise, he gave out the same text with a little addition, which was, "Thanks be to God which giveth us the victory."

On the demise of my beloved companion I felt very lonely; but one night I dreamed that I had a pleasing interview with her. I thought she came to me, and I knew that she was from the world of spirits, and that she was no more mine, but the Lord's.

I thought I would ask her some questions, and said to her, "I want to ask you some questions about the other world." I thought she said, "There are many questions that might be asked about that world, which might be very improper for me to answer."

I then said, "I want to ask a question about yourself: is it well with you?" She said, "It is well." I thought she then began to give me a description of heaven, of glory, and of the New Jerusalem; and as she went on to describe it, all appeared in sight. She said the New Jerusalem needed not the sun to enlighten it by day, nor the moon by night, for the glory of God was the light thereof.

She made use of such language as appeared to me peculiar to her state. At the time she conversed with me I understood it perfectly, but when awake there was but little of it I could get hold of; it appeared to be out of my reach; it was above me; I felt a struggle in my soul to attain unto it, but could not; I had to sink down and cry out, "It is not for mortals."

When I turned about to leave her, I had no disagreeable feelings—I thought she was no longer mine, but the Lord's; and, at the time of our interview, I thought my feelings were somewhat like what I suppose they will be in another world, when the ties of nature are all dissolved.

When I had gone a few steps from her, I thought I would go back and ask her one more question; so I went, and said, "My dear, I want you to answer me one more question, if it will not be offensive to God." I thought her countenance looked forbidding. I mentioned the name of a woman who was dead, and said, "Is she in heaven?" After a short pause she said, "I did not see her there."

I then turned about and awoke, and found it was a dream, but it left a pleasant sensation on my mind, and though I felt sensible of my great loss, I could not wish her back again, believing that her sufferings were all over, and that she had entered on her eternal rest.

Elijah and Electa had been married roughly ten years. The union produced no children. Three years later, in 1810, Elijah married Phoebe Wilson.

In the summer of 1816, Elijah participated in an important event in the history of the Methodist Church. The General Conference, which brings together representatives from the entire Church once every four years, was held that year in Baltimore, and Elijah had been among the 117 delegates elected to attend.

A few weeks earlier, the American Methodist Church had lost its founding bishop when Francis Asbury died on March 31 at the age of seventy-one. By that time, under his tireless leadership, Methodism had grown to become the country's largest denomination, with 214,000 members. By his own estimate, during his forty-five years on the circuit he had preached more than sixteen thousand sermons and had journeyed more than 275,000 miles on the back of a horse.

He never married, once referring to marriage as "a ceremony awful as death," and at his death his only worldly belongings fit into two saddlebags. But he had become the most famous preacher in America. In a fitting tribute, the General Conference of 1816 became his memorial service.

Elijah remembered it in his journal.

Our friends in Baltimore had heard that the bishop, in a former will, had bequeathed his body to his Baltimore friends, he having formed the first Methodist society in that place. They therefore petitioned the General Conference for permission to have his body taken up, and brought to their city.

The bishop had been buried in a private burying ground, about seventy miles from Baltimore—the friends in Baltimore wished him to be buried under the pulpit in the Eutaw church. Their request was granted, and they brought him to the city while the conference was in session; and although it was not publicized in any of the churches, I think there was the greatest concourse of people I ever witnessed.

He joined the sixty-plus preachers in attendance as they walked two by two behind the lead coffin into the church. William McKendree, who succeeded Asbury as bishop, presided over the funeral.

Elijah continued to ride the circuit for twenty-seven more years, most of the time in New York, until his retirement in 1843, when he and Phoebe moved to the village of Rye.

"Since I have lived in Rye," he wrote, "we have had some good revivals; although we have had some discouragements, yet amidst them all, we have kept our heads above the water."

He settled into a quiet life with his wife, attending church in Rye Village and in the nearby town of Milton. And he assumed the role of elder statesman, mentoring young preachers as they struggled with the rigors of the circuit, just as he had.

When our preachers are cast down I feel sorrow of heart, but when they feel encouraged then I rejoice with them; so I can "rejoice with them that rejoice, and weep with them that weep." But, I believe, when the members are all alive in religion, and striving for that mind that was in the Redeemer, we shall see good times; for we have the promise of God to that effect, and his promises will never fail.

He was asked to write a series of articles about his days on the circuits, which were later combined into the little book I bought on the Internet. It gave him the opportunity to reflect back on the hardships and pleasures of the life on the road.

It is very different now with the preachers from what it was in days gone by, for the time has been when it was thought almost a virtue to persecute the Methodists, especially in New-England, or Connecticut, for the Methodist preachers had to dispute every inch of ground.

Their circuits were very large, and they had to read their Bibles as they could, sometimes on horseback, and sometimes on their knees, and study their sermons while in bed or on horseback, for at many places they had but poor accommodations. I have had sometimes to travel forty miles in one day, and preach three times; but this was not grievous to me then, and it affords me great pleasure now to think how the Lord hath brought me through.

Sometimes, to be sure, I feel as if I were in the bloom of youth, but at other times I feel myself as on the brink of the grave, good for nothing. When I look forward I have nothing to fear, but much to hope. Thus I feel while I write.

It was to me a source of inexpressible satisfaction that I had been made useful to a few of my fellows . . . and the thought of meeting them on Canaan's happy shore, after the trials of life are over, and of greeting them as my spiritual children, often gilds the shadows of my supernumerary hours, and gives brilliancy to the rays of the descending sun.

Elijah Woolsey died in 1850. Despite the rigors of riding the circuit and the obvious toll it took on his health, he lived to the age of seventy-nine.

WHEN THE service at Harmony Hill ended, everyone headed to the Fellowship Hall next to the sanctuary, where there were sandwiches and slices of pie and coffee waiting for us. We stayed another hour and chatted with a few of Kem's "old timers." I asked them more questions about their church's history, and they asked me about Elijah.

Around noon we excused ourselves and left for Scout camp. We found that most of the rest of Chad's troop had already arrived. Everyone was busy unpacking and getting situated. I helped Chad set up his cot, and Cindy got him settled in the tent that would be home during his annual week in the wilderness. Before we left, I peered through the trees trying to imagine what this spot looked like two hundred years ago, and I wondered if a certain Methodist circuit rider ever rode through on his way to his next destination.

Cindy and Carlee headed home and I drove back to the church. I had an appointment with the people buried in the cemetery.

Harmony Hill's website quotes a passage from a book titled *History of Sussex County, New Jersey,* by James P. Snell (1981), about the founding of the church:

"What is now known as the Harmony Hill Methodist Church originated in a Methodist Episcopal Class organized in 1802 in Jacob Mains' log house by Revs. Elijah Woolsey and Gamaliel Bailey. There were twelve members in that class, but the names of only ten can be recalled: Jacob Mains & wife, Catharine Maines [sic], Christianus Mains, Abram Mains, James Egbert & wife, Mr. Kimball & wife. James Egbert was the leader. Among the earliest to join were Jacob Savercool, Jacob Banghart & wife, Conrad Hammond & wife, Samuel Lanney and wife."

I parked my car in front of the cemetery, got out with my camera, and walked among the headstones. Many of them have been worn down by the elements, rendering them unreadable. Those were the ones I focused on, because I suspected they marked the spots where the earliest members of this congregation were buried. Some of them might even have been original members, people who had actually heard Elijah Woolsey preach.

Elijah never had any children of his own, but he left behind a legacy that has lasted more than two hundred years. This little church is part of that legacy, and the handful of people with whom I spoke that morning were his spiritual descendants.

"I believe when the members [of a congregation] are all alive in religion," Elijah wrote at the end of his journal, "we shall see good times; for we have the promise of God to that effect, and his promises will never fail."

Chapter Eight

WASHINGTON, KANSAS,
1850 TO THE PRESENT

The Homesteaders

I MAY BE from Los Angeles, but my real homeland is a one-hundred-square-mile area in northern Kansas and southern Nebraska where my parents' families extend back three generations. On my father's side were the Griffeths and the Woolseys, and on my mother's side were the Norris and Benne families.

Home was the little town of Washington, Kansas. Mom and Dad grew up there, and my three sisters were born there before the family moved to California, where my brother and I were born. The values our parents instilled in us—the Protestant work ethic, an ever-optimistic pioneer spirit, and a quiet acceptance of God's will—were cultivated in the heartland like the crops that sustained the early pioneer families.

All of my Midwestern ancestors were godly people. They carried the banners of various denominations with them when they crossed the prairie in the middle of the nineteenth century. There were Methodists, Lutherans, Christians, and even a Catholic among them. Some, like my namesake maternal grandfather, David William Norris, were firebrands who raged with the ancient zeal of the Puritans. Others, like my maternal grandmother, Marie Benne Norris, embodied a more gentle faith.

When I was growing up, I spent many summers in Kansas with my parents visiting Grandma Norris and the many aunts and uncles and cousins who lived there. I stopped going after I graduated from high school. My last trip was in 1986, when Grandma died at the age of ninety-four. Now, after twenty years, I was returning to the prairie, the last stop of this three-year odyssey I had been on, to see once again the place where my ancestors had all come together.

I caught the last flight from Newark to Kansas City one Thursday evening. After it arrived at 11:00 P.M. local time, I picked up my rental car and drove to the hotel next to the airport, where I spent the night. Early the next morning I was heading west on Route 36 into Kansas. The road was straight and the terrain was flat. This was, after all, Kansas, so I had a view for miles all around me. It was a beautiful late-summer morning with bright blue skies and white, puffy clouds over-head. The cornfields with their bright green and gold stalks looked ready to be harvested.

Millions of years ago this land had been underwater, part of a huge inland lake bed, which helps explain the legendarily flat topography. The accumulation of dead plants and animals over the millennia created highly fertile soil. The result was more than 82,000 square miles of bottomland perfect for farming, and of gentle rolling hills suitable for grazing livestock.

Europeans first arrived here in the 1500s when the Spanish explorer Francisco Vásquez de Coronado led a gold-hunting expedition through the area. Then, in the spring of 1682, the territory was claimed for France by René-Robert Cavelier de La Salle, who had been sent by Louis XIV to establish fur-trading relationships with the natives who lived along the Mississippi River. It was La Salle who named the region Louisiana for his king.

In 1803, Thomas Jefferson bought the 828,000-square-mile parcel from Napoleon Bonaparte for less than three cents an acre. The Louisiana Purchase instantly doubled the size of the United States. When Louisiana became a state in 1812, the rest of the land was called the Missouri Territory, and St. Louis became its capital. Over the next forty years, portions were broken off to become states: Missouri in 1821, Arkansas in 1836, Iowa in 1846, and Minnesota in 1858.

The midsection of the country, the flatlands located between the Appalachian and Rocky Mountain ranges, had been designated as Indian Territory in the 1830s. In 1854, Congress created the Kansas-Nebraska Territory. By 1859 the process had begun to turn it into two states, but there was a major political obstacle: the slavery issue had become an obsession in Congress, and each time a territory was considered for statehood, inevitably the question was raised of whether it should be a slave state or a free state, and the horse trading would begin. In 1820, for example, a compromise was reached when Maine was allowed to enter the Union as a free state only if Missouri entered as a slave state.

Lawmakers tried to do the same with Kansas and Nebraska. A plan was devised in which Kansas would enter as a slave state and Nebraska would be a free state. But there were enough abolitionists living in Kansas to call the compromise into question. In 1860, militias both for and against slavery were formed, and fierce battles were fought for several months. Eventually the abolitionists won and Kansas entered the Union as a free state on January 21, 1861. Nebraska followed two years later. Though the Civil War officially began with the first shot fired at Fort Sumter on April 12, 1861, in fact the fighting had begun in earnest the year before in Kansas.

Washington, Kansas, c. 1900

Washington, Kansas, 2006

The town of Washington, Kansas, was incorporated in 1875 as the seat of a county that measured thirty miles square. Like virtually all of the communities in this part of the country, its birth was a direct result of the Homestead Act of 1862, and its prosperity was assured by the arrival of the railroad. Washington County's population in 1860 was only 383. Ten years later, though, after the act had been passed and the Civil War had ended, the number jumped to more than four thousand. And ten years after that, in 1880, it had surged to well over fifteen thousand.

I drove past the WELCOME TO WASHINGTON sign, turned off Highway 36, and began my tour of the town, past the house where Grandmother Norris lived, the high school my parents attended and the courthouse where they were married one summer afternoon in 1935, and the little white house where they first set up housekeeping.

On the east side of town, I found the old Episcopal church. It was abandoned when the congregation dwindled to just a few members and the sanctuary was turned into a meeting hall called Friendly Corners, where meals were served each day to the town's senior citizens.

Inside I found a diminutive, gray-haired woman in a white blouse and pink slacks setting tables. This was Mom's first cousin Helen. Mom was the eldest of a group of seven girl cousins who grew up in Washington in the 1920s, and Helen was the youngest. She and her husband, Floyd, lived on a farm west of Washington where they raised their five children, and at eighty she still worked at Friendly Corners.

We greeted each other enthusiastically, and she introduced me to her co-workers in the kitchen, who were busy preparing the day's meal just as the group of twenty men and women they would be serving streamed in through the front door and took their seats. Most of the men wore blue and white striped bib overalls and the women favored light-colored blouses and pale pastel pants. I didn't recognize any of these people, but I felt I knew them anyway. Like Helen, they were probably third- or fourth-generation residents whose great-grandparents had homesteaded here in the mid-nineteenth century.

It's a good bet they represented the spectrum of Protestant denominations. The harsh conditions on the prairie brought together people of various religious backgrounds. They supported each other by helping to bust sod and build shelters and fences. On Sunday, if they gathered for worship, services tended to be nondenominational. A pioneer woman named Lydia Murphy Toothaker, who lived with her husband and children just west of Kansas City in 1860, described a typical Sunday service in her diary:

"Irrespective of former religious affiliations, these new settlers came bringing all the family. There were the Bonneys, former Baptists, the Corliss[es], Unitarians, the MacDouglass[es] of Episcopal stock, the Plummers who in Kentucky had never attended a Methodist meeting.

"What fervent Amens rose during the sermon," she continued. "The walls of the house fairly shook with the Methodist hymns:

> *Let every mortal ear attend*
> *And every heart rejoice*
> *The trumpet of the gospel sounds*
> *With an inviting voice"*

Sermons often carried simple reminders about doing unto others and about cleanliness and godliness. In 1885, for example, a Methodist preacher named Samuel Porter Jones stood on a piano box in an open field one Sunday morning in Cincinnati and delivered a decidedly non-denominational message to his congregation.

"A good man goes to heaven because he is good," he declared, "and heaven is the center of gravity for all that is good; a bad man goes to hell because he is bad—that's the nature of the whole matter."

Helen walked to the middle of the room and asked everyone to stand. She led us in reciting the Pledge of Allegiance, and we sang the Doxology.

"Praise God from Whom all blessings flow. . . ."

It is a safe bet that wherever Protestants gather for some form of fellowship, they get around to singing this song, the only one that all denominations use. The tune was composed in the sixteenth century by a disciple of John Calvin's named Louis Bourgeois. It was originally called "Old Hundredth" because it was used with verses from the One Hundredth Psalm. More than a century later, in 1673, Anglican bishop Thomas Ken published a book of hymns he had written, some of which concluded with a four-line doxology, or song of praise:

> *Praise God from Whom all blessings flow*
> *Praise Him, all creatures here below*
> *Praise Him above, ye heavenly host;*
> *Praise Father, Son, and Holy Ghost.*

Eventually the words were married to the "Old Hundredth" and a tradition that has lasted for centuries was begun.

Lunch at Friendly Corners was oven-fried chicken, mashed potatoes with wonderfully thick country gravy made from drippings, corn, and a brownie for dessert. It was good hearty country fare, and it tasted delicious.

After everyone had finished eating and the servers had cleared the plates, I excused myself and told Helen that I would see her the next day, when we had plans to have dinner with her children and grandchildren.

I headed west out of town on Route 36 to begin my tour of the area and to reacquaint myself with the stories of my ancestors and the religious traditions they brought with them.

They were drawn to the area by the Homestead Act, which Abraham Lincoln signed into law in May of 1862. It was designed to draw settlers to the Great Plains, which, sixty years after the United States purchased the land, were still largely unpopulated.

Homesteaders had to meet certain qualifications: they had to be at least twenty-one years old or the head of a family, and they either had to be a U.S. citizen or to have filed a declaration of intent to become one.

For a fee of eighteen dollars, each homesteader could file a claim on a square tract of 160 acres. Eighty-acre tracts were also available in more desirable areas adjacent to railroad grants. Filers were required to work the land and to make it their permanent residence for five years. At the end of that period, they returned to the claims office with two witnesses who could vouch for the improvements made, and after paying one more fee of a few dollars, the land was theirs. By the end of the century, more than 80 million acres had been claimed by 600,000 homesteaders.

The first of my ancestors to move to the area were my great-great-grandparents Herman and Maria Benne, who migrated from Germany to America in 1849, around the time of the failed German Democratic Revolution. The year 1848 was one of great upheaval in Europe. In February, King Louis-Philippe of France was overthrown and the Second French Republic was formed. That inspired an uprising in the thirty-eight German states. In May the Frankfurt Assembly was convened to encourage Kaiser Wilhelm Frederick IV of Prussia to accept a unified Germany complete with a constitution and a national assembly. Almost a year later, in March of 1849, he rejected the idea and the revolution died. Thousands of German citizens who had grown tired of the oppressive monarchy fled to America.

At the time of their own departure, Herman and Maria had two children: three-year-old Ann and an infant son, Herman junior. The boy became ill and died during the voyage across the Atlantic, and he was buried at sea.

The Bennes settled first in Florence, Missouri, where my great-grandfather Henry was born in 1850. Seven years later the family—by then with two more sons—moved north to Minnesota, where they stayed for fourteen years. In November of 1871, when Maria's poor health could no longer take the extreme cold of that region, they came to Washington County, Kansas, where Herman homesteaded 160 acres and twenty-one-year-old Henry took out a claim on an eighty-acre tract nearby.

My great-uncle Erwin Benne—one of Henry's sons—who taught chemistry at Michigan State University for thirty-three years until his retirement in 1971, wrote a series of essays about the family's history. In one of these he described the hardships his grandparents faced the day they arrived in Kansas.

[It was] a sunny Indian-summer day, and they began immediately to prepare a dugout home, but during the night a cold northwest wind swept across the prairie, bringing with it stinging sleet and blinding snow. The wagons afforded only scant shelter for the family, and the horses had none.

However, unexpected help came to their rescue. A family that was settled on a claim about two miles away had seen the newcomers go by the day before, and in the spirit of pioneer hospitality, the husband made his way through the storm and invited them to share their dugout shelter.

The storm lasted three days while eighteen men, women, and children huddled in that dugout.

During that first winter, the family lived in almost total isolation . . . .Candles were their only means of artificial light. They had no clock, so time could only be estimated by the position of the sun in the sky. Their drab and limited clothing was largely homemade, and shoes were made to last as long as possible. Only home remedies were available for treating injuries or illnesses.

Theirs was a monotonous diet of corn bread, beans, potatoes and salt pork. When spring came, dandelions and lambs-quarters greens were eaten with relish since they added variety to their meals.

And things didn't get much easier for the next few years. Each spring Herman broke more sod and planted ever larger fields of corn, some of which he bartered for food and supplies, while the rest went to feed the livestock. It was a hard life for a couple who were already in their fifties.

I spotted a small cemetery next to the only Catholic church in the area, St. Peter and St. Paul, which was founded in 1887. This was where Herman and Maria were buried.

Herman was a Catholic and Maria was a Lutheran. When they arrived in 1871, there were only fifteen Catholic churches in the whole state of Kansas, with a membership of fewer than thirty thousand people. The closest one to them was 130 miles away, in Topeka.

Maria died in 1878 and was buried on the grounds of the family farm. When Herman died thirteen years later, in the spring of 1891, the family decided to bury them together in the new Catholic cemetery. But it wasn't going to be easy.

I pulled in to the church parking lot and walked to the back, where the cemetery was located. The fifty or so headstones inside were mostly located on the south side of the lot. I walked past them glancing at several names, but I knew that I would not find BENNE on any of them. Instead, I continued on toward a row of thick evergreen trees standing just inside the fence that formed the cemetery's northern border.

A hole had been cut in some of the trees' branches, forming what looked like the mouth of a cave, which I entered. Sure enough, just as I had heard, there at the foot of one of the trees, hidden from view, was a lone headstone.

BENNE

HERMAN   MARIA

1819–1891   1822–1878

I've heard at least two variations of the story about why they were buried in this out-of-the-way spot. One says that because Maria was a Lutheran, she was not welcome in the Catholic cemetery, and it was only after some protracted negotiations that the local priest, Father Alois Cihol, allowed them to be buried here where they wouldn't be seen.

The other variation blames Herman for their odd placement. The story goes that while he was on his deathbed, he refused the last rites from Father Cihol, and in retaliation the priest banished him and his Protestant wife to the cemetery's unhallowed ground.

Not much is known about Father Cihol. His name suggests that he was of Czech descent. In the 1850s, thousands of Czech citizens fled their homeland for America after the failure of the same Democratic Revolution that brought their German neighbors to the region. By 1874 the town of Wilson, located in central Kansas, had become the unofficial Czech capital of the state.

Is it possible there was bad blood between the German farmer and the Bohemian priest? Or was this simply a case of a Catholic clergyman trying to uphold Church tradition in a land where many traditions were disregarded in the name of community?

I bent down and swept away some of the dirt that had collected on the headstone. Through the opening in the trees I could see the rest of the cemetery. The other headstones, huddled as they were near the southern fence, looked like schoolchildren ignoring a couple of unpopular students.

I took a few photographs, breathed a brief silent prayer over the headstone, and returned to my car.

I DROVE north to the Greenfield Cemetery, roughly ten miles away in Lowe Township, where my maternal grandfather, Dave Norris, homesteaded in the 1890s. The gate across the entrance was locked. I pushed open a side gate and waded through the tall bluestem grass, waving off the swarms of grasshoppers that flew at me, and began hunting for his headstone.

My great-grandparents George and Sarah Norris migrated with their eight children from New Boston, Illinois, to Nebraska in the 1870s, when Grandpa Dave was a teenager. During the trip they met up with a wagon train headed north to the Dakota Territory, where gold was discovered in the Black Hills in 1874. The wagonmaster offered my grandfather a job as an Indian scout and, incredibly, his parents allowed him to take it. He left his family and continued on with the wagon train to Deadwood, which in its earliest days was a lawless mining camp of tents and lean-tos.

The Norris family belonged to the Christian Church (also known in some areas of the country as Disciples of Christ), a Protestant denomination that is uniquely American. It was founded in the early 1800s by four Presbyterian ministers from Kentucky and Pennsylvania. One of them, Barton Stone of Cane Ridge, Kentucky, sought unity among all Protestants, believing that denominations tended to divide the people arbitrarily. He proposed calling everyone Christians.

Stone and his colleagues preached basic principles: have faith in Jesus and live according to the Scriptures. There was no formal creed and no set order of worship. Church members were encouraged to read the Bible and to draw their own conclusions.

Great-grandma Sarah Norris home-schooled her children using the Bible to teach them to read, and her interpretation was a very conservative one. She would have been horrified to hear about the gambling, drinking, and carousing that her teenaged son was exposed to during his two years in Deadwood.

While Grandpa Dave was there, the first preacher to reach the Black Hills arrived in May of 1876. Methodist circuit rider Henry Weston Smith brought the word of God to the fortune hunters in Deadwood's mining camps, and on Sunday, May 7, he held the first service ever conducted in the area. According to a local merchant who was there, thirty men and five women attended. I have no way of knowing whether my grandfather was one of the men, but I have to believe that if he had heard about it he would have been there.

Preacher Smith based his sermon on a passage from the Old Testament:

"The Angel of the Lord encamps around those who fear him, and delivers them" (Psalms 34:1).

According to the local merchant who attended the service, Smith "preached a very interesting sermon. The congregation paid strict attention to the sermon except when there was a dog fight outside."

Preacher Smith worked during the week in a local sawmill, and on Sundays he conducted services on the streets of Deadwood and the nearby mining town of Crook City. On Sunday, August 20, after morning services in Deadwood, he tacked a note on the door of his cabin saying he was off to Crook City and that he would return later that day.

He never did. His body was found five miles out of town. He had been shot through the heart. His killer was never found.

Grandpa Dave left the Dakota Territory a short time later and rejoined his parents where they had settled in Ashland, Nebraska.

I found the headstone I was looking for almost immediately.

MARBLE
WIFE OF
D. W. NORRIS
1865–1913

DAVID W. NORRIS
1858–1946

In 1882, Grandpa Dave married Thalia Marble Richardson, and they had four children. Then, in March of 1899, the family bought a farm in Lowe Township, Kansas.

Each school season, from September to April, the young women who taught in the town's one-room schoolhouse traditionally boarded with the Norris family, because their farm was close by. Beginning in 1910, that young woman was Henry Benne's nineteen-year-old daughter, Marie.

Marble Norris died of stomach cancer on January 31, 1913. Eighteen months later, in June of 1914, her widower married the young schoolteacher. He was fifty-six and she was twenty-three.

The Norris and Benne families were scandalized. Grandpa Dave's children, some of whom were older than their new stepmother, all left the area. And my great-grandmother, Henry's wife, Bertha Benne, who was seven years younger than her new son-in-law, dismissed him as an "old fool."

Dave and Marie Norris had one child, my mother, Frances, who was born on the fourth anniversary of Marble's death. Mom remembered her father as a very stern man who rarely showed her any real affection. He apparently inherited his mother's strict religious tendencies, strongly disapproving of any social activity—most especially sporting events—that took place on Sundays. And he never allowed my mother to wear red dresses because they reminded him of the "ladies" who wore them in Deadwood.

In 1929 my mother was baptized at the age of twelve in the Christian Church in Washington. Members are baptized when they are old enough to profess their own faith. Each person is dressed in a special gown and immersed in a tub of water. When Mom sat down in the tub that had been placed in front of the congregation, the minister leaned over her, placed his hand on her head, and told her to hold her breath

as he pushed her under the water. Unfortunately she didn't take that breath until after she had been submerged, and she almost drowned. It was an unceremonious entrance into the family of Christ, and it caused her to develop an acute fear of water. She became a devout Christian, but she never learned to swim.

THE FIRST Methodist sermon ever preached in the Kansas-Nebraska territory occurred on Sunday, April 21, 1850, where Omaha is now located. The Reverend Harrison Presson was passing through on a wagon train heading west, and the settlers stopped just inside the territory's eastern border to observe the Sabbath.

Reverend Presson used an appropriate Old Testament verse as the basis for that sermon:

"The wilderness and the solitary place shall be glad for them; and the desert shall rejoice, and blossom as the rose" (Isaiah 35:1).

It was a passage of hope in which the prophet Isaiah looked ahead to the day in the eighth century B.C. when the Judeans would be released from captivity and their homeland could be restored to its original glory. The early prairie preachers of nineteenth-century America used it to forecast a bright future for the dusty plains of the heartland once the gospel had been planted like so many seeds of corn.

It was a prescient observation. By the middle of the 1860s, thousands of people had begun to head west, fleeing the political and economic chaos caused by the Civil War. The land rush was on.

President Teddy Roosevelt remembered that period in a speech he delivered in 1903:

The work of advancing our boundary, of pushing the frontier across forest and desert and mountain chain, was the great typical work of our nation; and the men who did it—the frontiersmen, plainsmen, mountain men—formed a class by themselves. It was an iron task, which none but men of iron soul and iron body could do.

The men who carried it to a successful conclusion had characters strong alike for good and for evil. If left to himself, without moral teaching and moral guidance, without any of the influences that tend towards the uplifting of man and the subduing of the brute within him, sad would have been his, and therefore our, fate. From this fate we have been largely rescued by the fact that together with the rest of the pioneers went the pioneer preachers; and all honor be given to the Methodists for the great proportion of these pioneer preachers whom they furnished.

Just as they had done in original colonies in the years after the Revolution, the Methodists moved aggressively into the rapidly expanding western frontier after the Civil War.

Census figures for 1870 detail the breakdown of denominations in Nebraska:

Methodists	10,150
Baptists	5,400
Presbyterians	3,125
Congregationalists	2,050
Lutherans	2,000
Episcopalians	3,500
Catholics	2,935

The 1890 census showed how successful the Methodists' campaign was:

Methodists	112,000
Baptists	36,500
Presbyterians	34,900
Congregationalists	32,000
Lutherans	49,900
Catholics	38,390

My great-great grandparents William and Martha Woolsey were among the first wave of postwar Methodist homesteaders to settle in Nebraska.

Just after their marriage in 1870, the Woolseys settled in Johnson County, near the town of Tecumseh. The county had been named for the war hero Richard M. Johnson, who was Martin Van Buren's vice president from 1837 to 1841. The success of Johnson's political career had been based largely on his claim that he had shot and killed the legendary Shawnee Nation leader Tecumseh in a decisive battle during the War of 1812. His catchy campaign slogan was "Rumpsey, Dumpsey, Colonel Johnson killed Tecumseh!"

The historian David Marquette wrote, "At that time Tecumseh itself was little more than a post office, the number of people never exceeding one hundred until after the war, when a number of old soldiers and others coming in, the town was incorporated in 1865."

William was one of those old soldiers. Because he had served more than two years in the Illinois Cavalry during the Civil War, the Woolseys were able to take advantage of a clause in the Homestead Act that allowed veterans to claim 160 acres of prime land next to lucrative railroad grants. A few years later the Atchison & Topeka Railroad rolled through and sparked an economic boom.

The Woolseys joined the Tecumseh Methodist Church, which was founded in 1857. The pastor who greeted them was probably the Reverend L. F. Britt, a charismatic former circuit rider from Tennessee who had made a name for himself in the South by riding the circuit on a white horse. Fellow circuit rider Andrew Cook wrote about his dynamic colleague:

"It was Brother Britt's custom to preach three times on Sabbath and many times through the week. His circuit seemed to have neither metes nor bounds, and the young man was in constant demand over a large area of country. It is well that he was put up as he was, for what was crushing troubles to many of us, was just food for amusement to him;

he not only carried his own troubles, but the troubles of others. It was only a young, vigorous mind and body that could stand the constant drain upon his cheery, happy nature."

William Woolsey's two years of military service were subtracted from the five years necessary to take full possession of his homestead, which meant that by 1874 he and Martha owned the land outright.

The homesteaders who were farming the Nebraska plains at that time never forgot the year 1874. During ten momentous days in July, a swarm of Rocky Mountain locusts in a formation estimated to have been roughly the size of California invaded the area, stripping the land of all vegetation. Scientists believe that as many as 12 trillion locusts made up that particular swarm. And there were others. From 1874 to 1878, swarms swept through most of the Great Plains each summer and devastated the economies of Kansas, Nebraska, Minnesota, and North and South Dakota.

In the epic novel *Giants in the Earth* (1927), about a Norwegian family's struggle to survive in nineteenth-century Minnesota, author

O. E. Rolvaag described in chilling detail the mysterious "layers of clouds" that approached from the west one summer afternoon.

"They had none of the look or manner of ordinary clouds; they came in waves, like the surges of the sea."

By the time the swarm had descended on the unsuspecting farmers, it was too late to do anything about it.

> From out of the sky gushed down with cruel force a living, pulsating stream, striking the back of the helpless folk like pebbles thrown by an unseen hand; but that which fell out of the heavens was not pebbles, not raindrops, not hail, for then it would have lain inanimate where it fell; this substance had no sooner fallen than it popped up again, crackling and snapping—rose up and disappeared in the twinkling of an eye; it flared and flittered around them like light gone mad; it chirped and buzzed through the air; it snapped and hopped along the ground; the whole place was a weltering turmoil of raging little demons; if one looked for a moment into the wind one saw nothing but glittering, lightninglike flashes—flashes that came and went, in the heart of a cloud made up of innumerable dark-brown clicking bodies!

The historian David Marquette described the strain the disaster placed on the local clergy:

> The crops were consumed and the people left destitute and helpless. They could not carry forward their Church enterprises nor support preachers, or even obtain for themselves the necessaries of life, and yet they needed the Gospel none the less for their misfortune; and the Church could not with honor, or with any Christian propriety withdraw from the field merely because the people had been unfortunate.
>
> And so these preachers went forth as representatives of a Gospel faith and of sacrifice and found the Divine assurance still in

practical force, "Lo, I am with you." Some of them have traveled their extensive circuits the whole year on foot, giving full proof of their ministry, and not neglecting the people in their underground cabins, who, in many cases, were kept at home for the want of clothing.

Hundreds of preachers headed east to get help, and they returned with donations of food, clothing, and cash. For thousands of farmers, it was too little, too late, and they boarded up their homes and left. That included William and Martha Woolsey, who took their four young children back to Knoxville, Illinois. When, after 1878, the plagues ended just as abruptly as they had begun, the Woolseys returned to Nebraska, where Martha gave birth to three more children.

William not only farmed, but worked for the railroad; for a time he owned a hotel, and in 1893 he was elected sheriff of Johnston County, a position he held for four years.

William and Martha Woolsey are buried in the Tecumseh Cemetery on the south side of town. Their large headstone is made of pink marble.

WILLIAM H.
June 15, 1848
Mar. 19, 1923
Co. D 7th Ill. Cav.

MARTHA A.
Nov. 22, 1850
Sept. 28, 1915

The obituary in the local newspaper, the *Tecumseh Chieftain,* dated March 24, 1923, called William "a man of genial disposition, absolutely unselfish . . . interested in his friends and devoted to his family."

Services were held in the Tecumseh Methodist Church, and he was given a formal military burial.

I HAD one last cemetery to visit.

The Ida Cemetery, roughly thirty miles west of Washington, has a fifteen-foot-high iron arch at the entrance that makes it visible on the open plains from miles around like an oasis in a field of prairie grass. I parked along the side of the road in front of it, and a chocolate-brown Labrador retriever emerged from under the arch and barked at me. Inside the cemetery, a man on a small tractor was mowing the grass between the headstones.

The man spotted me and cut the engine.

"Hershey!" he called to the dog. "Come here."

He and I waved at each other as I entered the cemetery. I patted Hershey on her side, and she walked beside me with her tail wagging.

"'Afternoon," I said as I walked up. "Any idea where the Griffeths are located?"

He shook his head.

"Sorry. I don't look at the names."

"No problem," I smiled. "I'll find them."

He started the engine and began to mow again while Hershey and I walked up and down the rows of headstones.

It wasn't a very big cemetery, maybe fifty yards square, so it didn't take me long to find what I was looking for.

GRIFFETH

MABELL L.	CURTIS O.
OCTOBER 14, 1892	OCTOBER 21, 1888
OCTOBER 28, 1991	OCTOBER 28, 1950

These were my paternal grandparents. Grandma Mabell was the granddaughter of William and Martha Woolsey. She had moved from Nebraska to Kansas with her parents and three siblings around 1900. Granddad Curt's grandparents left Illinois for Kansas in the late 1870s.

This headstone marked the intersection of ancient bloodlines that extended back to England in the 1500s, when this whole journey began with the English Reformation—a journey that never would have happened if Henry VIII's request for a divorce had been granted.

When my grandparents were married, on October 19, 1910, all sixty-eight of the ancestral families in my cousin LeAnne's fifty-page family tree converged. Nine generations of the Townes of the Massachusetts Bay Colony, ten generations of the Jenneys of the Plymouth Colony, and ten generations of the Woolseys of the New Amsterdam Colony came together.

Granddad Curt and Grandma Mabell had three sons (my father was the middle child). All three boys moved to California and, combined, they had eleven children. The family's journey continued.

I said good-bye to Hershey and her master, climbed into my car, and headed back the way I had come.

At long last, my journey was over.

BY FAITH ALONE

THE ELEVENTH CHAPTER of the book of Hebrews begins with the Bible's only explicit definition of faith, calling it "the assurance of things hoped for, the conviction of things not seen." It then races through a thousand years of history with a sweeping recap of some of the Old Testament's greatest epics. No more than a verse is devoted to most of the stories, and in each case it identifies faith as the driving force.

"By faith Abel offered to God a more acceptable sacrifice than Cain's."

"By faith Noah . . . built an ark to save his household."

And there were Isaac and Jacob and Joseph and Moses and David and so many others "who through faith conquered kingdoms, administered justice, obtained promises, shut the mouths of lions, quenched raging fire, escaped the edge of the sword, won strength out of weakness, became mighty in war, put foreign armies to flight."

Abraham gets the most attention, eleven verses in all, because he is where our collective journeys began. In an instant, this seventy-five-year-old farmer who is near the end of his life hears God's order to pull up stakes, move to an unknown land, and start all over again. And he does it, no questions asked.

"By faith, Abraham obeyed when he was called to set out for a place that he was to receive as an inheritance, and he set out, not knowing where he was going. . . . For he looked forward to the city that has foundations, whose architect and builder is God."

That is how the story began for our families. The English Puritans were looking for a city built by God, and those who chose to come to America probably took the more difficult path by giving up their homes for an unknown world, just as Abraham did. But they didn't see it that way. For them the more difficult choice would have been to stay in England, give in to the Church, and deny their faith.

They never looked back. Perhaps they were encouraged by Hebrews' description of the pilgrims who followed Abraham: "If they had been thinking of the land that they had left behind, they would have had opportunity to return. But as it is, they desire a better country, that is, a heavenly one. Therefore God is not ashamed to be called their God; indeed, he has prepared a city for them."

Faith. That's what this story was all about. There were times when I lost sight of it, when I was too busy making plane and hotel reservations, or making sure I got just the right photograph of this or that cathedral. But then it would come back to me at key moments: while I was kneeling before the altar at St. Nicholas Church in Great Yarmouth, England, or standing on the dock in Rotterdam, or in front of the witch trials memorial in Danvers, Massachusetts, or in the pulpit at Harmony Hill United Methodist Church in Stillwater, New Jersey, or on the open prairie in Kansas.

As exhilarating as it was to learn the names of my many ancestors and to retrace their long journeys, and as inspired and proud as I may have been by their achievements and their acts of courage, more than anything I was humbled by the depth of their faith, that mysterious, elusive force that comforts and motivates the people who have it, haunts those who desperately seek it, and agitates those who dismiss it.

Just as faith put Abraham on the road to Canaan, it also put the Townes, Woolseys, and Jenneys on those sailing ships to America and the Norrises and Bennes on those wagon trains to Kansas. It brought peace to Mary Estey during the Salem witch trials and gave Elijah Woolsey the endurance to ride the circuit for as long as he did.

I've always seen my life as a three-legged stool, those legs being Faith, Family, and Career. What I discovered during my three-year journey was that, to many of my ancestors, Faith *was* the stool.

Notes

"Where did you get all of your family information?"

I heard that question a lot while I was writing this book. What people were really asking, of course, was "How do I build my own family tree?"

My cousin LeAnne Eller, who assembled the fabulous tree that was my primary source, used the Mormon Church's legendary Family History Library. It was begun in 1894 to help members of the Church of Jesus Christ of Latter-day Saints do their own genealogical research. The main library building in Salt Lake City, Utah, has 142,000 square feet full of resource materials including the International Genealogical Index database, which contains hundreds of millions of names. There are also thousands of satellite locations, called family history centers, in eighty-eight countries (there was one located a few miles from my home in New Jersey, for example). More information can be found at www.familysearch.org.

Among the many genealogical websites on the Internet, the one I found most helpful was www.newenglandancestors.org, which is run by the New England Historic Genealogical Society in Boston.

Whenever possible, I tried to use at least two credible independent sources to confirm the names, dates, and locations in LeAnne's tree, including books, websites, and town and church records, and the one source I figured would be the most reliable—graveyard headstones.

The information on them is, after all, etched in stone. Ironically, the most glaring bit of misinformation I encountered came from a graveyard.

The very first one I visited while I was doing my research, the Bedford Union Cemetery in Westchester County, New York, where a handful of my ancestors are buried, included a large stone monument with the name WOOLSEY carved into it. The inscription on the monument began,

---

THIS FAMILY IS DESCENDED FROM
JOHN WOOLSEY OF IPSWICH ENGLAND,
FATHER OF CARDINAL THOMAS WOOLSEY . . .

This was very exciting news. From 1515 to 1530, during the reign of King Henry VIII, the cardinal held two very powerful positions simultaneously. He was both England's highest-ranking Catholic and its Lord Chancellor, making him the highest-ranking government official after the king. When Henry wanted to divorce Catherine of Aragon so he could marry Anne Boleyn, it fell to the cardinal to petition Pope Clement VII to give the Church's blessing. When the petition was denied, the king seized control of all church property, stripped the cardinal of his powers, and created the Church of England.

The cardinal's reputation today is uneven. One of his biographers concluded that he was "probably the greatest political genius that England has ever produced," while another called him arrogant, "more papal than the pope," and faulted him for using his ecclesiastic and political powers for his own personal gain.

A couple of private genealogical websites claimed my ten-times great-grandfather George Woolsey was the cardinal's great-grandson, which would have made him my thirteen-times great-grandfather. Five consecutive generations of my line of Woolseys named a son Thomas, the only male name to repeat that frequently, and a sixth generation actually named a son Cardinal. He was the younger brother of my great-great grandfather William Woolsey, born June 10, 1853, in Knoxville, Illinois, but he lived only eight years.

As impressive as it all seemed, after several months of research I concluded that there was no connection between the cardinal and my family. The monument in Bedford, New York, the websites, and many of my ancestors simply got it wrong.

First of all, there was the spelling of the last name. While my family has long spelled it *Woolsey,* the cardinal's last name was spelled *Wolsey.* Admittedly there were no hard and fast spelling rules around the time of the Reformation; that wouldn't happen until Noah Webster compiled his first dictionary, originally called *The Speller,* in 1783. Before then, a difference of one letter in a name was no big deal. In fact, the cardinal himself often signed his name *Wulcy.* But in this case the difference may have been significant, because single-O Wolseys generally hailed from Suffolk, England—the cardinal was born there, in the town of Ipswich—while double-O Woolseys came from Norfolk, where George Woolsey and his family lived in Great Yarmouth.

Biographers say Cardinal Wolsey fathered two children: a son, Thomas, and a daughter, Dorothy. Dorothy became a nun while Junior grew up to become something of a playboy who lived the good life on his father's power and income. After the cardinal's death, the younger Thomas vanished from public records, and I can find nothing anywhere to suggest that he had any children. If my ancestors had a record of some kind that connected us to the cardinal, it is lost to history.

What follows is an informal, chapter-by-chapter synopsis of the sources I found useful.

PART ONE. EUROPE

The books I found most helpful in summarizing the events before and after the Protestant Reformation in Germany and in England included Roland Bainton's classic biography of Martin Luther, *Here I Stand*

(1950); Patrick Collinson's *The Reformation* (2003); Erwin Doernberg's *Henry VIII and Luther* (1961); *The English Reformation, Religion
and Cultural Adaptation* (2002) by Norman Jones; and Alison Weir's
Henry VIII, The King and His Court (2001).

You will find an excellent treatment of the Thirty-nine Articles,
which formed the foundation of the Church of England, at http://
mb-soft.com/believe/txc/thirtyni.htm.

CHAPTER ONE. GREAT YARMOUTH

For my trip to Great Yarmouth, I packed lightly so that I could pass
more easily through airports. My first stop in England was a hotel in
London, where I stayed a few days while I visited Cardinal Wolsey's
Hampton Court Palace. When I arrived at the hotel, the clerk at the
front desk informed me that a package was waiting for me. I had forgotten that I had ordered an original copy of a history of Great Yarmouth,
published in 1772, from an English book dealer and asked to have it sent
to my hotel so that I could read it during my trip.

The book, *The History and Antiquities of the Ancient Burgh of Great
Yarmouth,* by Henry Swinden, turned out to be enormous. It measured eight by ten inches, ran almost one thousand pages, and weighed
five pounds. Because I literally had no room for it in my suitcase or
shoulder bag, I had to hand-carry it during my trip through England
and the Netherlands. But it turned out to be a wonderful resource that
helped me write my own brief history of Great Yarmouth. I also used
W. R. Richmond's *The Story of Great Yarmouth* (c. 1900) and *The History of Great Yarmouth* (1853) by Henry Manship, edited by Charles
Palmer.

For help with seventeenth-century wedding and baptismal ceremonies, I used the 1559 edition of the Book of Common Prayer.

The book I turned to again and again was William Bradford's
classic *Of Plymouth Plantation 1620–1647*. Perhaps the most author-
itative edition used by scholars today is the 1952 edition, edited by the

historian Samuel Eliot Morison. Purely for sentimental reasons, I chose to use a dog-eared old paperback copy published in the 1970s by Modern Library. I purchased it many years ago during my first visit to Plymouth, Massachusetts, back when I had no idea that my family had a connection to the colony.

CHAPTER TWO. THE NETHERLANDS

Bradford's account of the Separatists' years in Leiden is remarkable history. It was insightful and very readable. I highly recommend those chapters. I also found *The England and Holland of the Pilgrims,* by Henry Martyn Dexter and Morton Dexter, to be very helpful.

I found a few important references to the Jenney family on the Pilgrim Archives website, www.pilgrimarchives.nl. The physical archives are in Leiden.

PART TWO. AMERICA

The Pilgrim Hall Museum in Plymouth, Massachusetts, is a treasure. Officials there have carefully preserved many important documents and artifacts from the Plymouth Colony. Gaining physical access to the rare, fragile documents is not easy, but visiting the museum's website—www.pilgrimhall.org—is. A tour of the museum itself is well worth it.

CHAPTER THREE. PLYMOUTH, MASSACHUSETTS

In addition to my tours of the Pilgrim Hall Museum, the Plimoth Plantation a few miles south of town, and the wonderful Jenney Grist Mill, I relied a great deal on two books to help me understand the history of the colony. The first, of course, was Bradford's *Of Plymouth Plantation.* The other was *New England's Memorial,* Nathaniel Morton's own important history of the colony. When Morton was ten years old, he sailed from Leiden to Plymouth with the Jenney family on the *Little James* in 1623. He went on to become the colony's recording secretary. I purchased a 1772 edition of the book. I loved turning its surprisingly sturdy yellowed pages and seeing my ancestor John Jenney frequently listed next to the more famous members of the colony like William Brewster, John Alden, and Miles Standish.

I should also mention a book compiled by members of the Jenney family in 1988 titled *The Jenney Book: John Jenney of Plymouth, and His Descendants.* It contained a great deal of valuable information.

John and Sarah Jenney's wills are in the Pilgrim Hall archives. They can be accessed at www.pilgrimhall.org/WillJohnJenney.htm, and at www.pilgrimhall.org/WillSarahJenney.htm.

CHAPTER FOUR. NEW YORK

The Internet has a wealth of genealogical information, but not all of it is accurate, especially among private family websites where research standards are not very rigorous.

By far the best private genealogical site I found was administered by a distant Woolsey cousin of mine named Wilford Whitaker. We are both descendants of George and Rebecca Woolsey. His site, http://free pages.genealogy.rootsweb.com/~woolsey/www/woolgeo2nam.html, contained well-documented information, much of it from the Family History Library.

He and I independently came to the same conclusion that the Woolsey family is not related to Cardinal Thomas Wolsey. In fact, he has offered a tongue-in-cheek reward of $100 to anyone who can produce an official document proving otherwise.

Wilford and I differed on one minor point. He listed the birth of an eighth child to George and Rebecca Woolsey, a son named William, born October 12, 1655, but I did not find any other record to confirm it. One important source I used was the book *American Presbyterianism* (1885), written by a descendent of Rebecca Woolsey's, a professor of theology named Charles Briggs. In a footnote on pp. 102–3, he listed the children born to George and Rebecca Woolsey, quoting from "an ancient book of records handed down in the author's family." There is no mention of a William. George Woolsey's will does not list him, either. Wilford speculates that young William probably died at an early age. I agree, but neither of us found a death record confirming it.

Most of the details of the massive fraud perpetrated on thousands of "descendants" of Thomas Hall in the 1930s (which closely paralleled a scam to which my great-grandfather Charles Woolsey fell victim) came from an article in *Ancestry Magazine* by Delbert Hall called "The Hall-Edwards Estate: Fact or Fiction?" (11/1/95, vol. 13, no. 6).

Only a few months before I was scheduled to turn in my completed manuscript, I discovered a line of ancestors my cousin LeAnne did not have in her family tree: my ten-times great-grandparents Thomas and Rebecca Cornell, the parents of Rebecca Woolsey. The Cornells and their connection to the rebellious Ann Hutchinson and the rest of the dissident colony in Rhode Island deserved a chapter of their own, but there simply was not enough time to do it justice. I could not, however, leave out the bizarre story of Rebecca Cornell's mysterious death, because of the significant impact it had on the Woolsey family. Details of the inquest came from Jane Fletcher Fiske's *Rhode Island General Court of Trials 1671–1704* (1998). For more information about the incident and its aftermath, read Elaine Forman Crane's excellent *Killed Strangely: The Death of Rebecca Cornell* (2002).

CHAPTER FIVE. TOPSFIELD, MASSACHUSETTS

The citizens of Topsfield have done a wonderful job of preserving the town's history with its historical society. I'm grateful to society president Norman Isler for the resources he provided me. I also relied a great deal on the definitive *History of Topsfield, Massachasetts* (1940) by Norm's predecessor George Francis Dow, and on *The Descendants of William Towne* (1901), by Edwin Eugene Towne.

There is an active association of Towne family members that claims a membership in the tens of thousands. More information is available at www.townefamilyassociation.org.

CHAPTER SIX. SALEM, MASSACHUSETTS

First of all, I should mention that I found a variety of spellings of Mary Towne's married name—Easty, Esty, Estey—and in one document that Mary herself is thought to have written, it was spelled Estick. To be consistent, I chose one spelling: Estey.

The Salem witch trials of 1692 were well documented. The original documents are preserved in the Peabody Essex Museum in Salem. Many of them are reproduced in Boyer and Nissenbaum's thorough *The Salem Witchcraft Papers: Verbatim Transcripts of the Legal Documents of the Salem Witchcraft Outbreak of 1692* (1977).

A whole library of books has been written about the trials. I consulted a number of them. They are listed in the bibliography.

The full text of the Reverend Deodat Lawson's sermon that fanned the flames of the witch hysteria can be found at the Cornell University Library, http://historical.library.cornell.edu/cgi-bin/witch/docviewer?did=122.

All quotes from eyewitness Robert Calef came from the University of Virginia Library, http://etext.lib.virginia.edu/toc/modeng/public/Bur5Nar.html.

The full text of Increase Mather's "Cases of Conscience" can also be found at the University of Virginia Library, http://etext.lib.virginia .edu/salem/witchcraft/speccol/mather.

CHAPTER SEVEN. STILLWATER, NEW JERSEY

My most prized possession from my years of research is the fragile little volume of Reverend Elijah Woolsey's journals, edited by Reverend George Coles and published in 1845 as *The Supernumerary; or Lights*

and Shadows of Itinerancy, Compiled from Papers of Rev. Elijah Woolsey.
I found it after doing a search at www.abebooks.com, a wonderful
website that lists the inventories of thousands of used and rare book-
shops in the United States and in other countries. It was sitting on a
shelf in a small shop Cindy and I had visited years ago on Cape Cod, in
Brewster, Massachusetts. Abebooks.com became an invaluable reference. I found many out-of-print and hard-to-find books there.

Another book I turned to quite a bit for this chapter was *Beams of
Light on Early Methodism in America* (1887), which contained the journals of Elijah Woolsey's friend and mentor, Reverend Ezekiel Cooper.

Chapter Eight. WASHINGTON, KANSAS

This chapter was very much a collaborative family effort.

Much of the information about the Norris family came from my
mother, Frances Norris Griffeth. Benne family information came from
my cousins, Dr. Richard Benne—who first alerted me to the curious
circumstances of the burial of our ancestors Herman and Maria
Benne—and Helen Benne Elder, who is very active in the Washington
County Historical Society in Kansas. Some Griffeth family information came from my cousin Norma Olive, who plays a better game of
golf than I do.

A very helpful book was *A History of Nebraska Methodism,
1854–1904,* by David Marquette. The full text can be found online at
www.rootsweb.com/~nechurch/MECHURCH/hmec/index.htm.

The full story of Preacher Smith's adventures in Deadwood, South
Dakota, can be found at http://deadwood.govoffice.com. My wife
Cindy's family is from the Black Hills. Our grandfathers, Dave Norris
and Charles Haas, were contemporaries who were in Deadwood
around the same time. We often wonder if they knew each other.

Bibliography

Anderson, Robert Charles. *The Great Migration Begins: Immigrants to New England 1620–1633,* vols. 1–3. Boston: New England Historical Genealogical Society, 1995.

Bainton, Roland H. *Here I Stand: A Life of Martin Luther.* New York: Meridian, 1950.

———. *The Reformation of the Sixteenth Century.* Boston: Beacon Press, 1952.

Baker, Frank. *From Wesley to Asbury.* Durham, NC: Duke University Press, 1976.

Beale, David. *The Mayflower Pilgrims.* Greenville, SC: Ambassador-Emerald International, 2000.

Booty, John E., ed. *The Book of Common Prayer 1559.* Charlottesville, VA: University of Virginia Press, 1976.

Boyer, Paul, and Stephen Nissenbaum, eds. *The Salem Witchcraft Papers: Verbatim Transcripts of the Legal Documents of the Salem Witchcraft Outbreak of 1692.* New York: DaCapo Press, 1977.

Bradford, William. *Of Plymouth Plantation 1620–1647.* New York: Modern Library, 1981.

Briggs, Charles Augustus. *American Presbyterianism, Its Origin and Early History.* New York: Charles Scribner's Sons, 1885.

Brown, David C. *A Guide to the Salem Witchcraft Hysteria of 1692.* Self-published, 1984.

Burr, George Lincoln, ed. *Narratives of the New England Witchcraft Cases*. Mineola, NY: Dover Publications, 2002.

Campbell, Douglas. *The Puritan in Holland, England, and America*, vols. 1 and 2. New York: Harper and Brothers, 1892.

Coldham, Peter Wilson, ed. *The Complete Book of Emigrants 1607–1660*. Baltimore: Genealogical Publishing Co., 1987.

Coles, Rev. George. *The Supernumerary; or Lights and Shadows of Itinerancy, Compiled from Papers of Rev. Elijah Woolsey*. New York: G. Lane & C. B. Tippett, 1845.

Collinson, Patrick. *The Reformation*. New York: Modern Library, 2003.

Cooper, Ezekiel. *Beams of Light on Early Methodism in America*. New York: Phillips & Hunt, 1887.

Crane, Elaine Forman. *Killed Strangely: The Death of Rebecca Cornell*. Ithaca, NY: Cornell University Press, 2002.

Davies, Paul P. *The Priory and Parish Church of St. Nicholas Great Yarmouth*. Great Yarmouth, England: St. Nicholas Parish, 2004.

Defoe, Daniel. *A Journal of the Plague Year*. New York: Modern Library, 2001.

Demos, John. *A Little Commonwealth: Family Life in Plymouth Colony*. New York: Oxford University Press, 2000.

Dexter, Henry Martyn, and Morton Dexter. *The England and Holland of the Pilgrims*. Baltimore: Genealogical Publishing Co., 1978 (reprint of 1907 edition).

Dick, Everett. *The Sod-House Frontier*. Lincoln, NE: Johnson Publishing Co., 1954.

Doernberg, Erwin. *Henry VIII and Luther*. Stanford, CA: Stanford University Press, 1961.

Dow, George Francis. *History of Topsfield, Massachusetts*. Topsfield, MA: Topsfield Historical Society, 1940.

Evans, Thomas Grier, ed. *Records of the Reformed Dutch Church in New Amsterdam and New York, Baptisms from 25 December, 1639, to 27 December, 1730*. New York: New York Genealogical and Biographical Society (reprint by Bergen Historic Books, Inc., of 1901 edition).

Fiske, Jane Fletcher, transcriber. *Rhode Island General Court of Trials 1671–1704*. Boxford, MA, 1998 (self-published).

Gurney, Judith Jenney, ed. *The Jenney Book: John Jenney of Plymouth, and his Descendants*. Baltimore: Gateway Press, 1988.

Hall, David D., ed. *Puritans in the New World: A Critical Anthology*. Princeton, NJ: Princeton University Press, 2004.

Heath, Dwight B., ed. *Mourt's Relation: A Journal of the Pilgrims at Plymouth*. Bedford, MA: Applewood Books, 1963 (reprint of 1622 edition).

Hill, Frances. *The Salem Witch Trials Reader*. New York: DaCapo Press, 2000.

Hotten, John Camden, ed. *The Original Lists of Persons of Quality 1600–1700*. Baltimore: Genealogical Publishing Co., 2003 (reprint of 1874 edition).

James, Sydney V., ed. *Three Visitors to Early Plymouth*. Bedford, MA: Applewood Books, 1963.

Jewson, Charles Boardmen. *Transcript of Three Registers of Passengers from Great Yarmouth to Holland and New England 1637–1639*. Baltimore: Genealogical Publishing Co., 1964.

Jones, Norman. *The English Reformation: Religion and Cultural Adaptation*. Malden, MA: Blackwell Publishers, 2002.

Kammen, Michael. *Colonial New York: A History*. New York: Oxford University Press, 1975.

Kramer, Heinrich, and James Sprenger. *The Malleus Maleficarum*. New York: Dover Publications, 1971.

Lindsay, David. *Mayflower Bastard: A Stranger Among the Pilgrims*. New York: St. Martin's Press, 2002.

Ludwig, Charles. *Francis Asbury: God's Circuit Rider*. Milford, MI: Mott Media, 1984.

McMillen, Persis W. *Currents of Malice: Mary Towne Estey and Her Family in Salem Witchcraft.* Portsmouth, NH: Peter E. Randall, 1990.

Mead, Frank S., revised by Samuel S. Hill. *Handbook of Denominations in the United States,* tenth edition. Nashville: Abingdon Press, 1995.

Menetti, Monsignor Giancarlo, et al., eds. *All Popes in History: From Peter to John Paul II.* Bologna: Tu Es Petrus, 2000.

Miller, Perry, and Thomas H. Johnson, eds. *The Puritans: A Sourcebook of Their Writings.* New York: Harper & Row, 1938.

Morgan, Edmund S. *The Puritan Family.* New York: Harper & Row, 1966.

Morgan, Edmund S. *Visible Saints: The History of a Puritan Idea.* Ithaca, NY: Cornell University Press, 1963.

Morton, Nathaniel. *New England's Memorial.* Boston: S. Southwick, 1772.

New England Society of New York. *Plymouth Church Records 1620–1859,* vol. 1. Cambridge, MA: John Wilson & Son, 1920.

Palmer, Charles John, ed. *The History of Great Yarmouth by Henry Manship, Town Clerk.* Salem, MA: Higginson Book Co. (reprint of 1853 edition).

Reaney, P. H., ed., *The Dictionary of English Surnames.* Oxford, England: Oxford University Press, 1997.

Richmond, W. R., *The Story of Great Yarmouth.* London: Jarrold & Sons, c. 1900.

Roach, Marilynne K. *The Salem Witch Trials.* New York: Cooper Square Press, 2002.

Rolvaag, O. E. *Giants in the Earth.* New York: Harper & Row, 1927.

Schmidt, Gary D. *William Bradford: Plymouth's Faithful Pilgrim.* Grand Rapids, MI: Eerdmans Books for Young Readers, 1999.

Smith, John. *A Description of New England (1616).* University of Nebraska Online Electronic Text edition: http://digitalcommons.unl.edu/etas/4/.

Stanford, Miles J. *Fox's Book of Martyrs*. Grand Rapids, MI: Zondervan, 1967.

Stratton, Eugene Aubrey. *Plymouth Colony: Its History and People 1620–1691*. Salt Lake City: Ancestry Publishing, 1986.

Swinden, Henry. *The History and Antiquities of the Ancient Burgh of Great Yarmouth*. Norwich, England: John Crouse, 1772.

Taylor, Alan. *American Colonies: The Settling of North America*. New York: Penguin Books, 2001.

Tepper, Michael, ed. *American Passenger Arrival Records*. Baltimore: Genealogical Publishing Co., 1993.

Tepper, Michael, ed. *Passengers to America*. Baltimore: Genealogical Publishing Co., 1988.

Thacher, James. *History of the Town of Plymouth*. Salem, MA: Higginson Book Co. reprint, 1991.

Tocqueville, Alexis de. *Democracy in America*. New York: New American Library, 2001.

Towne, Edwin Eugene. *The Descendants of William Towne*. Newtonville, MA, 1901 (self-published).

Van Dael, P. C. J., and A. de Groot, eds. *The Pilgrim Fathers in Holland*. Amsterdam: Stichting Oude Hollandse Kerken, 2002.

Van der Zee, Henri and Barbara. *A Sweet and Alien Land: The Story of Dutch New York*. New York: Viking, 1978.

Van Deursen, A. Th. *Plain Lives in a Golden Age: Popular Culture, Religion and Society in Seventeenth-Century Holland*. New York: Cambridge University Press, 1991.

Warner, Michael, ed. *American Sermons: The Pilgrims to Martin Luther King Jr*. New York: The Library of America, 1999.

Weir, Alison. *Henry VIII: The King and His Court*. New York, Ballantine Books, 2001.

Weisman, Richard. *Witchcraft, Magic and Religion in 17th-Century Massachusetts*. Amherst, MA: University of Massachusetts Press, 1984.

Wigger, John H. *Taking Heaven by Storm: Methodism and the Rise of Popular Christianity in America*. Chicago: University of Illinois Press, 2001.

Woolsey, C. M. *History of the Town of Marlborough, Ulster County, New York*. Albany: J. B. Lyon Co., 1908.

Acknowledgments

So many people to thank, so little space.

First of all, the sincerest of thank-yous to my cousin LeAnne Eller for the incredible job she did in building a fabulous family tree. There would have been no book without it.

A big thank-you to my wonderful editor, Julia Pastore, who "got" this book right away and kept me focused on its mission.

To Larry Kramer, my friend and agent (in that order, I'm happy to say), who cheerfully endured many dinners listening to all of the book ideas I have had over the years. He enthusiastically shepherded this project from start to finish.

To Dan Strone, my literary agent. After Larry sent Dan my proposal for this book, we arranged a meeting in Dan's palatial office in New York City, which is lined with shelves filled with hundreds of best-selling books by important authors he has represented over the years. I was truly humbled by Dan's excitement about this project and at how hard he worked to find the perfect publisher for it. I can't thank you enough, Dan.

To the many people I met along the way who were so helpful, including Norm Bendroth, Norm Isler, Leo and Nancy Martin, and Kem Monk.

To my personal board of editors who read portions of the manuscript and gave helpful suggestions: Greg Lee, Dan Clark, and most especially Alison Tepper Singer.

To my mother, Frances Griffeth; to my cousins Dick Benne, Helen Elder, and Norma Olive, our families' official historians, for generously sharing family stories; and to my distant cousin Wilford Whitaker, who painstakingly assembled one of the best-documented genealogical websites on the Internet: http://freepages.genealogy .rootsweb.com/~woolsey/index2.html.

Finally, a big hug to my family: to my wife, Cindy, who had to talk me down from more than a few ledges when I was convinced this book would never be finished on time (she designed the family tree at the front of the book); and to Chad and Carlee, who cheerfully put up with all of the trips to churches and graveyards in Europe and America.

Index

About the Author

────────

BILL GRIFFETH is a fifth-generation Methodist, born in Los Angeles. In high school he narrowed his career choices to journalism and the ministry. Journalism won, but he remained active in the Methodist Church. Even as he built a successful career as a TV news anchor, first at the Financial News Network (FNN) and then at CNBC, he served a number of positions at his home churches in California and New Jersey, including Lay Leader and Administrative Council Chair. He has also been a guest lay preacher at several churches around the country. He and his family live in New Jersey. Visit him at BillGriffeth.com.